# DISTRICT DEVELOPMENT PLANNING

# DISTRICT DEVELOPMENT PLANNING

(A Case Study of Two Districts)

TARSEM LAL

CONCEPT PUBLISHING COMPANY, NEW DELHI

First Published 1986


Tarsem Lal (*b*. 1938- )

*Published by*

Naurang Rai
Concept Publishing Company
H-13, Bali Nagar
NEW DELHI-110015 (India)

*Printed in India by*

Bharat Enterprises
*at* Chetna Printers
Shastri Marg-3
Mauzpur, Shahdara, Delhi-110053

*In Search of Alternatives*
*for a better Tomorrow*

## FOREWORD

In all developing countries, planning has been given substantial importance as a key input for the achievement of the developmental goals of nation building and economic growth. The governments in these countries are providing increasing financial resources to formulate and implement numerous anti-poverty programmes and other incentives to encourage human resource development. Looking to the result, it is becoming evident that something is wrong in the existing planning policies and processes which create bottlenecks in reaching the targets. Serious search for alternative planning framework is, therefore, necessary to provide avenues enabling the poor and disadvantageous sections of the society to meaningfully participate in the planned development process and exploiting optimum potentialities of the limited but scarce resources.

The policy makers and others involved in the planning process have been faced with the task of evolving and applying criteria by which to determine the total resources required for various development programmes and the justifiable distribution and utilization of these resources over various activities and levels of planning. With the avowed policy of the present Prime Minister to take India into the twenty-first century, apart from advancement in science and technology, decentralized planning system has also to be institutionalized on a firm footing towards achieving an egalitarian and modernized society.

Dr. Lal has made an excellent indepth study of district level planning process with a view to provide an understanding of the variety of considerations important to the philosophy and methodology of local level planning. He has also critically analysed the reasons for the persistence of certain inbuilt problems leading to non-fulfilment of several of the important objectives of district planning and made valuable suggestions to bring about better integration and coordination in planning and implementation of various development programmes. His rich administrative experience at the field level and intimate involvement with numerous programmes in various capacities has helped him to make pragmatic suggestions to improve the mobilization and allocation of resources, involvement of democratic institutions and development agencies as well as streamlining the administrative procedures. Based on a rigorous research methodology, the conclusions have been scientifically deduced, logically argued and cogently presented.

Dr. Lal has essayed a useful study of the district planning patterns with their operational aspects in a district each in the states of Maharashtra and Haryana. He has appreciated the merits of the Maharashtra pattern and its working, while pointing out the salient features with shortcomings in the Haryana pattern and its working. At the same time he has drawn attention to the declining in the participation of the panchayati raj institutions in the Maharashtra pattern and its operations.

The contemporaneous challenges faced by developing countries are numerous, and without institutionalized local level planning framework, it may not be possible to evolve rational public policies, much less to alleviate the sufferings of those who are at the brink of extinction. Dr. Lal has, therefore, rightly focussed his lens on the key organizational and administrative issues, thereby looking at the grassroot problems and initiatives in a detailed but objective manner. The penetrating eye of the researcher has brought to surface many intricate issues, which if rightly tackled, can be of immense help to the policy makers and others interested in seeing better tomorrow in a world full of rising expectations but shrinking resources. By making this thought provoking contribution, the author has done yeoman's service not only to India, but to the developing world at large. I congratulate him for this painstaking research effort and wish that the recommendations of the study be seriously pursued by planners and policy makers. The alternatives suggested by the author need further exploration and adoption to suit the changing requirements. I highly appreciate the positive and constructive approach of the author who with his inborn optimism thinks that removal of backwardness and poverty is not a lost case. Such a treatment is reassuring and full of hope in an environment of misery, deprivation and dejection.

N.R. INAMDAR

Tilak Professor and Head,
Department of Political Science
and Public Administration,
University of Pune,
PUNE-411007

# CONTENTS

# LIST OF MAPS AND CHARTS

# LIST OF TABLES

# IMPORTANT ABBREVIATIONS

| | |
|---|---|
| AAP | Annual Action Plan. |
| AGA | Additional General Assistant to Deputy Commissioner. |
| ARC | Administrative Reforms Commission. |
| BDPO | Block Development and Panchayat Officer. |
| CADA | Command Area Development Authority. |
| CEO | Chief Executive Officer. |
| CPM | Critical Path Method. |
| DCC | District Consultative Committee. |
| DCP | District Credit Plan. |
| DDP | Desert Development Programme. |
| DIC | District Industries Centre. |
| DLRM | District Level Review Meeting. |
| DPAP | Drought Prone Area Programme. |
| DPB | District Planning Board. |
| DPDC | District Planning and Development Council. |
| DPO | District Planning Officer. |
| DRDA | District Rural Development Agency. |
| DRI | Differential Rate of Interest. |
| EC | Executive Committee. |
| FFDA | Fish Farmers Development Agency. |
| GSDA | Ground Surface Drilling Area. |
| HYVP | High Yielding Variety Programme. |
| IAAP | Intensive Agricultural Area Programme. |
| IADP | Intensive Agricultural Development Programme. |
| ICDS | Integrated Child Development Scheme. |
| KVIC | Khadi and Village Industries Commission. |
| IRDP | Integrated Rural Development Programme. |
| ISB | Industry and Small Business. |
| MAIDC | Maharashtra Agro-Industries Development Corporation. |

| | |
|---|---|
| MFALA | Marginal Farmers and Agricultural Labourers Agency. |
| MNP | Minimum Needs Programme. |
| MPBCDC | Mahatma Phule Backward Classes Development Corporation. |
| MSEB | Maharashtra State Electricity Board. |
| MSFC | Maharashtra State Financial Corporation. |
| NABARD | National Bank of Agricultural and Rural Development. |
| NREP | National Rural Employment Programme. |
| PERT | Programme Evaluation and Review Technique. |
| PLO | Petrol Lubricant and Oil. |
| PS | Primary Sector. |
| SEC | Special Executive Committee. |
| SLBC | State Level Banks Committee. |
| SSC | School Standard Class. |
| TASP | Tribal Areas Sub-Plan. |
| TRYSEM | Training for Rural Youth for Self Employment. |
| UNCRD | United Nations Centre for Regional Development. |

# PREFACE

AT the threshold of Independence, India mutilated and partitioned, inherited a colonial legacy punctured by devastations of the Second World War with a backlog of chronic poverty and severe sense of deprivation. Based on serious handicap and shaky foundations, the edifice of planning exercises started on a modest and unpredictable note but slowly geared itself to effectively meet the emerging challenges of socio-economic development. The mid-term appraisals and other evaluation studies testified that there were areas of excellence and promising performance as well as some pockets of vested interests and exploited under-privileged groups. The net result has been that inspite of the persistent and serious efforts of planners and policy makers to tackle the problems of underdevelopment and poverty, much ground yet remains to be covered. Basic minimum human needs have been identified and efforts are being concentrated to satisfy them but the overall impact in real terms cannot be measured only in statistical terms. Quantitative achievements, even if impressive, cannot compensate for the qualitative gains. Therefore, the focus should be both on quantitative and qualitative aspects.

In every developing country, development has been regarded as an all pervasive activity with multi-dimensional thrust in economic, political and social spheres. The emerging developmental scenario is facing serious environmental and societal challenges, making the task of transformation ticklish. For majority of India's population, the Government means the district administration and as such centralised planning which is in vogue in India has no relevance to the backward areas and the target groups for whom the planning is being undertaken. District planning, except a few oasis, has failed to emerge as a possible alternative to centralized planning on various grounds but it must succeed to serve the majority of the people not only to banish poverty from the country but also to improve the quality of life of those who are across the poverty line and waiting for better days. To prepare India to enter the twenty-first century with optimism and confidence, there is a need to institutionalize decentralized planning as a system on a priority basis and rejuvinate other development institutions like Panchayati Raj, local bodies, cooperatives banks, etc. Its in this faith, that this research effort touches on some of the key conceptual, procedural, financial, administrative and organisational issues in the field of development administration. Based on an indepth study of two districts—Karnal in Haryana State and Thane in Maharashtra State—the present book is a condensed version of the doctoral thesis on "*District Development Planning: A Study of Two Districts*" *awarded by the Panjab University, Chandigarh, in March 1985*. The manuscript has been vetted and edited to make it more readable free from statistical and technical jargons. Some of the parameters discussed are of a universal nature, posing serious challenges to the developing world at large. If this study initiates thinking and encourages debate and dialogue ultimately culminating in action in furthering the cause of district development planning as a system, the efforts of the author will be amply rewarded. However, it may be mentioned here that no financial assistance was secured from any quarter with the result that this project is the outcome of years of labour of love and patience undertaken to operationalize district development planning as a viable discipline within the framework of multilevel planning to achieve the objective of a balanced socio-economic development of the district with special inbuilt package for the poor to lift them above the morose poverty on a viable lasting footing.

Prof. N.R. Inamdar, Tilak Professor and Head, Department of Political Science and Public Administration, University of Pune, has been very kind to add to very thought provoking 'Foreword'. I am grateful to him for sparing his valuable time and appreciating this effort.

I must place on record my deep sense of gratitude to Dr. S.K. Sharma, Professor of Public Administration, Panjab University, Chandigarh, for his having supervised this thesis.

He initiated me into this and provided valuable guidance throughout the period of the study untiringly despite his heavy schedule of work. To the Panjab University, I owe an unrepayable debt and to the Department of Public Administration, my sincere gratitude for all the help, guidance and facilities without which this effort would have remained only a dream. Throughout my involvement in this work, Mrs. Ravi Lal, my wife, had to take care of many things and she, therefore, deserves a share of whatever pleasures and satisfactions are there in the completion of this project. So many colleagues, well-wishers and friends have helped me in so many ways, both in Haryana and Maharashtra, as also in Chandigarh, that it will be embarrassing for me to omit some names and the list, however, exhaustive, cannot include all. I, therefore, thank them individually and collectively for all that they did for me enabling me to complete the study within the stipulated period of 3 years. However, I alone am responsible for all that I have written in my individual capacity and the views expressed do not represent the views of any Government or Institution. Lastly, Mr. Naurang Rai has put in his best to bring this book in the market in a record time for which he deserves my appreciation.

TARSEM LAL

# 1

# INTRODUCTION, SCOPE AND METHODOLOGY

AFTER Independence, with the transformation of the law and order state into a welfare state, the emphasis shifted from regulatory administration to development administration. A gradual process of planned development started in 1951, through a series of Five Year Plans and annual plans. With the setting up of the Planning Commission, planning became an integral part of the federal economic system. Planning was conceived in comprehensive terms and targets in various fields were laid down, both at the Central and the State levels. Resources were allocated to various sectors and to schemes within each sector.

The planning process continues to be centralized despite the oft-repeated demand for decentralization. The unsatisfactory performance of the centralized planning has often been highlighted and at the same time there is a need to harmonize plans of local agencies and also to ensure consistency between local and national plans. Complete decentralization has also been disfavoured and it has been accepted that planning exercises should be carried out at several levels with appropriate links between them. The multi-level planning framework has implications of its own but the studies conducted so far have pointed out that such a framework has yet to become fully operational.

Despite more than three decades of planning history of India, about 50 per cent of its population mostly comprising small and marginal farmers, landless agricultural labourers, Scheduled Castes, Scheduled Tribes and rural artisans have been living below the poverty line continuously over a long period.[1] The

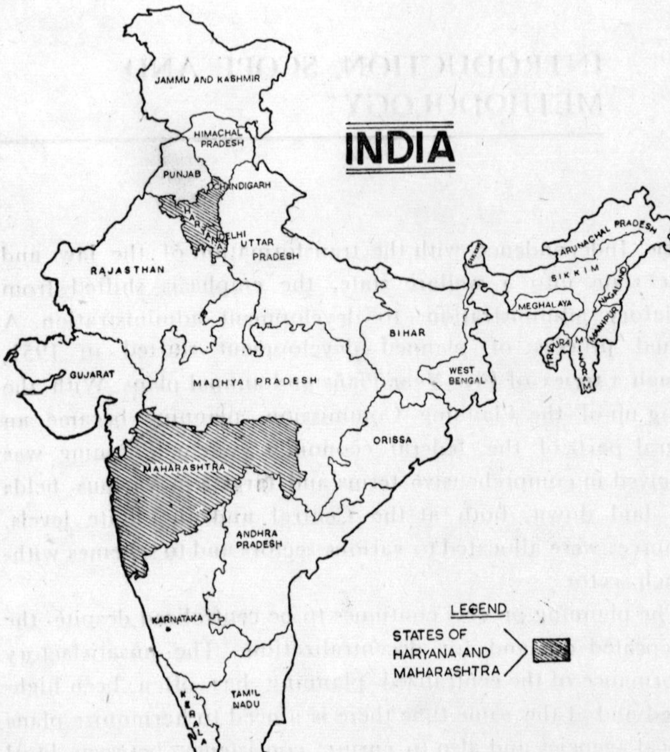
INDIA
JAMMU AND KASHMIR
HIMACHAL PRADESH
PUNJAB
CHANDIGARH
HARYANA
DELHI
UTTAR PRADESH
RAJASTHAN
GUJARAT
MADHYA PRADESH
BIHAR
WEST BENGAL
ORISSA
MAHARASHTRA
ANDHRA PRADESH
KARNATAKA
TAMIL NADU
KERALA
ARUNACHAL PRADESH
SIKKIM
NAGALAND
MEGHALAYA
MANIPUR
TRIPURA
MIZORAM
LEGEND
STATES OF HARYANA AND MAHARASHTRA

expectation that planning would raise the living standards of the millions of this country is far from being fulfilled . . . . Problems of poverty and unemployment not only seem to defy all solutions, but also have assumed larger and more complex dimensions.[2] This has caused a great deal of concern to Government, planners, academicians and social reformers. The community development and other programmes launched by Government of India since early fifties did not result in improving the socio-economic condition of weaker sections of society as their benefit could not percolate to this category of persons and was mostly cornered by the comparatively affluent sections. Realising this lop-sided development and the urgency to afford benefit to small and marginal farmers and landless agricultural labourers, Government initiated a number of special programmes such as, the Small Farmers Development Agencies (SFDA) Marginal Farmers and Agricultural Labourers Agencies (MFALA), Tribal Area Programme, Hill Area Programme, and Drought-Prone Area Programme[3] towards the beginning of seventies. These programmes aimed at providing financial assistance to the target groupsby way of not only raising institutional loans but also by providing subsidy[4] to them for undertaking various programmes like land development, soil conservation, minor irrigation and subsidiary occupations.

Even these programmes failed to create any visible impact on the weaker sections. Only small fraction of the rural poor who had some land could be effectively covered and the bottom deciles without any land had in most cases been left untouched.[5] A Conference of the State Ministers on Rural Development, Community Development and Panchayati Raj reviewed the working of these programmes in 1975 and came to the conclusion that certain inherent weaknesses in the system were responsible for undermining the stipulated achievements. The major common defects observed in the implementation of these programmes were:[6] (a) lack of synchronization of normal state plan activities and the activities of these programmes, (b) absence of integrated and coordinated planning and execution by dovetailing the plan resources with the funds of these agencies, (c) lack of acceptance of role and responsibility by different offices at the district level towards these special programmes, (d) inadequate involvement of the heads of departments concerned with various aspects of these programmes, and (e) inadequate involvement of the block development machinery and the Panchayati Raj institutions in implementing the programmes.

All these programmes did not get integrated with the district level programmes through a planning process and tend to hang loose from the state level programmes. The package of a 'New Deal' originally envisaged did not reach the poor as they were neither specifically owned, nor groomed by any department at the district level. Moreover, each project was provided with a skeleton nucleous staff, and states were required to strengthen the extension machinery which was seldom done as experience shows.[7] The existing extension agency of the state did not reach the poor target groups to provide them necessary inputs and package of practices. Thus, they continued to grow the traditional varieties of crops despite the availability of irrigation facilities and were not even covered under the normal programmes in the district. In this situation, only a small fraction of the rural poor has been covered effectively by these poverty-amelioration programmes. Even amongst those covered, a sizeable portion is of those who had some land,[8] and the benefits of these programmes did not trickle down to the landless.

About 3,000 development blocks out of 5,004 in the country were covered by one or more of the above mentioned special programmes but none of these programmes covered the entire country, though a large number of blocks in the country had more than one of these programmes operating simultaneously in the same area for the same target groups. This multiplicity of programmes and agencies in the same area created various problems and difficulties. In practice, these programmes were "reduced to mere subsidy giving programmes shorn of any planned approach to the development of the rural poor".[9] In view of the above, a single programme known as the "Integrated Rural Development Programme"[10] had been launched in 1980 throughout the country to raise the standard of living of those families living below the poverty line.

In the past, systematic planning in India remained confined

at the national level and to some extent at the state level and only sectoral approach to planning was adopted which merely stressed upon economic sectoral planning without giving any importance to the social justice and not much has been done to operationalize planning at the district level except in Maharashtra and Gujarat.

Development planning is in vogue in the less developed countries in Asia, Africa and Latin America and it is found in its most articulate form in India. All these countries are characterized by low labour productivity and low per capita income, small industrial sector, low level of living, undesirable (from the developmental angle) attitudes and pattern of performance in life and at work and institutional barrier to change, as a result of which poverty, unemployment and inequality assumed formidable dimensions in these countries. Development Planning should, therefore, aim at changing all these simultaneously, through a policy intervention and action programmes at the level at which these barriers, physical and mental, to development halt the development process. This change can be achieved effectively by mobilizing total resources, human and material, through the action-oriented administrative system.

India is committed to a policy of growth with social justice. It has necessarily to devise policies and programmes so that the benefits of development should flow in equitable and just manner to all groups and communities for reducing socio-economic cleavages. The Constitution of India declares in the Preamble that it aims at securing for its citizens: "Justice, social, economic and political, equality of status and opportunity, to promote among them all, fraternity assuring the dignity of the individual and the unity of the nation." In the Directive Principles of State Policy, it is stated that "the state shall strive to promote the welfare of the people by securing and protecting, as effectively as it may, a social order in which justice, social, economic and political, shall inform all the institutions of national life." Article 46 of the Constitution of India further states that "the state shall promote with special care the educational and economic interest of the weaker sections of the people, and, in particular of the Scheduled Castes and the Scheduled Tribes, and shall protect them from social injustice and all forms of exploitation." Therefore, besides economic growth, social justice is equally an important theme as envisaged in the Constitution, and the clientele which requires this justice is physically present within the territorial boundaries of the districts further sub-divided into blocks and clusters of villages, and they and their problems can be visibly seen from a close range at the district level. Thus the topic selected for research is of great importance in view of constitutional commitments.

## DISTRICT AS A PLANNING UNIT

India is a sub-continent, and in terms of division of the functions of the Government, there are three main tiers, viz., the Union, the State and the District, and the District is further divided into blocks for the implementation of development programmes. There is, however, no provision in the Constitution for planning at the district level but the plan documents attach great importance to operationalize planning at this level.

D. R. Gadgil emphasized that the lowest stratum of governmental authority in India is the district. Planning from the bottom has, therefore, to be chiefly associated with the district development effort but he further argued that it (district) is ordinarily too large and hetrogeneous, it would be difficult to formulate the integral plan directly for the entire district. Therefore, while some elements of activities and some integrating factors would operate only at the district level, for the bulk of the activities in relation to primary production, dispersed industry, rural trading and transport or urban activities oriented towards serving the rural economy, etc., the district has to be divided into convenient areas for the formulation of an integrated plan for the lowest level area unit and he advocated the concept of the "mandi area" as the most appropriate for this purpose.[11] V. Nath, on the other hand, argued that the emphasis on resource development activities and provision of more advanced services makes the district a more important unit of planning than the block.[12] There are others who are of the strong view that the district is the ultimate reducible viable unit of planning in terms of data collection, planning machinery and infrastructural facilities, marketing and services, as also the availability of officers of various disciplines at the district headquarters.[13]

The need for making district the major unit of local planning is also felt for other reasons. Effective district development planning will require considerable measure of decentralization of decision making from the state level to the district level. Such decentralization is more feasible at the district level than at the block level. There are several reasons for this. Firstly, the district has the full complement of district level officers who can provide the specialist assistance needed for drawing up plans. On the non-official side, the Zila Parishad has the top level leadership of the district. Secondly, for reasons of administrative feasibility, especially maintaining effective communication between the state and local levels, the district is more suitable than the block as a unit of local planning.

Regional planners have also been making a strong plea for introducing regional planning in India. In the past, full-fledged regional planning was not attempted in India as an integral part of the Five Year Plans because of the absence of well-defined regions which correspond with the politico-administrative units. Even in future, we cannot think of full-fledged regional planning in India because of the (a) impracticability of adjusting the boundaries of the states with the natural boundaries of homogeneous regions and (b) the ineffectiveness of formulation and implementation of full-fledged regional plans if their boundaries cut across state's boundaries. In this situation, planning has to be attempted at the sub-regional levels within the well defined jurisdiction of the states. Sub-regional planning unit should normally satisfy such criteria as (a) contiguous geographical area, (b) homogeneous administrative machinery capable of formulating and implementing integrated area plans, (c) reliable statistical data base, (d) existence of nodal regions, i.e., growth poles, and growth centres, and (e) amenability to adjustment of boundaries to make them as far as possible homogeneous natural boundaries.[14]

If we apply these criteria, states as units of regional planning automatically fall outside the purview. The village and the block do not fulfil the second, third and fourth criteria. So, in between these, we have the districts which satisfy, by and large, most of these criteria, and we can attempt sub-regional planning at the district level in India.

The above discussion reveals that this issue is quite subjective but because of the unsatisfactory performance of the centralized planning and heavy industry-cum-trickle down development strategy pursued so far in this vast country, the balance of arguments seems to be tilting in favour of district as a unit of development planning especially due to availability of: (a) data, (b) planning machinery, (c) implementing agencies; (d) local leadership and local government institutions, (e) financial institutions, and (f) availability of infrastructural facilities, marketing and services at the district level. Above all, increased scope of plan activities at the district level and the emphasis on area development approach tend to make the argument stronger in favour of the district development planning.

The Planning process in India, by and large, is centralized and has become more or less a routine, stale and prisoner of its own premises; unable to cope with the changing realities. Lessons from the past experience have not been fully utilized to solve the present day problems and planners continue to defend themselves despite their proven irrelevance and ineffectiveness.[15] The Sixth Plan document while highlighting the achievements has admitted of a "limited success in redistributing assets", slower pace of generation of employment opportunities and inability of large segments of the population to share in the benefits of progress or participation in the process of development.[16] Thus, there is a need for a thorough review of the basic premises, assumptions and working processes of planning in this country so as to make it more effective.

The subject of planning covers a wide variety of problems. Therefore, the literature relating specially to Indian economic problems has centered round planning from one point of view or another. Studies relating to planning organization in the period before the Planning Commission was set up in 1950 were prescriptive rather than empirical in character. Later, a number of administrators and academicians attempted various kinds of organizational analysis or critical evaluation of the manner in which the Planning Organization and procedures had worked in actual practice. The importance of developing well equipped sectoral planning agencies in Central Ministries was emphasized by the Planning Commission only in the Third Plan document.

Very few attempts have been made in studying the Planning Organization at the state level. There are half a dozen studies relating to various types of analysis of organizational and procedural devices for planning at the state level. There have also been a few occasional articles but a fairly detailed enquiry about how the planning machinery in various states is being undertaken has been provided by A.R.C. Study Team Report on the machinery of planning published in 1967.

As regards district planning, the concept was not clearly developed or its application analysed for a long time except through research papers. Panchayati Raj began to be emphasized as the main focus of rural development, planning at the block and district levels came to receive added attention. D.R. Gadgil was very emphatic in propagating the importance of using the district as a unit for effective planning. The Wardha Plan while reflecting his thinking attempted to provide a pattern for such efforts. In addition to a number of articles on the subject, a study *District Planning: Moradabad* (1968), by the National Council of Applied Economic Research provided some valuable insights. A study by the Programme Evaluation Organization (Planning Commission) regarding *Study of Development Staff at the District and Lower Levels* (1968) examined the problems of development staff at the district level. The A.R.C. Study Team on the *Machinery for Planning* (1967) as well as A.H. Hanson, *The Process of Planning* (1968) have devoted special chapters to reviews of district and grassroot planning. There are also a couple of studies sponsored by the R.P.C. which deal with individual case studies of planning at the district level. In 1969, Planning Commission framed *Guidelines for the Formulation of District Plans* which dealt in detail with the concept of district planning, preparing district plans, assessing existing levels of development, and planning for development. Lal Bahadur Shastri National Academy of Administration organized a Seminar on "District Planning" in 1973 in which the researcher also participated. The papers presented at the Seminar as well as the proceedings were brought out in a special issue of the Journal of the Academy in 1975. There have been some studies relating to Multi-level Planning. There was a Special number of the *Indian Journal of Public Administration*, July-September, 1973 devoted to this theme. A paper on District Planning in Maharashtra by Prof. N.R. Inamdar and "The District as a Planning Unit: Style and Locus" by Rakesh Hooja touched only some aspects. Again, *Multi-level Planning in India* (1979) by Y. Venugopal Reddy dealt with various issues of planning at all levels. Only the last chapter regarding Formulation of a District Plan for Hyderabad has been of some relevance to the present study.

Sudipto Mundle in *District Planning in India* (1977), deals with integrated spatial planning and with the reasons why the approach has fallen short of expectations. The author has tried to organize observations from the field into a firm theoretical formulation. K.N. Kabra, in *Planning Process in a District* (1977), examines one aspect of the planning process and identifies the gaps—social, economic, organisational and administrative which are required to be plugged in order to lift district planning exercise from its formal character to a full-blooded, meaningful component of planning for social development. The Planning Commission has set up a Working Group under the Chairmanship of Dr. C.H. Hanumantha Rao to prepare guidelines for planning at the district level.

Most of the literature available in the area of district planning tends to be broadly descriptive. Most of the papers and articles in various high class periodicals describe the cumulative experience in regard to the formulation and implementation of some select aspects of district plans. They contain useful inferences to serve as guidelines for future action in regard to the need for decentralized planning but are inadequate to present an integrated picture of all the aspects of district development planning in particular socio-economic settings. Thus, while all the above studies were useful in assessing the extent and magnitude of the problem, their approach and coverage were limited to certain aspects. After their perusal, it was felt that there was a big research gap in this important area because district still continues to be a nodal point where all the policies and programmes of the government converge. It was with this intention that the present attempt was undertaken in two districts in two states of India, viz., Thane district in Maharashtra and Karnal district in Haryana.

## Profile of Maharashtra with special reference to Thane district

Maharashtra with 30 districts and 3.08 lakh square kilometres of area has a total population of 6.28 crores according to 1981 census. The average density of population works out to 204 persons per square kilometre against an all India average of 221. The sex ratio has been 937 females per thousand males and urban population amounts to 35.05 per cent of the total population. The level of literacy has been 47.2 per cent against 36.08 per cent for the country as a whole with literacy among males being 58.79 per cent and among females 34.78 per cent. The percentage of Scheduled Castes and Scheduled Tribes population is 16.3 per cent.

The total number of workers in the state as per 1981 census was 24,302 thousand which constitute 38.8 per cent of the total population. Cultivators accounted for 35.1 per cent of the workers, agricultural labourers 26.6 per cent, household industry workers 2.6 per cent and other workers 35.7 per cent. There were in all 2,416 thousand (3.8 per cent) marginal workers and 36,066 thousand (57.4 per cent) non-workers in the state.

During 1981-82, the state income of Maharashtra was Rs. 15,886 crores and the per capita income Rs. 2,519 at current prices against Rs. 1,750 in India. The share of primary sector in Net State Domestic Product at current prices during 1981-82 was 28.3 per cent, of secondary sector 35.2 per cent and of tertiary sector 36.5 per cent.

The contribution of agriculture to Net State Domestic Product at current prices during 1981-82 was 26.4 per cent. The state ranked second in net area sown and third in gross cropped area in 1978-79 accounting for 13 per cent and 11 per cent of the respective areas in India. On the industrial front, the state accounted for nearly a sixth of productive capital as well as of employment and nearly a fourth of gross value of output and value added by manufacture by the organized industrial sector in the country.

**Thane district**

Thane is one of the 30 districts in Maharashtra. The total geographical area of this district is 9,558.00 square kilometres of which 44.6 per cent is under forests. The district has 13 Talukas[17] and 1,622 villages. The population of the district according to 1981 census is 33.52 lakh persons comprising 53.1 per cent males and 46.9 per cent females giving a sex ratio of 883 females per thousand males. Rural population accounts

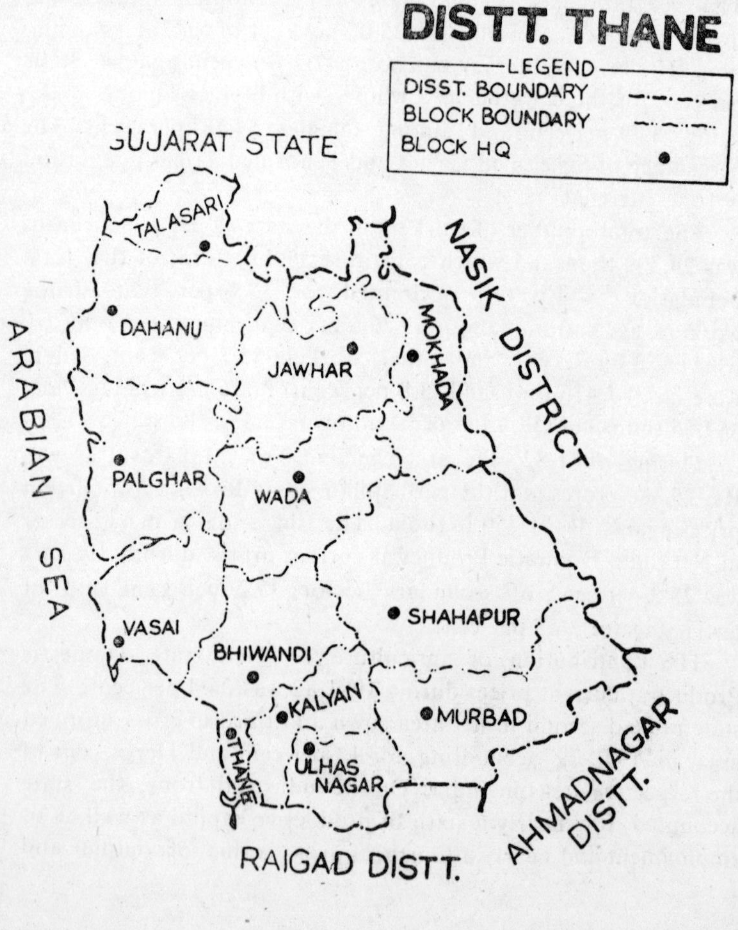

for 55.6 per cent and urban population 44.4 per cent. The density of population in the district is 351 persons per square kilometre. The percentage of literacy in the district is 50.51 with male literacy amounting to 59.86 and female literacy 40.14. Scheduled Castes and Tribes account for 24 per cent of the total population.

According to survey conducted by District Rural Development Agency, Thane, during the period April 1982 to June 1983, the total number of rural households in the district was 2,31,757 out of which 1,39,025 (60 per cent) were those who were below the poverty line. Of these, the number of Scheduled Tribe households was 83,648 (60 per cent), Scheduled Castes 5,742 (4 per cent) and others 49,635 (36 per cent).

The total number of workers in the district according to 1981 census is 1,268 thousand of which 28 per cent are cultivators, 13 per cent agricultural labourers and the rest are engaged in other occupations.

The cultivable area in the district during 1977-78 is 385 thousand hectares. The net sown area is 267 thousand and gross sown area is 276 thousand hectares. The cropped area under foodgrains is 195 thousand hectares. The net as well as gross irrigated area is 7 thousand hectares.

The total number of Industries in the district as on 31-12-1979 was 1,249 having average daily employment of 133 thousand workers.

The total number of cooperative societies in the district during 1979-80 was 2,470. These had a membership of 3.31 lakh. The working capital of these societies was 0.37 crore. The total amount of loan advanced by them was 0.53 crore and the loan advanced by agricultural credit cooperative societies alone was 0.39 crore.

The district had in all 10 hospitals and 50 dispensaries during 1978-79. The total number of beds available in hospitals was 2,890.

There were 2,429 primary institutions, 233 secondary institutions and 13 higher education institutions in the district during 1979-80. The district was also well served with transport, communication, post and telegraph facilities.

**Profile of Haryana**

Haryana comprises of 12 districts which have been further divided into 36 tehsils, 95 blocks and 6,731 inhabited villages. The total population of the state according to 1981 census is 128.51 lakh persons comprising of 68.46 lakh males and 60.05 lakh females. The sex ratio comes to 877 females per thousand of males. The percentage of rural population is 78.12 of the total population. Scheduled Castes account for 19.07 per cent. Literacy rate in the state is 38.84 per cent.

The total number of workers in Haryana according to 1981 census was 3,588 thousand which constitute 27.92 per cent of the total population. Among the workers, 45.0 per cent were cultivators, 16.4 per cent agricultural labourers, 3.4 per cent engaged in household industry and 35.2 per cent other workers. There were 727 thousand marginal workers and 8,537 thousand non workers which accounted for 5.65 per cent and 66.43 per cent respectively of the population.

During 1980-81, the state income of Haryana was Rs. 2,972 crores and per capita income Rs. 2,335 at current prices. The share of primary sector in Net State Domestic Product at current prices was 54.6 per cent, of secondary sector 18.5 per cent and of tertiary sector 26.9 per cent.

The contribution of agriculture and animal husbandry to Net State Domestic Product at current prices during 1980-81 was 53.8 per cent. The net area sown and the area sown more than once were 3,602 and 1,860 hectares respectively. The state produced 5,533 tonnes of cereals and 503 tonnes of pulses during 1980-81. The total irrigated area in the state was 2,133 hectares.

On the industrial front, the state had 3,303 registered factories during 1981-82. The estimated number of workers employed in these factories was 182.7 lakh. The state also had 440 hospitals and dispensaries having a total bed strength of 8,765 as on 31.12.1981. The state was also well served with educational facilities. During 1980-81, the number of universities was 3, colleges 147, higher secondary schools 1,475, middle and primary schools 5,825. The total number of co-operative societies in the state during 1980-81 was 9,557. These had a membership of 19.49 lakh and had advanced total loan amounting to Rs. 158 crores. The total length of metalled roads in the state during 1980-81 was 18,260 kilometres and almost all the villages in the state had been linked with pucca roads.

**Karnal district**

Karnal is one of the 12 districts in the state and consists of 9 development blocks. The total population of this district according to 1981 census is 13.23 lakh persons comprising of 7.14 lakh males and 6.09 lakh females. The sex ratio works out to 863 females per thousand males. The total geographical area of the district is 3,721 kilometres which gives density of population of 356 persons per square kilometre. The percentage of rural population to total population is 73.82. Scheduled Castes form 17.96 per cent of the population. The level of literacy in Karnal district is 36.42 per cent with rural literacy accounting for 29.30 per cent and urban literacy 56.42 per cent.

According to survey conducted by DRDA, Karnal in 448 villages out of 595 in the district, there were in all 1,48,323 families out of which 47,660 (32 per cent) were having per capita annual income upto Rs. 700/-. These families were considered to be below the poverty line. Of these, 20,383 (43 per, cent) were Scheduled Castes families.

The distribution of families below the poverty line according to per capita annual income reveals that 4,548 (9.5 per cent) were having per capita annual income upto Rs. 175/-, 15,349 (32.2 per cent) between Rs. 176-350, 15,773 (33.1 per cent) between Rs. 351-525 and 11,990 (25.2 per cent) between Rs. 526-700. Again 4,503 families (9.4 per cent) were small farmers, 4,090 (8.6 per cent) marginal farmers, 25,110 (52.7 per cent) landless agricultural labourers, 12,069 (25.3 per cent) non-agricultural labourers and 1,888 (4.0 per cent) rural artisans.

The total number of workers in the district according to 1981 census is 3.81 lakh of which 36.73 per cent are cultivators, 22.92 per cent agricultural labourers, 4.09 per cent engaged in household industry and 36.26 per cent other kinds of workers.

The total cultivable area in the district during 1980-81 is 348 thousand hectares out of total of 394 thousand hectares. The net sown area is 324 thousand hectares and the total

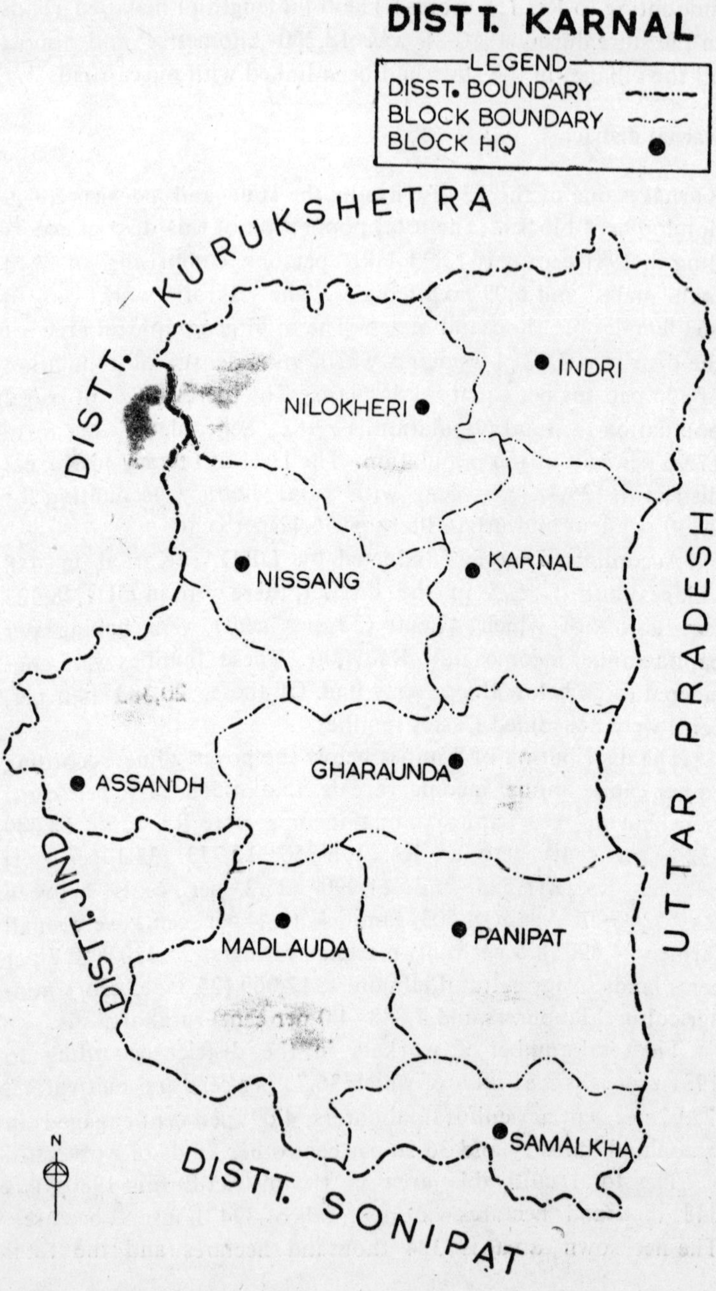
DISTT. KARNAL
LEGEND
DISST. BOUNDARY
BLOCK BOUNDARY
BLOCK HQ
DISTT. KURUKSHETRA
INDRI
NILOKHERI
NISSANG
KARNAL
UTTAR PRADESH
ASSANDH
GHARAUNDA
DISTT. JIND
MADLAUDA
PANIPAT
SAMALKHA
DISTT. SONIPAT
N

cropped area 494 thousand hectares. Wheat and rice are the the principal crops grown in the district. During 1980-81, the total production of wheat was 511 thousand tonnes and of rice 402 thousand tonnes. The total foodgrain production during 1980-81 was of the order of 946.4 thousand tonnes. The total net area irrigated in the district during 1980-81 was 290 thousand hectares which constitute 89.5 per cent of the net area sown.

The total number of registered factories in the district during 1981 was 485 employing a total number of 11,301 workers. The total number of cooperative societies in the district during 1980-81 was 1,093. These had a membership of 2.27 lakh. The working capital of these societies was 7,794 lakh. The total number of commercial banks in the district as on 31.12.1982 was 130 and the population per bank office amounted to 12,800.

The district had 36 hospitals and dispensaries as on 31-12-1982. The total number of beds available was 491 with 36 beds per lakh of population.

The district has also adequate education facilities and contains good number of institutions, technical and non-technical. The district is also well served with transport, communication and postal facilities.

## OBJECTIVES OF THE STUDY

District Development Planning in this study has been conceived as a deliberate and scientific exercise in rational and optimum utilization of available resources—physical, financial and human—for achieving pre-determined socio-economic goals within the multi-level planning framework during a specific period. Broadly, the study deals with select issues relating to plan formulation, mobilization of resources, Government grants and loans, development administration, coordination, monitoring and evaluation with a view to ensuring the benefits of planning efforts to the people of the area in general and the target groups in particular.

In particular, an indepth study has been made to:

(a) provide an understanding of the variety of considerations that are important to the philosophy and methodology of district level planning,

(b) look into the reasons for the persistence of certain inbuilt problems leading to non-fulfilment of several of the important objectives of district planning,

(c) suggest ways and means to bring about better integration and coordination in planning and implementation of various development programmes,

(d) make suggestions to improve the resource allocation and mobilization, involvement of democratic institutions and extension agencies as well as streamline the administrative procedures involved in implementation, and

(e) offer general suggestions to improve and operationalize planning at the district level.

In making this study, an attempt has been made to proceed on the hypothesis that better the understanding of the variety of constraints and considerations which go into integration and coordination in planning and implementation of various development schemes at the district level, greater will be the utility of the schemes in the context of the development effort of the state. Poor conception of various dimensions of district plans results in the failure of the achievement of the various objectives of the development schemes and subsequent loss of resources—both natural and human.

## Research methodology

To look into some of the issues, outlined above as objectives of the study, an exhaustive study of Government policies in respect of the district planning in Haryana and Maharashtra with special reference to study districts have been made. Relevant documents, guidelines, reports and instructions issued by the Planning Commission and State Governments have been carefully studied and analysed. This reading was further supplemented by making several personal field visits to both the districts. After preparing the first draft, the data was checked and cross-checked by intensive interviews with the district officers and others involved in the process. A schedule of detailed questions was prepared and the replies have been analysed in the relevant chapters. The tools employed for collection of data have been the schedule, interviews, participant's observations and detailed discussions with the field officials.

As an incharge of various assignments, the researcher was himself involved in implementing a number of development schemes and projects as Sub-Divisional Officer (Civil), Chief Executive Officer and Additional Deputy Commissioner of various projects such as Small Farmers Development Agency, Marginal Farmers and Agricultural Labourers Development Agency, Drought Prone Area Programme, and Command Area Development Agency. Later on, as Deputy Commissioner, the researcher was also Chairman of the Drought Prone Area Programme and Small Farmers Development Agency which was later on named as District Rural Development Agency entrusted with the planning and implementation of Integrated Rural Development Programme in the district. At the secretariat level, the researcher had the opportunity of working in the department relating to the implementation of not less than 50 such development projects and programmes. Working in various corporations such as the Haryana Agro-Industries Corporation, Haryana Economically Weaker Sections Kalyan Nigam and Haryana Harijan Kalyan Nigam as Managing Director helped researcher to look into various development schemes initiated to help the poor. The experience of the researcher for about two decades in senior managerial positions was very helpful to look into some of the issues closely related to the objectives of the study.

The researcher attended a number of refresher courses, training courses, symposia and seminars arranged in India and abroad. A Seminar on "District Planning" organized in the Lal Bahadur Shastri National Academy of Administration, Mussoorie was also attended which was really useful for understanding the concept, significance and limitations of district planning. A mention may also be made of a very useful six month course on Planning for Integrated Regional Development, which the researcher attended at the United Nations Asian

Development Institute, Bangkok (Thailand) and the United Nations Centre for Regional Development, Nagoya (Japan). These exposures were very helpful in providing a theoretical base.

The researcher has interviewed more than two hundred serving officials of various ranks for obtaining their opinions and views on various aspects. These interviews have given first hand account into the actual working and problems being faced in formulation and implementation of schemes. Besides being interesting, they generated a sense of realism and offered meaningful insights. Secondary sources include the published books and articles having direct bearing on this subject.

### A schematic view

The study has been divided into ten chapters. The first chapter outlines the methodology of research, including the objectives and scope of the study, profile of the districts studied and methods applied for collecting data and the review of the existing literature. Chapter II deals with the meaning of development and planning concepts, evolution and objectives of district planning in India in general and Maharashtra and Haryana in particular with special reference to Thane and Karnal districts. Chapter III examines the scope of district planning and the criteria for the identification of district level schemes. Chapter IV gives a detailed account of the process of district planning, indicating therein various stages through which the district plan has to undergo. It also indicates the proposed model of process of district planning. Chapter V identifies the resources for financing the district plans. Important matters such as allocation of funds to the districts on the basis of a well established formula and utilization of government grants under plan and non-plan are discussed at length. Besides government grants, chapter VI concentrates on the mobilization of loans from the commercial and cooperative banks for financing the bankable schemes, and also formulation of District Credit Plan and Annual Action Plan, mechanism for achieving coordination between the bankers and the district administration as well as the need for integrating the credit plans with the district development plans. Chapter VII covers matters like strengthening and institutionalization of development administration at the district level. Coordination is no less important an issue at the district level and the same is being discussed in chapter VIII. The next chapter underlines the need for monitoring and evaluation of district level schemes so as to ensure timely follow up to remove the bottlenecks in the implementation of the schemes on one hand, and ensuring benefits of planning to the common man, on the other. The suggestions and conclusions of the study are presented in the last chapter.

## REFERENCES

1. Planning Commission, Sixth Five Year Plan (1980-85), 1981, p. 51.
2. Kamta Parsad, Planning in India: Some Basic Issues relating to Operational and Strategic Aspects (Presidential Address), The Indian Economic Association, 66th Annual Conference, Banglore, December 28-30, 1980, p. 1.
3. Beneficiary-oriented programmes were launched in the country in the early seventies to provide financial assistance and a package of inputs to improve the socio-economic conditions of the small and marginal farmers and landless labourers. Under these projects, a small farmer is described as a cultivator with a land-holding of 2 hectares or below and marginal farmer is a cultivator with a land-holding of 1 hectare or below.
4. Subsidy was provided to the small farmers @ 25 per cent of the total financial requirement for taking up various schemes, and 33 per cent to marginal farmers, and landless labourers, and remaining financial assistance was arranged as loans from the cooperative and commercial banks. This pattern of financial assistance still obtains even under the IRDP.
5. Sixth Five Year Plan, op. cit., p. 159.
6. Conference of the State Ministers on Rural Development, Community Development and Panchayati Raj was held in New Delhi on the 8th May, 1975.
7. In Haryana, the existing extension machinery was not strengthened and the existing staff was required to carry out the additional duties connected with these programmes. It, therefore, remained busy in its normal programmes and paid lip service to provide technical know-how to the poor. For instance, if a small or marginal farmer was provided a loan, and a subsidy for the installation of a tubewell under the SFDA programme, the file of such a beneficiary was closed with the disbursement of subsidy so far as the Agency was concerned.

8. Sixth Five Year Plan, op. cit.
9. Ibid., p. 170.
10. The salient features of the Integrated Rural Development Programme are: (a) a target-group based apprcach which identifies the poorest of the poor and helps them to acquire productive assets, technology and skill so as to enable them to cross the poverty line, (b) subsidy-cum-credit pattern of providing financial assistance based on identification and development of economically viable schemes, (c) a household rather than an individual approach followed implying that the economic upliftment of the household will be sought through a package of activities involving all working members in the family. (d) due importance will be given to the development of secondary and tertiary activities and a certain proportion of expenditure will be specially used for them, and (e) cluster approach.
11. D.R. Gadgil, *District Development Planning*, Gokhale Institute of Politics and Economics, Poone, 1967.
12. V.Nath: Area Development: Planning at District and Block Levels: *Indian Journal of Public Administration: April-June. 1965, p, 185.*
13. Refer Sudipto Mundle, *District Planning in India*, Indian Institute of Public Administration, New Delhi, 1977.
14. District as a Unit of Sub-Regional Planning in India (Mimeo), Sardar Patel Institute of Economic and Social Research, Ahmedabad, 1981, p. 6.
15. "The most important objectives of planning have not been achieved, the most cherished goals seems to be as distant today as when we set out on the road to planned development. "Draft Five Year Plan, 1978-83, p. 2.
16. Sixth Five Year Plan, op. cit., p. 10.
17. Taluka boundaries are co-terminous with the boundaries of Block or Tehsil in Maharashtra.

2

# EVOLUTION AND OBJECTIVES

## MEANING OF DEVELOPMENT AND PLANNING

"DEVELOPMENT" is a multi-facet concept aiming at the socio-economic transformation of a traditional society into a modern one whereas planning is a blueprint for action to translate the development concept to achieve the pre-determined goals. In recent years, the developing countries especially in the Third World[1] have taken to planning as an important aspect of economic development. Even the developed countries have to resort to development planning to give specific directions to their economies, as also to provide socio-economic benefits to the less-privileged.

There is a lot of discussion about the content and meaning of the concept of "development". Traditionally, development was considered synonymous to "economic growth", or "rapid aggregate economic growth", and planning approaches in the Third World conform practically to this traditional model of development from the year 1950 to 1970, as a result of which poverty, inequality, unemployment and rural stagnation, by and large, plagued these countries. Development for the past two decades has also meant the capacity of a national economy, whose initial economic condition has been more or less static for a long time, to generate and sustain an annual increase in the gross national product at rates of perhaps 5 to 7 per cent or more.[2] Paul Streeten thinks that early thinking and policy making was dominated by economic growth as the principal performance criteria of development, not so much because growth was regarded as an appropriate objective in itself, but because it was thought either that its fruits would rapidly "trickle down" to the poor, or that corrective governmental action would be relied upon to redistribute them, or that inequality and poverty are essential for growth (which through accumulation by the rich, would first have to create the productive base from which to launch the attack on poverty).[3] However, it was soon evident that none of these three assumptions was valid. It became clear that growth in many countries remained concentrated on a narrow enclave of modern, organized, urban industry; that governments often were unwilling or incapable of using taxes and social services to offset growing inequalities; and that the concentration of income in the hands of the rich was not a necessary condition of development.[4] Thus, the traditional model of development merely reckoned development synonymous to economic growth considering that the benefits of it will trickle down to the poor, and it did not have any concern for distributive justice. Its main emphasis, by and large, was economic aspect of development rather than social, political or cultural aspects which are equally important. Therefore, the developing countries, inspite of serious efforts, failed to tackle the problems especially of poverty, unemployment and inequality, as also of growth in general as the poor could not participate in the development process in these countries because of inadequacy of specific policy directions and programmes to uplift their socio-economic conditions.

To explain the rising concern for the removal of poverty, development was related to transforming the entire society enmeshing together its economic, social, political and administrative aspects for an all round balanced upward change.[5] Development during the Seventies was redefined in terms of reduction or elimination of poverty, inequality, and unemployment within the growing economy. Redistribution with growth became a common slogan.[6] In fact, development is considered as a process of social transformation from a traditional society to a modern society.[7] Development, therefore, is not merely an exercise in growthmanship but means and includes (a) social justice, and (b) growth. Professor Dudley Seers raised the following basic questions about the meaning of development:

"The questions to ask about a country's development are, therefore, what has been happening to poverty? What has been happening to unemployment? What has been happening to inequality? If all three of these have declined from high levels, then beyond doubt this has been a period of development for the country concerned. If one or two of these central problems have been growing worse, especially, if all three have, it would be strange to call the result "development" even if per capita income doubled".[8]

Development has to tackle all the three basic issues of poverty, unemployment and inequality besides achieving economic growth. Therefore, economic growth alone is not development but it is more than that. In a U.N. document, development was regarded as a complex phenomenon. It implied a quantitative concept that might be understood as economic growth and a qualitative concept, rendered fairly accurately by the idea of "well-being". Economic growth is a phenomenon measurable in terms of increasing national income or per capita income. While the "well-being" of the population indicates a higher standard of living—a complex notion difficult to quantify which encompasses such various factors as the level of satisfaction of the needs of the population, in terms of food and nutrition, housing, health, education, recreation, security, spiritual satisfaction, etc.[9] In the same tone, Michael P. Todaro observed that development must, therefore, be conceived of as a multi-dimensional process involving major changes in social structures, popular attitudes and national institutions, as well as the acceleration of economic growth, the reduction of inequality, and the eradication of absolute poverty. Development, in its essence, must represent the entire gamut of change by which an entire social system, tuned to the diverse basic needs and desires of individuals and social groups within that system, moves away from a condition of life widely perceived as unsatisfactory and towards a situation or condition of life regarded as materially and spiritually "better".[10] The new approach to development relied heavily on planning as an important input.

**Role of planning**

It may be recalled that when the USSR introduced Five Year Plan, planning was "denounced as the road to "serfdom" by the First World but now the planning has become a way of life in almost all the countries. Jawahar Lal Nehru, the Chief Architect of Indian Planning, observed that planning is an exercise of intelligence to deal with facts and situations as they are and find a way to solve problems. It is also defined as an activity directed towards the conscious and deliberate choice of economic priorities by some public authority.[11] Todaro defined the term planning as under:—

Economic planning may be described as a deliberate governmental attempt to coordinate economic decision making over the long run and to influence, direct and in some cases even control the level and growth of a nation's principal economic variables (income, consumption, employment, investment, saving, exports, imports, etc.) in order to achieve a predetermined set of development objectives. An economic plan is simply a specific set of quantitative economic targets to be reached in a given period of time. The planning process itself can be described as an exercise in which a government first choose social objectives, then sets various targets, and finally organizes a framework for implementing, coordinating, and monitoring development plan.[12]

Planning may also be described as the process of rational decision making, and it has come to be used . . . to refer to the technical elaboration of the means that should be employed to attain certain goals expressed in policies woven into strategy.[13] The term planning, therefore, consists of (a) means, (b) goals, (c) policies, and (d) strategies.

In most of the countries of the Third World, development plans are formulated within the framework of mixed economy.[14] Despite a few decades of planning, most of these countries have not been able to achieve both the accelerated growth and social justice.

India has evolved its development philosophy and is the fore-runner of development planning in the Third World. During the freedom movement, Mahatma Gandhi, the champion of the cause of the down-trodden, and other national leaders advocated planning for development to ameliorate the socio-economic position of the teeming millions groaning under the weight of abject poverty. Development as envisaged by the Indian leaders finds its place in the Preamble to the Constitution of India as well as in the Directive Principles of State Policy, as also in all the Five Year Plans documents. The Preamble of the Indian Constitution sets out the basic objectives of the new social and economic order which the nation has solemnly resolved to bring into existence viz., to secure to all its citizens; justice, social, economic and political; liberty of thought, expression, belief, faith and worship; equality of status and of opportunity and to promote among them all fraternity assuring the dignity of the individual and the unity of the Nation.[15]

Thus, the Preamble is the foundation-stone of the development philosophy of the country. Further to it, the Directive Principles of the State Policy contain a set of positive directions spelling out the charter of socio-economic democracy. These Principles envisage that 'the State shall strive to promote the welfare of the people by securing and protecting, as effectively as it may, a social order in which justice, social, economic and political, shall inform all the institutions of national life'.[16]

In view of the above, planning in India has been regarded as a panacea, especially after Independence. However, actual planning process started with the launching of the First Five-Year Plan in 1951, and now the Seventh Plan (1985-90) is being implemented in the country. Although the immediate objectives of the Indian Plans have varied from plan to plan in the light of the prevailing economic situation yet "economic growth" and "social justice" have always remained the basic objectives of all the plans. Initially, the emphasis in development planning was on the achievement of high growth rates of total gross domestic products or national income.[17] Therefore, planning in India, in fact, followed the traditional model of development from 1951 to 1970, in which development was taken synonymous to economic growth and the teeming millions did not derive tangible benefits from the planning efforts during this period primarily due to lack of appropriate emphasis in the shape of specific policies and programmes for the poor and the less privileged. This fostered a centralized planning with concentration of efforts on the high growth modern sectors of the economy. Adoption of this policy was based on the consideration that increased growth *per se* would ultimately benefit all sections of the population through "essential spread effects". As this 'top down approach' did not result in any percolation of benefits but only accelerated the existing disparities in income or levels of living among people, distributional equity, therefore, became an important issue in development planning.[18]

In the year 1952, a bold attempt was made by launching the Community Development Programme with a view to reducing the poverty especially in rural India but this programme, with a very thin financial base, did not achieve the intended results. However, development administration was brought into existence as an agent of change[19] in the Community Development Programme. The subsequent programmes of national importance, like the Intensive Agricultural District Programme (IADP), Intensive Agricultural Area Programme (IAAP) and High Yielding Varieties Programme (HYVP) were launched in the selected districts in the country with a view to achieving self-sufficiency in foodgrain production. A cursary glance of the first four plan documents and these programmes would reveal that there was no inbuilt mechanism in these programmes to reduce or eliminate poverty amongst the target groups comprising small farmers, marginal farmers, landless agricultural labour, Scheduled Castes and Scheduled Tribes, and small artisans, as a result of which the winds of development bypassed the abject poor, and the main benefits of the infrastructural and institutional framework developed during the first four plans were mainly reaped by the well-to-do sections of the society especially having land or capital base whereas the poor, whether rural or urban, got only periphery benefits.

The year 1970-71 became a turning point in the history of development planning in the country with the launching of beneficiary-oriented projects such as (a) Small Farmers Development Agencies (SFDA), (b) Marginal Farmer and Agricultural Labour Agencies (MFALA), and subsequently other special programmes viz., (a) Drought-Prone Areas Programme (DPAP), and (b) Command Areas Development Programme

(CADP). These programmes, however, could not make a dent on the poverty front mainly due to haphazard planning, lack of coordination at the district level, lack of strengthening of development administration at the district level, non-involvement of the district officers in these programmes, inadequate institutional support, lack of integration of these programmes with the other on-going programmes and projects in the districts.[20] Although these programmes failed to achieve the desired objective yet these generated a kind of biased development philosophy in favour of the poor. Now, the Integrated Rural Development Programme (IRDP) has been launched in the country with a bias in favour of the rural poor, and it seeks to provide them necessary package of development inputs including infrastructure with the objective of generating more income and employment opportunities. The overall strategy is to create assets for the rural poor which will ensure steady flow of income to them. This "New Deal" is designed for those families which are living below the poverty line of Rs. 3500/- per annum. This is a welcome biased attempt in favour of the rural poor but the urban poor, who are also the outgrowths of the rural areas, are left high and dry. T.N. Chaturvedi, while discussing the problems of rural development, points out that there is no point in making dichotomy of rural and urban poverty, as it does not reflect the socio-economic reality. It is the landless labourer or the agriculturist with a small plot of land, who is not in a position to earn his livelihood in the village, moves to the cities which may be called as "slums of hopes". Poverty in this country constitutes a continuum and has to be looked at from this stand-point. This will help in ensuring institutional relationship with the rural economy and the relationship of the village economy with environment outside.[21] In the light of the above, continuous and consistent but steady efforts are necessary to ensure that benefits of development reach all the poor and less privileged without any differentiation over rural or urban basis.

## EVOLUTION

India began the process of planned development, nearly thirty-five years ago with the start of the First Five Year Plan in April 1951 and ever since it has remained a "growing concern".[22] The manner in which this purpose has been translated into specific objectives, has varied over the years. However, in a broad sense, the basic objectives of planning in most of the developing countries are the same. In one form or another but possibly with varying emphasis, these objectives reflect the views of all sections of the population and represent a national consensus. India is a vast country and multi-level planning[23] has been regarded as an important mechanism to ensure development. Development of man as a member of the growing society has to be attempted at a level of administration at which he, his problems and difficulties could be seen, identified and solved rather than at the national or state level. The process of planning at the district level has to be strengthened to ensure alround area and human resource development. Whereas flexibility and diversity to suit varying needs and circumstances are welcome, stress on coordination of efforts, resources and programmes of different sectors will remain important till the eradication or elimination of poverty, inequality and unemployment. Looking in the historical perspective, the basic form of the district as a unit of administration has a remarkable continuity. It has not changed substantially from the time of Manu.[24] Every effort, therefore, at development and planning must converge at this areal unit before it percolates below at block and village levels.

The economic development of a district is a complex process in which economic and uneconomic factors are closely interwoven. It can best be defined by its major objective, viz., the exploitation of all productive resources in order to expand real income of the district and eventually of the state. The district development will concern itself not only with man's material needs, but also with the improvement of the social conditions of his life. Development is, therefore, not only economic growth but growth plus change—social, cultural and institutional as well as economic.[25]

The First Five Year Plan recognised the importance of district plans[26] but practically little was done to concretize the concept. In fact, the preparation of the First Five Year Plan in the states took place mainly at the State headquarters.[27] The Second Plan further emphasized that when the Planning is undertaken on a national scale, a careful view has to be taken as to which programmes should form part respectively of the national, state and district plans. Besides this, the Second Plan also made a mention of the main programmes and activities for the formulation of district plans, inter-alia, providing for the setting up of the district development councils to coordinate the work of various agencies concerned with development.[28] However, nothing was achieved in this direction during the Second Five Year Plan. Practically, the Plans of the States had been prepared independent of local plans during the Second Plan.[29] The Third Plan too gave considerable importance to district level planning and also identified district level programmes and schemes which were similar to the activities outlined in the Second Plan.

The Fourth Plan (1969—74) laid down more and more stress on social justice and equality as well as the problems of weaker sections, Scheduled Castes and Tribes, and landless labour, as also on local and district planning to solve their problems. It further recognized that if the state plans are to succeed, their formulation in relation to physical features and resources and the institutional organizations in each area is the first requirement. Development needs not only financial resources and material inputs but personnel and the right kind of institutions. This requirement has to be worked out for each operational area. The natural corollary of beginning to plan realistically and from the bottom is to recognize that planning is not something that comes from outside or the above but what each state, district, locality and community does to develop its own resources and potentialities.[30] In the year 1969, the Planning Commission firmly recommended district as the unit of planning and implementation and also issued 'Guidelines for the Formulation of District Plans'.[31]

The resolution adopted by the National Development Council at its meeting held on March 18-19, 1978 approved the objectives of removal of unemployment, reduction in poverty and inequalities and continued progress towards "Self-reliance", and the Draft Five Year Plan 1978-83 too gave a lot of importance to district level planning, and stipulated that the district plan will have to be both a resource development as well as infra-structure plan for supporting the production-cum-employment thrust of the block level planning, and it will also take into consideration the institutional support available, inputs, services, and the marketing facilities that have to be developed.[32]

The Sixth Five-Year Plan (Revised) 1980-85 also envisaged important role for planning at the local level in agriculture, minor irrigation, animal husbandry, fisheries, marketing and processing, cottage and small-scale industries, local infrastructure and social services including water supply, housing, health, education, sanitation and local transport.[33] The Planning Commission further renewed its faith in the decentralization of planning to achieve the twin objectives of effective implementation of the anti-poverty programmes and a balanced regional development.[34]

In view of the need and importance of district development planning, most of the states have created the planning machinery at the district level. District planning Boards or Committees have been set up in Haryana, Punjab, Himachal Pradesh, Gujarat, Jammu and Kashmir, Karnatka, Madhya Pradesh, Maharashtra, Meghalaya, Nagaland, Rajasthan, Tamil Nadu, Uttar Pradesh, and West Bengal for the formulation of district plans, and the work of these Boards or Committees is looked after by the Collector in these states.

Having dealt with the evolution of district development in general, it is now proposed to deal with the objectives of district development planning.

## OBJECTIVES

Multi-level planning[35] has come to stay in India, and district as a unit of local-level (area) planning has a great role to play for achieving the dual objectives of increased production and equitable distribution within the policy frame of the state as well as of the Government of India. The objectives of district development planning, by and large, must emanate and conform to the objectives of national as well as state plans.

Thus, the broad objectives of district development plan have to be in conformity with the objectives of the national and state plans. It will be necessary to integrate the national and state objectives into the long term development potential of the district. Therefore, the initial general objectives which are in conformity with macro-plan objectives may be considered as the broad objectives of a perspective plan of the district. The specific objectives of a Five Year Plan of the district have to be formulated on the basis of an assessment of the immediate specific needs of the people of a district. In this exercise, the objectives of a district plan will be broadly identical with the macro-plan objectives though the programme of district plan will differ from district to district, depending upon their resource, potential and priority need.[36]

In view of the prevailing conditions, India has accepted area planning approach with weightage to target groups such as small farmers, marginal farmers, small artisans and landless labour. In this context, commonly accepted objectives of a target-group-oriented anti-poverty strategy[37] are: (a) higher productivity and increase in production or growth in GNP, (b) distributive justice or equity in sharing, or distribution of benefits of development, (c) employment, (d) people's participation, (e) self-reliance, and (f) maintenance of an ecological balance between the man and nature. These goals are not only interdependent and inter-linked but must be looked upon as a single package[38] to achieve integrated development.

The main objectives of the national planning are removal of unemployment, reduction in poverty, and inequality and continued progress towards self-reliance, and the state and district plans have to emulate these objectives keeping in view the potential, need and aspirations of the people. Depending upon the nature and characteristics of the district, objectives of a district plan would vary in emphasis from one district to another. An irrigated district will have a greater potential for crop production whereas a dry district would have potential for animal husbandry, sheep and goat rearing, sericulture, soil conservation and other activities allied to agriculture.

Thus, the main objectives of planning at the district level are firstly to achieve maximum benefits out of plan expenditure on the basis of past experience of local potential, needs and aspirations of the people, and secondly, to remove disparities in the level of development between different sub-regions of the district.[39] The objectives of district planning have been further elaborated as doubling the per capita income, provision of full employment, maximum utilization of available resources both human and material, opening up of backward areas, provision of basic minimum needs such as food, drinking water, health, housing, education, and cultural activities.[40]

A historical review of the planning process in India also shows that district planning has been consistently advocated, from one plan to another, as a means of achieving one or more of the following objectives: (a) ensuring local participation and local enthusiasm; (b) mobilizing local resources; (c) obtaining feed-back in terms of field level experiences for making planning process at the state level more realistic; (d) facilitating integrated physical planning to establish closer correspondence between resource endowment and potentials of an area and the contents and magnitude of development programmes taken up therein and greater complementarity between inter-dependent programmes falling within the sphere of different departments; and (e) accelerating the development of backward groups, areas, identifying growth inhibiting factors and counter-acting stagnation by providing for measures, facilities, and incentives specifically suited to the particular physio-geographic and socio-economic situation.[41]

In the paper entitled "Towards an Approach to the Fifth Plan," the Planning Commission has identified two major objectives of planning: (a) economic growth with distributive justice and (b) to provide minimum basic needs to the maximum number of citizens. Planning Commission has also recognized the need for micro-level planning to achieve these objectives.

Guidelines for the Formulation of District Plans issued by the Government of Haryana spelt out the following four inter-related objectives to be kept in view while preparing the district plans: (a) increase in the productivity per unit; (b) better utilization and conservation of natural resources; (c) more equitable distribution of the benefits of development between different areas and communities through more rational location of facilities and services; and (d) the expansion and diversification of employment opportunities.[42]

Following the guidelines of the Planning Commission, Maharashtra decided to adopt the district as the unit of planning and to formulate the perspective plans for each district with the twin objective of giving opportunity to all the districts to attain full development in keeping with their resources and of removing the imbalances in development as between districts and areas within the same district to the extent possible.[43] Now, the position in this regard in Thane and Karnal districts is presented below.

**Thane district**

District development planning was introduced in Thane district[44] as also in other districts in Maharashtra in its most rudimentary form in 1972, and it picked up subsequently. The policy of district planning was pursued vigorously by the State Government from 1974-75 i.e., with the commencement of the Fifth Five-Year Plan to achieve the following objectives: (a) securing full development of natural and other resource potential of a district, and (b) attaining parity in the matter of certain social and economic infrastructural facilities over a period of 15 to 20 years so that the disparities in levels of development as between different districts as also between different areas within the same district are ironed out during the period of the perspective plan.[45] Major factors responsible for the introduction of district planning in Thane district as also in other districts in Maharashtra have been:

(a) setting up the Planning Sub-Committee of the Cabinet under the chairmanship of the Chief Minister to take decisions on various vital issues such as allocable funds between the state and district sector schemes, and approval of formula for allocation of funds amongst the districts;

(b) identification of state and district sector schemes by the state government, and laying down of priorities for various schemes to be included in the district plans;

(c) determination of shares of state and district schemes out of the state plan;
(d) existence of a strong planning organization at the state level headed by the Planning Minister to provide technical advice and guidance in the formulation of plans at all levels.
(e) communication of financial ceilings to the DPDCs by the Planning Department;
(f) preparation of a separate Tribal Areas Sub-Plan (TASP) within the prescribed financial ceilings;
(g) setting up of the District Planning and Development Council, its Executive Committee and Special Executive Committee for formulation and monitoring of the district plan as well as to bring about coordination between various implementing agencies at the district level;
(h) appointment of the Collector as the Member Secretary of the DPDC, to look after the work of formulation, monitoring and evaluation of the district plan;
(i) setting up of the district planning unit to attend to the work of the district plans; and
(j) evolution of certain imaginative and innovative procedures under the district planning process in Maharashtra in order to make district planning a realistic and effective process. Some of these are discussed below:

*Release of grants*

The administrative departments concerned with the provision in the budget voted by the State Legislature directly release the funds to the district level officers responsible for implementing schemes under intimation to the Heads of the Departments instead of channelizing such releases to the district officers through the Heads of Departments. This has served to cut down the delays in the release of funds to the district level.

*Reappropriation*

In order to ensure that the financial allocation made available to each district for its annual plan is utilized in the same district, the DPDC has been given the freedom to recommend reappropriation of savings within the district itself, subject to certain limitations relating to the programmes in the core sectors. It has also been laid down that the reappropriations approved by the DPDCs should be given effect to by the Heads of Departments.

*Accountability of the district officers to the DPDC*

Orders have been passed by the State Government specifying that the district level officers are accountable to the DPDC for the implementation of the programmes at the district level. The progress of schemes is also being reviewed by the "Executive Committee" as also by the Special Executive Committee of the DPDC. During these meetings, district officers are given appropriate directions for better implementation of the schemes.

*Incorporation of the district plans in the state plan*

Various stages through which the District Annual Plans are finalized are prescribed by the Planning Department so as to incorporate the district plans in the state plan in time. The district plans so finalized are integrated in the state plan for seeking the approval of the State Legislature and thereafter communicated to the DPDC for being adopted as a final district plan.

**Karnal district**

In 1972, Government decided to constitute District Planning Advisory Boards in all the districts[46] in the State. District Planning Advisory Board, Karnal, was constituted under the chairmanship of the Deputy Commissioner, Karnal to advise the district authorities about the programmes to be taken up for systematic socio-economic development of the district. Guidelines for the formulation of district plans[47] were sent to the Deputy Commissioner, in 1972, and he was asked that these should not be construed as exhaustive or final in any respect. He was accordingly charged with the responsibilities of drawing up the plan for the district.[48]

A separate district plan unit was also set up in the

Planning Department to coordinate as well as to give technical guidance to the concerned district officers. This unit was to be headed by the District Planning Officer. The Government decided in 1972 to appoint a District Planning Officer, Karnal, alongwith the supporting staff. In 1972, an HCS Officer was posted as District Planning Officer who relinquished the charge on 27.12.72. Thereafter, the post of the District Planning Officer was not filled up, and the planning work was entrusted to the Additional General Assistant to the Deputy Commissioner in 1973 in addition to his normal duties. Subsequently, this work was entrusted to the District Statistical Officer, Karnal with effect from 18.4.1974 in addition to his own duties.

The constraints which thwarted the evolution of district development planning in Karnal[49] as also in other districts of Haryana are: (a) lack of mechanism to provide authenticated guidance to district level authorities in matters regarding classification and reclassification of state and district sector schemes, and sharing of funds between the state and district sector schemes, (b) lack of a formula for the distribution of funds among the districts, (c) non-existence of the district planning unit, (d) non-communication of firm financial ceilings to the district authorities, (e) ineffective district planning bodies, and (f) lack of mechanism for dovetailing the district plans in the State Plan.

## OVERVIEW

Development may be viewed as a multi-dimensional concept encompassing the acceleration of economic growth on the one hand; and elimination or reduction of poverty, inequality and unemployment on the other. It also involves major changes in social structures, nation building institutions, values, attitudes, and beliefs of the people so as to uplift them towards condition of life perceived as materially and socially better than the existing one. However, development concept in itself cannot lead a country towards better life. The nation has to take a series of actions to achieve the development so conceived, and these may be designated as the Planning Process.

Planning may be defined as a process of rational decision-making to achieve certain pre-determined goals in the long run, say five or ten years. Planning is, therefore, an exercise in which the government have to (a) choose objectives, (b) arrange resources, (c) spell out policies, strategies and targets, and (d) organize a framework for implementing, coordinating, and monitoring the plan.

The dual goal of development planning is (a) economic growth, and (b) development of man in the growing society but it cannot be achieved through the instrumentality of central planning as is being generally done in India. In fact, development of man as a member of the growing society has to be principally attempted from a level of administration from which he, his problems and difficulties could be seen, identified and sorted out. It is a well-established fact that the objects of planning, that is, the poor, are found in the villages and towns within the district, and as such the development planning process has to be brought to the district level or below to solve their problems so as to enable them to participate in the process of socio-economic development. That is why, the importance of district planning is emphasised in all the plan documents to achieve better results. The district planning system cannot be transplanted in any state but has to be evolved by consistent and steady efforts of the administrative leadership which is expected to bring the results of planning to the doorsteps of the poor and the less privileged.

In Thane district as also in other districts in Maharashtra, the district planning process has been conceptualised, evolved and operationalized over a period of time and the main factors that really gave shape to it, apart from political commitment, are: setting up of a high-powered Planning Sub-Committee of the Cabinet Committee headed by the Chief Minister, defining the scope and contents of a district plan, measures for the disaggregation of allocations, constitution of the DPDC and of the planning machinery, and delegation of administrative and financial powers. Moreover, formulation of district plans is not the privilege of bureaucracy alone at the district level but of the DPDC on which both officials and non-officials are represented. This body is headed by the designated Minister of the district and responsible for the formulation of district annual plans and monitoring their implementation. Therefore, the district planning system, as evolved, has become a "growing concern" in Thane and other districts of Maharashtra.

The experience of Karnal, as also in other districts in Haryana, on the other hand, shows that the district development planning remained mostly a concern of the officer of the rank of the Deputy Plan Advisor in the Planning Department at the state level, as a result of which, it did not get going at the district level where even the regular District Planning Officer could not be posted to look after the plan work. The District Planning Advisory Board, the District Planning Committee and the District Planning Executive Committee had rarely met for the purpose for which they were constituted. These planning bodies like many other bodies merely remained ornamental. The planning process in Karnal did not take off because most of essential prerequisites obtaining in Thane were missing here.

In view of the need and significance of district planning within the multi-level planning frame, it appears imperative to conceptualize and operationalise the district planning process as a system. The main issues that require close examination in this regard are: what range of activities should be included in the district level schemes? Is the existing model of district planning process as contained in the "Guidelines" of the Planning Commission adequate? What should be the criteria for the allocation of funds to the state and district level schemes and what should be the formula for their reallocation amongst the districts? What mechanism can be devised to secure effective people's participation? Should the Collector continue to play key coordinating role? How can monitoring and evaluation be made effective instruments to remove bottlenecks in the successful implementation of the district level schemes? Some of these issues have been discussed in the succeeding chapters.

## REFERENCES

1. The Third World stand for the developing countries of Asia, Africa and Latin America whereas the economically advanced capitalist countries led by USA are in the First World and the socialist countries in the Second World.

2. Michael P. Todaro, Economic Development In The Third World; Longman, London 1981, p. 68.
3. Paul Streeten, Development Perspective, Macmillan Press Ltd; London, 1981, p. 108.
4. Ibid.
5. S.K. Sharma, Development Administration in India, Theory and Practice, International Book Co., Jullundur, 1971, p. 4.
6. Michael P. Todaro, op. cit., p. 68.
7. S.K. Sharma (ED), Dynamics of Development: An International Perspective (Vol.I), Concept Pubilshing Company, Delhi, 1978, p. 2.
8. Dudley Seers, The meaning of development, Eleventh World Conference of the Society for International Development, New Delhi (1969), p. 3.
9. United Nations, Integrated, Approach to Rural Development in Africa, New York, 1971, p. 1.
10. Michael P. Todaro, op. cit., p. 70.
11. K. Pattarswamaiah, Aspects of Planning, Oxforda nd IBH Publishing Co., New Delhi, 1977, pp. 1-2.
12. Michael P. Todaro, op. cit., p. 430.
13. S.K. Sharma (Ed), Dynamics of Development: op. cit., p. 280.
14. Mixed economy is characterized by the existence of an institutional setting in which part of the productive resources are privately owned and operated while the other part is controlled by the public sector.
15. Refer Constitution of India, Preamble.
16. Refer Constitution of India, Article 38.
17. Tripathy, Rao and Thupliyal, A Manual for Formulation and Implementation of Block Plan, National Institute of Rural Development, Hyderabad, 1981, p. 2.
18. Ibid., p. 2.
19. P.R.Dubhashi, Administration And The Task of Nation-Building in India: Public Administration Journal, Dec., 1981, Published by the Public Administration Campus, Institute of Management, Tribhuvan University, Dillibazar, Kathmandu, Nepal, p. 5.
20. Conference of the State Ministers of Rural Development, Community Development and Panchayati Raj held at New Delhi on 8th May, 1975.
21. T.N. Chaturvedi, Challenges to Rural Development (Mimeo) University Grants Commission Seminar from February 13th-15th, 1982, Punjabi University, Patiala, p. 4.
22. Ministry of Education and Social Welfare. The Gazetteer of India, Vol. III, Economic Structure and Activities, New Delhi, 1975, p. 1222.
23. India is a vast country and have multiple units of Administration such as national, state, division, district, tehsil, block and village. In view of its vastness, it is necessary to have effective planning at all these levels.
24. B. Mehta, District Administration in the Past and in Future, *The*

*Indian Journal of Public Administration*, (July, Sept., 1971), IIPA New Delhi, p. 522.

25. B. Venkatappiah, Member, Planning Commission, District Development and District Administration: Address delivered on August 23, 1968, under the auspices of the Indian Institute of Public Administration, Mysore Regional Prant, Banglore.
26. Government of India, Planning Commission, First Five Year Plan, New Delhi, 1952, p. 140.
27. Planning Commission, Second Five Year Plan, New Delhi 1956, p. 150.
28. Second Five Year Plan, p. 158.
29. Planning Commission, Third Five Year Plan, p. 334.
30. Planning Commission, Fourth Five Year Plan (1969-74), p. 111.
31. Planning Commission issued these guidelines to the States and Union Territories for the formulation of district plans in the year 1969. The main idea behind this was that the states should adopt district as the unit of planning and take suitable steps towards decentralized planning at the district level. However, states were free to adopt these guidelines for the formulation of district plans or evolve their own guidelines by modifying these guidelines.
32. Five Year Plan 1978-83, p. 160.
33. Sixth Five Year Plan (Revised) 1980-85, p. 93.
34. The Approach to the Seventh Five Year Plan (1985-90).
35. Multi level (area) planning refers to planning at various levels such as national, state district, town, block, cluster of villages, and even a village.
36. G. Thimmaiah, District as a unit of Sub-Regional Planning in India (Mimeo), Training Programme on District and Block Level Planning (June 22-July 11, 1981), Sardar Patel Institute of Economic and Social Research, Ahmedabad, p. 11.
37. Refer R.C. Malhotra, (Ed.), Local Level Planning and Rural Development Alternative Strategies, Concept Publishing House, New Delhi, 1980, pp. 18-20.
38. Ibid., p. 21.
39. Tribhuvan Prasad: Concepts, significance, and limitations of District Planning (Mimeo), Background Paper No. 2 on Seminar on District Planning, June 3-June 10, 1973, Lal Bahadur Shastri National Academy of Administration Mussoorie, p. 1.
40. K.A. Sundaram: District Development Planning in Tamil Nadu (Mimeo), Seminar on District Planning, June 3-June 10, 1973, Lal Bahadur Shastri National Academy of Administratian, Mussoorie, p. 1.
41. Anand Swarup: Development Planning for Integrated Development (Mimeo), Seminar on District Planning (June 3-10, 1973), Lal Bahadur Shastri National Academy of Administration, Mussoorie, p. 1. Also see District Planning, Special Issue, (Spring 1975), Journal

of The Lal Bahadur Shastri National Academy of Administration, Mussoorie, p. 11.

42. Government of Haryana, Guidelines for the Formulation of District Plans, 1972, p. 21.
43. Government of Maharashrta, Resolution GAD/No. FD/SPM/ 1072, dated 20-10-1972, p. 1.
44. This information has been condensed from the Govt. resolution, letters and circulars issued from time to time from 1972 to 1983.
45. Government of Maharashtra, Planning Department, Note on Planning Process and Planning Organization in Maharashtra for use of the proposed Conference of State Planning Ministers at New Delhi on the 4th April, 1981 pp. 12-13. Also see paper on District Planning in Maharashtra presented in the workshop on Seminar on District and Block Level Planning from 27th to 29th April, 1983, p. 2.
46 No. ESA (DP)-80/21696, dated 10th September 1980 from the Economic and Statistical Advisor to the Government of Haryana to the Commissioner and Secretary to Government of Haryana, Planning Department.
47. These guidelines are issued in the form of a booklet and are based largely on the guidelines for the formulation of district plans issued by the Planning Commission.
48. D.O. Letter No. 36 (17)-pg. (h)-72/32107, dated 3rd October, 1972 from Shri N.N. Kashyap, ICS, Financial Commissioner, Revenue, Haryana to Shri H.V. Goswami, I.A.S., Deputy Commissioner, Karnal, p. 1-2.
49. Based on personal interviews with the district level officers, as also with the state level officers dealing with the work of district planning.

# 3

# SCOPE OF DISTRICT PLANNING

DISTRICT planning is likely to remain a dream in the absence of a clear delineation of the scope of activities which could be planned and implemented at the district level. The Government of India and the State Governments can formulate plans on various subjects falling in the "Union List" and "State List" respectively. As far as subjects in the "Concurrent List"[1] are concerned, both the Union and the States are competent to formulate plans but the Union Government have over-riding authority over the states. Thus, there is no constitutional provision enabling the "Local Units" such as districts and blocks to formulate their development plans. In this way, local level planning can not be undertaken at the district or lower levels unless this function is delegated by the state in favour of such levels. In view of this, the state Government has to take a "hard decision"[2] to demarcate the state and district sector schemes if it has to go in for district level planning.

Despite the fact that there is no 'district list' in the Constitution authorizing the districtsto plan their development activities, even then the need to undertake planning at these units has always been emphasised, especially in view of the big size of the country. The planners realized the significance of districts development planning from the very inception of the planning era and rightly made a mention of it in all the plan documents without any exception. The First Five Year Plan emphasized the importance of district plans within the frame of the state plans but nothing was done to concretize the concept. As a result, the formulation of the First Five Year Plan in the states was done at the state headquarters.

The Second Five Year Plan showed a concern for district development planning[3] and included the following main activities in the ambit of district plan: (a) the community development and national extension programme; (b) social welfare extension projects; (c) agricultural production programme and allied activities in the field of rural development such as animal husbandry and soil conservation; (d) development of cooperatives; (e) village panchayats; (f) village and small industries; (g) schemes for utilizing effectively resources developed through state projects for irrigation, electricity, communication, industrial development and expansion of trainning facilities; (h) housing and urban development; (i) the programme of small savings; ( j) aiding construction projects through labour cooperatives and sharamdan; (k) programme for the welfare of backward classes; (l) programme in rural and urban areas relating to social services, especially expansion of education at primary and secondary levels, health units, health education, sanitation, malaria control, and family planning; (m) utilizing and assisting voluntary organizations engaged in constructive social work; (n) land reforms; (o) prohibition work; (p) dissemination of information about programmes of national, state, regional and local development.[4]

Thus, the Second Plan made an attempt to demarcate the activities which could be planned and implemented with advantage at the district level but practically nothing was realized out of this concept due to lack of experience in this regard as well as its newness to the planning culture which stood for centralized planning only at the centre and states.

The Third Plan gave considerable importance to local level planning, and suggested that in the following fields, proposals for the Third Plan should be drawn up by states on the basis of district and block plans: (a) agriculture, including minor irrigation, soil conservation, animal husbandry, and dairying, (b) development of cooperatives, (c) village industries, (d) elementary education, specially provision of school buildings for local communities, (e) rural water supply, and programme of minimum rural amenities, including construction of approach roads linking each village to the nearest road or rail head, and

(f) works programmes for the utilization of manpower resources in rural areas.

The scope of the district plan as defined in the Planning Commission's Memorandum on the Fourth Five Year Plan was also similar to that of the Second Five Year Plan.[6] The scope of activities outlined in the Guidelines for the Formulation of District Plans issued by the Government of Haryana in the year 1977 was also quite close to the scope of district planning propounded in the Second and Fourth Plans.[7]

There have been different views about categorization of schemes[8] and some scholars would like the planning responsibilities at the district level to be limited to only select aspects.[9] Others would like greater emphasis to be placed on potential aspects while formulating local plans[10], but the underlying concern everywhere is the effective utilization of resources.[11] The first step in the formulation of a district plan is the demarcation of development activities which should go into the district plan.[12] Such a demarcation is necessary because the district level plan is one of the four recognised levels of planning in India and this step alone will bring the planning process to the district level.

In a conceptual framework, the scope of district planning can be examined under two possible approaches, namely (a) demand and supply approach; and (b) potentiality approach.

According to the first approach, the district should plan only for such sectors for which the order of consumption (demand) and production (supply) is likely to be in equilibrium. This approach stresses the point that a district will not find it feasible to plan for such sectors whose demands originate outside the district and, therefore, a district should limit its planning responsibility to such sectors which serve the local market. According to this approach, major irrigation projects, power, and state highways would fall within the state sector schemes; and land development programmes, family planning, and primary education will fall within district sector schemes. Since "backward and forward linkages" for most of the development activities generally lie outside the district, it would, therefore, neither be desirable nor practicable to adopt this approach in planning at the district level.

According to the second approach, a district should plan around its potentialities determined on the basis of resource endowment, manpower specialization, and infrastructure.[13] In this case, development of an "export sector" is a pre-condition for the development of a district and, therefore, utmost attention to planning of this sector should be given in the preparation of plans for the districts. This approach relies on the operation of market mechanism for bringing about equilibrium in the demand and supply of goods not at the district level but at some higher level of geographical aggregation. In this approach, the district will plan comprehensively for the total economy keeping in view the potential but certain activities such as major irrigation and power generation would be indicated for state level planning.

Thus, a clear distinction is required to be made between the state and district sector schemes. Schemes such as research and training in agriculture, surveys for ground water, major irrigation projects, power generation, large and medium industries, university education, and major water supply schemes for the cities, are included in the state sector schemes whereas all other activities are included in the district sector schemes.[14]

In the District Planning Guidelines[15], the Planning responsibility at the district level has been looked at both from the points of view of the district as well as the state. Decisions in respect of (a) rural and panchayat roads, (b) elementary and secondary education, (c) welfare of educationally and socially backward classes, (d) social welfare, and (e) training for farmers, craftsmen and artisans can be wholly taken at the district level and planning of: (a) agriculture production, minor irrigation development, and soil conservation; (b) animal husbandry including dairying and milk supply; (c) forestry; (d) community development and cooperation; (e) village and small industries; (f) road transport; (g) warehousing and marketing; (h) health and family planning; (i) housing-urban and rural; and (j) town planning and urban development can be planned at the district levels within the constraints of state policies whereas planning in respect of (a) agricultural education; (b) veterinary education; (c) medical education; (d) technical education; (e) university education; (f) medium irrigation, ayacut development, soil conservation, river valley projects; (g) inland waterways; (h) large and medium industries, large scale cooperative processing units, power development; (i) water supply schemes, and (j) tourism will be done by the state Government.

State plan schemes have been demarcated into district sector schemes and state sector schemes. Agricultural production, soil conservation, forests, fisheries, animal husbandry, marketing, minor irrigation, ayacut development under minor irrigation projects, primary and secondary education, district and village roads, health, water supply and sanitation, urban development, welfare of backward classes, social welfare, housing and cooperation fall within the district sector schemes; and the schemes like generation and distribution of power, major and medium irrigation projects, major and medium industries and investment in corporate bodies, university education, professional and technical education, surveys, research and training, state highways, ayacut development under major and medium projects, ports and inland waterways are the state sector schemes.[16]

Now, the experience with regard to the scope of district development planning in both the study districts in Haryana and Maharashtra is being discussed.[17]

### District level schemes in Karnal[18]

In the earliest document available, the state plan included two kinds of schemes: (a) state schemes, and (b) local schemes. In the first category were the schemes which though located in a particular district benefitted the whole state. As many as 270 schemes were included in the state schemes in the Second Five-Year Plan (1956-61).[19] In the second category were schemes which served local needs even though some of them covered more than one district.[20] In this district, as many as 134 local schemes were included in the scope of district plan in the Second Five Year Plan (1956-61). Main categories of schemes included in the local schemes were (a) agriculture production, (b) minor irrigation, (c) consolidation of holdings, (d) animal husbandry, (e) fisheries, (f) community projects and national extension service, (g) cooperation, (h) village panchayats, (i) Bhakhra Nangal Project, (j) major and medium irrigation projects, (k) power projects, (l) industries, (m) education, (n) roads, (o) road transport, (p) development of national and regional languages, (q) health, (r) housing, (s) labour and labour welfare, (t) welfare of Scheduled Castes and other backward classes, (u) removal of untouchability, (v) welfare of Criminal Tribes, (w) social welfare, (x) development of mandis and factories, (y) statistics, and (z) publicity.[21]

In another Five Year Plan of Karnal,[22] the schemes which were included in the scope of district plan were divided under two categories (a) Agriculture Production Plan, and (b) Other Sectors. The following schemes were included in the Agriculture Production Plan[23]: (a) inputs such as irrigation, water management, cropping pattern, fertilizers and other inputs; and (b) infrastructure comprising of farm credit, storage, drainage, power, roads and administrative support. The other sectors consisted of (a) cattle development, and (b) forests only.[24] Therefore, the scope of schemes included in Fourth Five Year Plan of this district was confined to agriculture and allied sector with added emphasis on irrigation schemes to increase agriculture production.[25]

In the Fifth District Plan, the schemes included were mostly those for which districtwise break-up had been possible. State level projects like power and irrigation did not figure in the draft as they benefitted more than one district and bifurcation in respect of these projects was not available easily.[26] Development plan of this district (1974-1979) included in it the following main categories of schemes[27]: (a) agriculture, (b) irrigation, (c) animal husbandry, and dairy farming, (d) forests, (e) industries, (f) cooperation, (g) education, (h) industrial training, (i) medical and health, (j) roads, (k) labour welfare, (l) social welfare, (m) welfare of Scheduled Castes, (n) public health, (o) panchayats, (p) drainage, (q) tourism, (r) housing, (s) fisheries, (t) town and country planning, and (u) publicity.[28]

Now, the experience of Thane district in Maharashtra is being discussed at length highlighting therein the criteria adopted for the identification or classification of the district level schemes and the activities actually classified as district level schemes from time to time.

**District-level schemes in Thane[29]**

In Maharashtra, district level planning was pursued vigorously from 1974-75. The State Government had identified the state and the district sector schemes. The criteria for determining whether a scheme belongs to the state or district sector is based on its location and the area to be benefitted. Based on this criteria, schemes like (a) generation and distribution of power, (b) major irrigation projects costing over Rs. 5 crores, (c) investments in corporate sectors and other institutions, (d) surveys, research and training programmes, (e) administrative and residential buildings, (f) universities including agricultural universities and institutions of professional education like engineering and medical colleges, but excluding arts, science and commerce colleges and polytechnics, (g) the state and national highways and (h) ports, are categorized as state level schemes. These schemes are formulated at the state level and their implementation is entrusted to the directorates through their field staff. Generally, these schemes are located and implemented in more than one district or a group of districts or the whole state, and their benefits accrue to more than one district or a group of districts or the whole state. In some cases, the state level schemes may be located or implemented in one district, but their benefits may accrue to a group of districts or the whole state. For instance, medical college may be located in a particular district but its benefits will accrue to the whole state as the admission of candidates in such a college is done on merit from throughout the state.

Programmes like (a) agricultural production, (b) medium minor irrigation, (c) soil conservation, (d) ayacut development, (e) animal husbandry, (f) dairy development, (g) forest, (h) fisheries, (i) warehousing and marketing, (j) cooperation and community development, (k) small scale industries, (l) education, (m) social welfare, and (n) backward classes are categorized as district level schemes. The district sector is really the residuary sphere and whatever is not specifically included in the state sector belongs to the district sector.[30]

In the Fourth and Fifth Five Year Plans of Thane district, the district level schemes were broadly grouped as (a) agricultural production programme, cooperation and community development; (b) irrigation and power; (c) industries, mining, transport and communication; and (d) social welfare.

During the course of the Fifth and Sixth Five-Year Plans, distinction between the state and district level schemes had been further sharpend, and a third category of schemes known as "state pool schemes"[31] had also been evolved. Therefore, the schemes are now reclassified as: (a) state level schemes; (b) state pool schemes; and (c) district level schemes. Schemes such as power, major irrigation projects costing over Rs. 5 crores, investment in corporate sectors and other institutions, research, state and national highways, are state level schemes while the following district level schemes are being financed from the state pool in this district[32]: (a) employment guarantee scheme, (b) horticulture, (c) social forestry, (d) forest: (i) wild life and nature conservation, and (ii) protection of forests, (e) dairy development, except dairy cooperatives; (f) Bhatsa medium irrigation project, (g) road development: (i) infrastructure facilities for state transport services, and (ii) Sakar special programmes for district roads, (h) schemes relating to control of communicable diseases: (aa) control of malaria, (bb) control of Falaria, (cc) control of I-B. (including BCG vaccination), (dd) cholera control programme, and (ee) V.D. control programme.

As far as the identification of district level schemes is concerned, it has been done fairly over a long period from 1974 to 1983. The district level schemes were standardized and consolidated by the Planning Department in the year 1977-78 and sent to the DPDCs for the formulation of district annual plans for 1978-79.[33] Broadly, all these schemes are grouped under six main groups[34] as: (a) agriculture and allied services,[35] (b) cooperation[36], (c) water and power development,[37] (d) industry and mining,[38] (e) transport and communication,[39] and (f) social and community services.[40]

The final position as to the number of standardized district level schemes included in the district annual plan in Maharashtra and Thane district in particular is given below:

**District sector schemes (Non-Tribal and Tribal) in Maharashtra***

| Group | Total no. of district sector schemes | Non-Tribal schemes provided for from column 2 | Tribal schemes provided for from column 2 |
|---|---|---|---|
| 1 | 2 | 3 | 4 |
| Agriculture and allied services | 136 | 114 | 76 |
| Cooperation | 38 | 17 | 22 |
| Water and power development | 173 | 152 | 19 |
| Industry and mining | 15 | 14 | 1 |
| Transport and communication | 19 | 19 | 8 |
| Social and community services | 201 | 183 | 75 |
| Total: | 582 | 499 | 201 |

**District sector schemes (Non-Tribal and Tribal) in Thane***

| Group | Total no. of district sector schemes | Non-Tribal schemes provided for from column 2 | Tribal schemes provided for from column 2 |
|---|---|---|---|
| 1 | 2 | 3 | 4 |
| Agriculture and allied services | 87 | 74 | 51 |
| Cooperation | 16 | 8 | 7 |
| Water and power development | 6 | 5 | 5 |
| Industry and mining | 9 | 6 | 3 |
| Transport and communication | 10 | 10 | 6 |
| Social and community services | 129 | 123 | 63 |
| Total: | 257 | 226 | 135 |

**Explanation*: Some of the schemes are common for both Tribals and Non-Tribals, and occur under columns 3 and 4. Hence, their totals do not tally with the grand totals in col. 2.

It is clear from the above tables that as many as 582 schemes under six groups are categorized as district level schemes in Maharashtra besides 18 such schemes being financed from the state pool.[41] In Thane, 257 schemes (refer Appendix I) are categorized as district level schemes[42] besides 8 such schemes being financed from the State pool. 226 district level schemes are formulated under the Non-TASP and 135 under the TASP[43] in this district. Therefore, the scope of the district level schemes to be included in the district plan is clearly defined for Thane district, as also for other districts in Maharashtra, and the DPDC constituted under the Chairmanship of the designated Minister formulates the district plan every year in respect of these schemes within the financial ceiling communicated to it by the Planning Department.

The scope of district planning in Thane has two major limitations and constraints. These are; (a) that the DRDA schemes are outside the scope of the district planning, and (b) that the planning of pool schemes is also kept out of the scope of district plans. DPDC Thane is required to make provision of funds in respect of the DRDA schemes from its financial ceiling and formulation of schemes is done by the DRDA, Thane[44] and the DPDC has no say in planning these rural development schemes. The State Government wanted to bring the formulation of these schemes in the fold of the DPDC but the Government of India did not agree to deviate from the all India pattern,[45] as a result of which this important programme is kept out of the scope of the district planning.[46] Pool schemes[47] are also district level schemes but planned by the concerned directorates at the state level and financed from the state pool.[48] Therefore, these schemes are also kept out of the scope of district planning.

## OVERVIEW

District planning is one of the most vital links in the multi-level planning system, and the starting point is to clearly identify the activities and schemes which can be planned and implemented at this level within the indicative financial ceiling. There is no constitutional provision or any other legal sanction to initiate the process of planning at the district level, and as such district planning has to emanate from the "political will" to be demonstrated by the political leadership taking a firm decision to initiate a delegated planning process at this level. Decentralized planning is an article of faith, and requires the leadership to take a hard decision to identify district level schemes by shedding its authority to that extent, and that too without abdicating its overall responsibility.

The scope of district planning, duly backed by political will and financial ceiling, has been clearly demarcated in Maharashtra by way of classification and reclassification of district level schemes. This step alone has given realism to the district planning as a concept, and district plans cease to be mere shopping lists or catalogues of demands. Thane district has adopted suitable schemes having potential in the district. Keeping in view the list of schemes being included in the district plan of Thane district, it is clear that potentiality approach has been adopted there, and the schemes which directly benefit the district have been classified as district level schemes. In Haryana, standardization of the district level schemes has not been done primarily because of lack of mechanism for the classification of state and district sector schemes, as a result of which the scope of district planning is what the district level officers think of, and that too without any indication of financial ceiling. Therefore, district planning process remained a non-starter in Karnal district.

Identification of district schemes, though a prerequisite to operationalize the district planning, is not enough in itself. It will also be necessary to evolve a sound process of district planning for the formulation of district plan, and as such this vital aspect is being examined in details in the next chapter.

## REFERENCES

1. Refer Constitution of India, Seventh Schedule.
2. Taste of power is really very sweet, and the authorities at the state level would not like to delegate administrative and financial powers to its constitutents that is, district and block levels as it involves

sheding of their own powers to that extent. Recent trend in the states is towards centralization instead of decentralization in favour of district level. If the political leadership at the state level has to introduce planning at the district level, then it has to take firm decision without yielding to any pressure from any quarter including from within which is generally irresistable.

3. The idea of district planning is as old as the planning history of India. The First Five Year Plan referred to district plans, and the role of the local institutions in the planning process. It was symbolized by the phrase "planning from below".
4. Planning Commission, Second Five Year Plan, 1966, pp. 156 and 158.
5. Planning Commission, Third Five Year Plan, p. 334.
6. Planning Commission; Memorandum on the Fourth Plan, New Delhi, 1964, pp. 80-81.
7. Refer Chapter III and IV of Guidelines for Formulation of District Plan, Government of Haryana, Chandigarh, 1972.
8. Refer Tribhuvan Prasad, Concepts, Significance and Limitations of District Planning (Mimeo), Seminar on District Planning, June 3-June 10, 1973, Lal Bahadur Shastri National Academy of Administration, Mussoorie, pp. 5-6.
9. Refer S. Chakravarti, The Planning Process in India; An Appraisal and a Framework (Mimeo), Planning Commission, New Delhi: 1972.
10. Local plans refers to district and block plans, as also village production plans.
11. Government of India, Planning Commission: The Planning Process.
12. G.Thimaiah, District As a unit of Sub-Regional Planning in India, Training Programme on District and Block Level Planning (June 22-July 11, 1981), Sardar Patel Institute of Economic and Social Research, Ahmedabad, p. 10. Also refer Om Parkash Mathur, Planning For Districts: Some Problems in Developing An Analytical System, Journal of the Lal Bahadur Shastri National Academy of Administration, Mussoorie, p. 28.
13. Ibid., p.30.
14. In Andhra Pradesh, this is the pattern of demarcation of state and district sector schemes.
15. Madras State Planning Commission, District Planning Guidelines to District Collectors.
16. Refer Planning Commission's No. PC(P) 27/2/82-MLP, dated 2.6.1982. Also see District Planning in Karnataka, IIPA-First Course on Planning for Rural Development Feb. 7-19, 1983, New Delhi, pp. 1-2
17. This information contained in the ensuing paragraphs is condensed from the Government Resolutions, Circulars, Notifications, and letters issued from time to time.
18. This information is summarized from the official record and plan document of Karnal district.

19. Second Five Year Plan: Punjab State: District Karnal (1956-61), Controller of Printing and Stationery, Punjab 1958, Part IV, pp. 27-41.
20. Ibid., p. 2.
21. Ibid., pp. 15-27

    Although a large number of "local schemes" were provided for in the Second Five Year Plan of Karnal yet the planning exercises were not undertaken at the district level. Local level schemes alongwith financial provisions were merely culled out of the state plan abstracts.
22. Fourth Five Year Plan Of Karnal District (Haryana), A Draft Outline (prepared by the Deputy Commissioner, Karnal, Haryana Dairy No. 27, D.P.O. Karnal, dated 22.8.73).
23. Ibid., pp. 16-127.
24. Ibid., pp. 128-153.
25. The District Plan Karnal was not integrated with the State Five Year Plan and as such schemes included in this district plan were not backed by financial sanctions.
26. Government of Haryana, Development Plan of Karnal District (Fifth Plan and Perspective), Chandigarh, p. 2.
27. Ibid., p. 3.
28. This Plan document could not be integrated in the State Five Year Plan, and as such the schemes included in it were not backed by financial sanctions through budgetary mechanism.
29. This information is based on letters issued by the Govt. of Maharashtra from time to time. Detailed Statements Of Outlays Provided For District Level Schemes In The Annual Plan, 1981-82, 1982-83, and 1983-84, and personal interviews with the State and district level officers in Bombay and Thane districts respectivcly.
30. Planning Commission's No. PC (P) 27/2/82-MLP, dated 2.6.1982.
31. State Pool schemes are district level schemes which are formulated and finalized at the state level and funds required therefore are taken out of the total allocations for district level schemes. The aggregate amount so taken out constitutes a state level pool, out of which these schemes are financed. However, the funds so incurred are finally shown against the district in which these schemes are implemented.
32. This information is collected from the office of the District Planning Officer, Thane.
33. Circular No. DPC-1078/PRG-B, dated 29-8-1977, Planning Department, Government of Maharashtra, Bombay, pp. 17-27.
34. Refer Detailed Statements Of Outlays Provided For District Level Schemes In The Annual Plan For 1983-84, pp. i-xxvi.
35. Refer Detailed Statements Of Outlays Provided For District Level Schemes In The Annual Plan, 1983-84, Government of Maharashtra, Bombay, 1983, pp. i-x.

36. Ibid., p. x.
37. Ibid., pp. i-xii.
38. Ibid., pp. xiii-xiv.
39. Ibid., pp. xiv-xvi.
40. Ibid., pp. xvii-xxiv.
41. Circular No. DPC-1082/Desp-17, dated 5.10.82 issued by the Planning Department, Government of Maharashtra, Bombay, regarding the formulation of District Annual Plan, 1983-84, Annexure II.
42. This figure is culled out of Detailed Statements Of Outlys Provided for District Level Schemes In The Annual Plan, 1983-84.
43. In Thane district, separate Tribal Area Sub Plan (TASP) and General Plan also known as Non-TASP are formulated within the financial ceilings communicated by the Planning Department, and finally dovetailed in the district Plan.
44. DRDA Thane is a registered society under the Indian Societies Registration Act, 1860 and provides subsidy to the small farmers @ 25 per cent as well as to the marginal farmers and landless labourers @ 33 per cent of the total financial requirement of the scheme, and the remaining amount is raised as loan from the commercial and cooperative banks. It has two bodies, that is, Governing Council (which functions under the chairmanship of the Chief Executive Officer, Zila Parishad, Thane from 1.6.1982 instead of the District Collector): and the General Body (whose meetings are presided over by the designated Minister) that are responsible for planning the schemes in the district. Accordingly, the schemes of the DRDA Thane are approved by these bodies subject to the final approval of the State Level Committee.
45. Based on my personal interviews with the Project Officer of the DRDA Thane.
46. However, the implementation of all the schemes of the DRDA Thane is reviewed by the DPDC Thane or its Execntive Committee.
47. Pool Schemes are district level schemes but planned by the concerned directorates and financed from the state pool and implemented through the state sector officers. These are generally new plan schemes to which the Government attached more importance. If these schemes are left to the DPDC, these schemes, being new and difficult to push through, are likely to be ignored and neglected by the DPDC in making financial provisions. Some of these projects are inter-district, and the requirement of funds for their successful implementation from the Government as well as from the commercial banks and other financial institutions like the Life Insurance Corporation and Rural Electrification Corporation is quite heavy, and also require sophisticated planning to attract these institutions to extend financial assistance. As soon as the total allocation for the

district plan schemes is decided, the amount required for the district level schemes which are to be planned and funded from the state pool, is deducted and the remaining amount is distributed amongst various districts as per formula approved by the Government.

48. The implementation of the pool schemes is also done by the officers responsible to the concerned directorates.

# 4

# PLANNING PROCESS

PLANNING Process[1] is a multi-facet mechanism which gives practical shape to plan formulation at any level. District Planning as a system is required to evolve the process[2] for the formulation of district plans failing which these plans are likely to remain mere "catalogue of demands" rather than implementable plans. Process of plan formulation at the district level can be divided into 5 stages, viz., (i) resource inventory, (ii) study of on-going efforts, (iii) overall strategy and sub-regional strategies, (iv) plan framework, and (v) programmes.[3]

The main features of the process of district planning are[4] (a) collection, scrutiny, corelation and interpretation of available data and its representation on a series of overlay maps; (b) listing of the lacunae and inadequacies of the on-going schemes; (c) identification of potentials which are being underutilized and misutilized; (d) enunciation of a broad strategy for increasing incomes and augumenting employment through alternative projection of production and other activities; (e) enumeration of the measures required for the application of the strategy in terms of extension of infrastructure, provision of financial and material resources, organization of technological support, modification or innovation of existing programmes and pricing, fiscal and other policies; (f) validation of the proposed strategy and its operational implications through consultations with the state level planners, financial and promotional institutions, committees of district level officers, panels of knowledgeable farmers, and entrepreneurs; and (g) preparation of specific inter-related schemes indicating measures of promotion, implementation, financial assistance, extension, incentives and disincentives in consonance with local experiences, requirements, trends and preferences within the parametres defined by the state Government.

## PLANNING COMMISSION'S MODEL

The methodology of Indian planning has acquired many new dimensions like district level planning in the course of its practical evolution for more than three decades. Accordingly, the importance of district planning was emphasized since the inception of planning era particularly from the Second Five Year Plan. However, it is difficult to come across effective steps taken towards district planning prior to the Fourth Five Year Plan. In fact, there was little scope for the planning at the district level as the central assistance to the states was tied down to certain programmes, and the only option to the states was either to accept or reject them. It was at the formulation of Fourth Plan that a clear stand was taken by the Planning Commission when it issued a set of guidelines[5] suggesting therein the planning process for the formulation of district plans. It was the first official attempt to evolve a model of process of district planning which consists of the following steps:—

(a) The district officers incharge of various activities are required to fill up various statistical tables and prepare notes on the guidepoints.[6] In brief, district level officers are expected to prepare comprehensive notes on these guidepoints analysing the problems and varieties of conditions in different blocks setting forth the success as well as shortcomings of the on-going development schemes,[7] and suggest the supplemental action to be taken during the next five years or one year period. These tables and notes will provide the raw material for the formulation of the district plan.

(b) The next step in the process of district planning is the study and integration of those notes and tables into a broad statement listing the resources, problems and prospects and setting forth the priorities to be accorded to different activities.[8] This broad statement may be called as the preliminary framework of the district plan.

(c) Thereafter, a series of meetings are required to be

organized to obtain the reactions of the officials and non-officials in respect of the proposals contained in the preliminary framework of the plan,[9] and the following meetings are envisaged:—

(aa) The first meeting in the series is to be with the block and district level officers to discuss the preliminary framework as well as determine the inter-se priorities of different blocks in respect of various indicators, viz., (i) availability of marketing facilities, (ii) communication facilities, (iii) linking of villages with mandis, and with block headquarters, hospitals, veterinary dispensaries, etc., (iv) availability of irrigation facilities, (v) position of sub-soil water, (vi) availability of power, (vii) extent of industrial activity, (viii) level of development of agriculture and industrial sectors, and (ix) overall economic condition of the area.[10]

This meeting will give an overview of the variety of conditions existing in the district and would help determining the interse position of different blocks in respect of the above mentioned indicators. It will also help in assessing (a) the performance of cooperatives, panchayati raj and other institutions regarding provision of services, participation in plan formulation and programme implementation and raising of local resources, (b) the projections in respect of the demand for agriculture inputs such as fertilizers, seeds, pesticides, tractors and also for credit for the above items, as also for minor irrigation and rural electrification, and (c) possibility of raising local resources for village roads, school buildings, location and opening of high schools and colleges, and the augmentation of medical facilities.

(bb) The next round of meeting is to be arranged with the "advisory panel" of progressive farmers and entrepreneurs to ascertain their views about the activities contained in the preliminary frame. The idea of presenting the preliminary framework to this panel is not really to obtain their endorsement but to stimulate them to articulate their perceptions about the problems and prospects of development of various blocks and to obtain their views about the feasibility of approaches set forth in the framework.[11]

(cc) The third meeting is to be held with the representatives of the cooperatives, local self government bodies, banks and

Panchayati Raj institutions to obtain their views about the proposals contained in the preliminary framework and to assess the quantum of resources likely to become available for the district plan within the district.[12]

(d) The next step is to revise and enlarge the "preliminary framework" in the light of the above discussions and this is to be done by the District Planning Officer under the overall supervision of the Collector or any other authority entrusted with this work. This revised framework would form the basis for detailed and more specific discussions with individual district level officers for the purpose of defining the lines of approach to be adopted for the solution of the problems posed by them or the representatives of different institutions and functional groups.[13]

(e) The next link in the process of district planning is to call a meeting of all district level officers to lay down the long term perspective of development as well as the integrated strategy to be followed in the short-term plan under preparation.[14] In addition, the objectives and guidelines to be adopted for different programmes is also to be laid down in this meeting to furnish a basis for the drawing up of detailed schemes for inclusion in the plan of the district. These guidelines are to indicate firm inter-sectoral and programme objectives, stipulate the lines on which new schemes should be drawn up, existing scheme should be modified and clarify the manner in which the development of backward areas or communities would be undertaken.[15]

(f) Then, the district level officers are required to formulate different schemes, specifying in each case (a) the objectives; (b) the activities envisaged; (c) the financial, physical and personnel inputs required; (d) the physical results expected from year to year; (e) the quantum of private and institutional resources likely to become available towards its execution; and (f) the manner in which the scheme would be reviewed, coordinated and synchronized with other schemes and evaluated from time to time.[16]

(g) After the district level officers have formulated schemes in their respective fields, these schemes have to be presented in the form of an integrated and operational plan. This is to be done in a meeting of the district level officers and reprsentatives of various institutions. As a result of this meeting, the district plan will emerge. The plan so formulated will also reflect the physical and financial targets proposed to be achieved during a particular period.

(h) The plan emerging at the district level may be very ambitious in financial and physical terms,[17] and may need "an exercise in prunning." It is very important that this exercise should not be undertaken at the state level in a mechanical fashion without consulting the departmental officials and others who have participated in the formulation of the district plan.[18]

The process of district planning envisaged as above in the Guidelines of the Planning Commission is a mere recommendatory model and the State Governments are required to adopt or modify it according to their own requirement. The intended model touched on various steps in the process of planning, and also emphasized the importance of categorization of schemes into state and district sectors as well as distribution of resources between the state and district sectors and also amongst the districts in the state but it left to the states to evolve or develop their own formula or criteria in this regard, as a result of which most of the states could not evolve a sound process of district planning. Now, it is proposed to examine this model in the light of the experiences gained in the study districts.

### Karnal

Planning process in Karnal was initiated right from the Second Five Year Plan, as also in the Fourth Five Year Plan but nothing tangible came out of these exercizes.[19]

Fourth Plan (1969-74) of Karnal district was prepared at the district level by the then Deputy Commissioner, Karnal who edited the proposals of district level officers intelligently and gave it a shape as a plan document. It had no backward and forward linkages in the process of planning, and as such this plan did not become an integral part of the budgetary mechanism.

Guidelines for the Formulation of District Plans issued by the Planning Commission in September 1969 were accepted in full by the Government of Haryana and the same were circulated to the Deputy Commissioners in the state in 1972.[20] For the formulation of Development Plan of Karnal (Fifth Plan and Perspective 1974-1979), the following process which is in no way even near the Guidelines on the subject was observed: (a) District Planning Officer, Karnal, on receipt of Guidelines from the Government[21], invited the schemes from the concerned district level officers, (b) the schemes received from the district level officers were compiled by the District Planning Officer and the first draft of the district plan was sent to the Planning Department for "perusal and comments"[22], and (c) final draft district plan was sent by the Deputy Commissioner to the Commissioner and Secretary, Planning Department.[23]

The process of planning in Karnal could not become opreational due to the following reasons[24]: (a) there was no high powered body of the Cabinet as in Thane to give authenticated guidance to the field levels in vital matters relating to the formulation of the district plan, (b) the district level planning process remained a concern of the junior level officers at the headquarter, (c) no attempt was made to demarcate the district sectors schemes, as a result of which the district level officers formulated their proposals according to their own understanding, (d) firm financial ceilings were not communicated to the district, (e) the priorities as to core and non-core programmes were not indicated, (f) the planning staff at the headquarter and in the field was not adequately strengthened[25], (g) the directorates were not involved in the process of decentralized planning and they continued to plan in respect of the schemes which could have been possibly planned at the district level, (h) sectoral guidelines were not issued to the district level officers by the concerned directorates, (i) there was no high powered body to scrutinize and approve the district plan, and (j) the district plan could not be integrated with the state plan through the budgetary process[26]. These constraints need attention and corrective action.

It is clear from the above that the process of district planning actually followed in Karnal was altogether different from the one contained in the guidelines circulated by the Planning Department.

**Thane**

In Maharashtra, a serious attempt had been made to give practical shape to the process of planning at the district level, as a result of which it evolved the planning process. As soon as the Government of Maharashtra decided to adopt the district as the unit of planning, steps were taken to formulate perspective district plans for 15 years for each district of the state.[27] It was, however, clarified that the work will be done in four stages,[28] viz., (a) data collection and analysis, including resource inventorying and assessment of levels of development reached by each district; (b) consultation with local people to assess the development needs and priorities; (c) resource estimation for the 15 year perspective plans of the district in consultation with the finance department; and (d) plan finalization.

The work relating to the perspective plan was not pursued beyond the first stage as the state's perspective plan was not ready as well as due to uncertainty about the resource position. However, during the first stage, the Government took the following steps that gave fillip to the process of district planning:[29]

(a) The Government appointed technical resource survey teams in the major fields of primary production, such as agriculture, animal husbandry, dairying, fisheries and forest to assess the present level of development in each district and prospects of growth based on the physical resources of the districts and to make constructive and realistic recommendations in this regard. These reports provided a technical framework for formulating projects based on local resources for inclusion in the district plan and may be regarded as valuable reference documents for district planning.

(b) Efforts were made to collect statistical and economic data for ascertaining the level of development reached in each district. A publication called 'Districtwise Statistical Information' was published in 1973 by the Planning Department, which provides information on various aspects of development in the districts for three time periods—1951, 1961 and 1969-70.

(c) On the basis of the statistical data and the resource survey, an 'indicative framework' of the proposed perspective for 'district development' was also prepared. This indicative framework provides information on various socio-economic indicators of development, highlighting the position of the district, vis-a-vis other districts and the state as a whole, and as such helped evolving the planning process at the district level.

The above steps could be regarded as a preliminary work in the direction of district perspective planning, which also laid the ground for the formulation of the district five year plans.

Before the commencement of the fifth plan, steps were taken by the Government to prepare five year plans for all districts in the state. The following procedure was indicated by the state Government to the district planning body as guidelines[30] for the preparation of the draft fifth plan of Thane district as also for other districts in Maharashtra:

(a) Updating of the resource surveys, statistical economic data and socio-economic indicators of development.

(b) Scrutiny of the existing schemes in regard to their relevance and recommendation as to their continuance or withdrawal.

(c) Preparation of a list of schemes and a ranking according to their priorities.

(d) Preparation of a master plan for the district, showing a list of productive and labour intensive works. While some of these works could be included in the district plan, depending upon their priority, the remaining works were kept as 'stand by works' for each block in the district for an emergency situation, i.e. in the event of any natural calamity.

(e) Finalization of an integrated plan of the district.

The draft district five year plans (1974-79) were formulated by the District Planning Boards in the state, keeping in view the above guidelines but these plans were not given final shape because the clear resources position of the State Five Year Plan was not visible. The district planning record reveals that the District Planning Board of Thane finalized the Fifth Five Year Plan (1974-79) of this district with an outlay of Rs. 54.74 crores[31] and sent it to the State Government for approval. However, this district five year plan was not approved by the Government. The available record and the practice reveal that now neither the perspective plans are prepared, nor are the district five year plans formulated. Since 1974-75, only district annual plans are being prepared in Thane, as also in other districts of Maharashtra. In view of the above, process of planning in formulating the district annual plan in Thane district is discussed in the succeeding paragraphs.

During the Fifth Five Year Plan as well as in the first 4 years of the Sixth Plan from 1974-75 to 1983-84, only district annual plans were formulated in Thane district, as also in other districts in the state, for which systematic planning process had been evolved. The process of planning for the formulation of the district plan can be divided into two phases: (a) first phase from 1974-75 to 1976-77, and (b) second phase from 1977-78 to 1983-84.

The process of district planning observed in Thane in the first phase could be summed up as: (a) the Planning Department issued general guidelines to the district planning body for the formulation of district annual plan[32] indicating therein the financial ceiling as well as priorities to be accorded to the "core programmes" relating to agriculture, irrigation, industries and power development,[33] (b) all the district level officers were asked to prepare and send their proposals to the Member-Secretary, (c) the compilation of the proposals was done schemewise, sectorwise and sub-sectorwise by the District Planning Officer, (d) consolidated draft proposals were placed before the district planning body for consideration and approval, (e) thereafter, draft plan was sent to the Planning Department with copies to the Heads of Departments and Administrative Secretaries, and (f) then, the draft plan was finalized in the state level meeting presided over by the Planning Minister, and incorporated in the state plan.

In the first phase, planning process for the formulation of the district annual plan was evolved quite elaborately, and the same had been further refined in the second phase. The process of planning adopted in this district for the formulation of district annual plan in the second phase is detailed below:[34]

(a) The Planning Department issues exhaustive guidelines

indicating the policies, priorities and programmes of the Government for the formulation of district annual plan.[35]

(b) Planning Department, with the approval of the Planning Sub-Committee of the Cabinet, communicates the financial ceilings for the district annual plans sometimes in the month of August every year. Financial ceilings as indicated in Table 4.1 for the district annual plans of Thane district for a period of 5 years[36] has given realistic touch to the process of planning at the district level.

TABLE 4.1: **Financial ceilings for the district annual plans**

*Rs. in crores*

| Year | Total plan funds earmarked for the district annual plans in the state | Financial ceilings for Thane | | |
|---|---|---|---|---|
| | | General Plan | Tribal Areas Sub-Plan | Total |
| 1979-80 | 233.14 | 4.57 | 8.42 | 12.99 |
| 1980-81 | 225.00 | 5.15 | 6.50 | 11.65 |
| 1981-82 | 285.00 | 5.81 | 8.54 | 14.35 |
| 1982-83 | 386.88 | 6.39 | 9.40 | 15.79 |
| 1983-84 | 445.00 | 9.16 | 13.45 | 22.61 |

(c) Then the implementing officers are asked to prepare and send the proposals which are compiled by the District Planning Officer.

(d) A small team consisting of the District Collector, Chief Executive Officer, Zila Parishad, President, Zila Parishad, and 2-3 non-officials examine the plan proposals of the implementing officers.[37]

(e) The next stage in the planning process is discussions of the Senior Officers of the Planning Department on the draft annual plan proposals with the small team. Senior officers of the Department examine the proposals to find out as to whether these are in conformity with the policies, priorities and programmes of the Government.

(f) After these discussions, the proposals are consolidated

by the District Planning Officer under the overall supervision of the Collector and placed before the DPDC for consideration and approval.

(g) In the light of the discussions of the DPDC, the draft district annual plan is prepared and sent to the Planning Department with copies to the Heads of the Department and Administrative Secretaries. The main recommendations made by the DPDC, Thane, both under Non-TASP and TASP to the Government for a period of 5 years are given in Table 4.2.

TABLE 4.2: **Total outlay recommended by the DPDC**

*Rs. in crores*

| Year | Non-TASP | TASP | Total |
|---|---|---|---|
| 1979-80 | 4.57 | 8.42 | 12.99 |
| 1980-81 | 5.15 | 8.83 | 13.98 |
| 1981-82 | 5.96 | 8.75 | 14.71 |
| 1982-83 | 6.40 | 9.72 | 16.12 |
| 1983-84 | 9.16 | 13.45 | 22.61 |

(h) The draft annual plan received from the DPDC is then discussed in the State level meeting with the Executive Committee and Special Executive Committee held under the Chairmanship of the Planning Minister. This meeting is also attended by the Secretaries and Heads of Departments and all the ticklish and important issues are resolved and the plan is finalized in this meeting.[38]

(i) The district plan, finalized at the state level meeting, is then incorporated in the draft annual plan of the state to be submitted to the Planning Commission and the Central Ministries.

(j) Modifications, if any, suggested by the Planning Commission and Ministries are carried out at the state level by the Planning Department.

(k) Planning Department sends the so finalized Annual Plan to the Finance Department for being built into the budget.

(l) After dovetailing the Plan into the budgetary process,

the Finance Department seeks the approval of the State Legislature.

(m) After its approval by the Legislature, the Planning Department publishes the "Detailed Statements of Outlays Provided for District Level Schemes", and sends it to the DPDCs and all other concerned for being adopted as final plan. Total plan outlay approved by the Government in favour of Thane district for a period of four years are shown in Table 4.3.

TABLE 4.3: **Total outlays approved for Thane**

*Rs. in crores*

| Year | NON-TASP | TASP | Total |
|---|---|---|---|
| 1979-80 | 6.69 | 7.82 | 14.51 |
| 1980-81 | 5.74 | 9.55 | 15.29 |
| 1981-82 | 6.00 | 10.19 | 16.19 |
| 1982-83 | 7.41 | 10.61 | 18.02 |

The above table shows that the Government provides substantial funds separately both for Non-TASP and TASP every year and this step alone has made the process of planning at the district level realistic.

(n) A new procedure for release of grants is being followed. According to this, the administrative departments concerned with the provisions in the budget voted by the State Legislature, directly communicate to the officers responsible for implementing schemes at the district level, the budget grants placed at their disposal instead of channelizing such releases to the district officers through the Heads of Departments. This has served to cut down delays in the release of funds to the district level.[39]

## A COMPARATIVE VIEW

Planning Commission, ever since it came into being, recommended to states the adoption of the district as the unit of planning and repeated references to it are found in almost all the plan documents from 1951 onwards. In September, 1969, it designed Guidelines detailing therein the process of planning for the formulation of district plans and circulated these to the states. The process of planning for the formulation of the district plans, as fathered by the Planning Commission, is quite comprehensive and innovative but it was merely a suggestive or recommendatory in nature. The plain reading of the guidelines for the formulation of the district plans reveals that the Planning Commission emphasized the need for the (a) demarcation of schemes into state and district sectors, (b) allocation of resources between state and district sectors and among districts, and (c) incorporation of district plans in the state annual plan through the budgetary mechanism. However, it left to the states to adopt the guidelines of the Commission or evolve or develop their own criteria and procedures in all these vital matters, as a result of which the planning process did not graduate in most of the states in the country.

The experience in Karnal reveals that the process of district planning was initiated without any policy frame and as such it remained a mere paper exercise primarily due to lack of politico-administrative initiatives[40] to take firm decisions on certain vital issues such as (a) criteria for the classification of state and district sector schemes, and (b) formula for transfer of financial resources in favour of the district. In fact, it suffered, by and large, from the same infirmities as the one recommended by the Planning Commission in its guidelines for the formulation of district plans.

In Thane, the process of district planning was initiated since 1972 with the setting up of the District Planning Board under the Chairmanship of the Revenue and Civil Supplies Minister, and subsequently this Board was substituted with the DPDC, for the formulation of (a) Perspective Plan, (b) Five Year Plans, and (c) Annual Plans of the district. Perspective and Five Year Plans are no longer prepared in Thane,[41] as also in other districts of the state. However, an elaborate process of planning has been evolved only for the formulation of district annual plans. The experience reveals that the Government has clearly demonstrated "political will and commitment"[42] in evolving the process of district annual planning by giving a policy frame without which decentralized planning cannot become operational.

In Maharahstra, a high powered Planning Sub-Committee of the Cabinet has been constituted under the Chairmanship of the Chief Minister to provide authentic guidance on important issues such as allocation of funds, and classification and reclassification of district level schemes which have made the process of district annual planning a meaningful exercise. Not only this, the Government of Maharashtra has further demonstrated its political will and commitment by creating the planning machinery known as DPDC, consisting of officials and non-officials under the Chairmanship of the District Minister, that finally approves the district annual plan.

The process of district planning in Thane district, as also in other districts in Maharashtra, passes through various inter-related stages such as: (a) issuance of guidelines indicating therein the financial ceilings, policies, plan priorities and programmes by the Government for the formulation of district annual plans, (b) preparation of sectoral schemes by the implementing officers, (c) examination of the schemes by the small team, (d) discussions with the senior officers of the Planning Department, (e) consolidation of draft plan proposals by the District Planning Officer under the overall supervision of the District Collector and the member Secretary of the DPDC, (f) approval of the draft annual plan by the DPDC, (g) submission of the draft district plan to the Planning Department with copies to the Heads of Departments and the Administrative Secretaries, (h) finalization of the draft district plan in the state level meeting headed by the Planning Minister, and (i) finally integration of the district annual plan in the state annual plan for seeking the approval of the Planning Commission and of the State Assembly.

The idea of setting up of a small team in the second phase to examine the proposals of the individual district level officers is certainly an improvement on the process of planning in the first phase but it does not help in having an integrated view of one department with the other connected departments, apart from appreciating their constraints in respect of availability of finances, administrative bottlenecks, and other management problems. The small team is a non-technical body and finalizes sectoral proposals without establishing any linkages with the proposals of other departments. For instance, the success of schemes of agriculture sector depends upon (a) the availability of loans for the purchase of inputs, (b) regular supply of electricity for the running of the tubewells and pumping sets, (c) supply of seeds, fertilizers and pesticides, (d) irrigation facilities, and (e) a large number of other linkages with other departments. The small team, while finalizing the proposals of agriculture sector, do not take into consideration the valuable views of the other officers who are expected to provide these enabling services. Therefore, the process of planning as outlined above, although quite elaborate, does not provide for inbuilt suitable mechanism for proper examination and integration of various sectoral schemes through inter-departmental technical deliberations of all the concerned departments.

Despite the above weakness, the process of district planning is an article of faith in Thane and other districts of Maharashtra and it has greatly been possible due to politico-administrative initiatives, improvisations and interactions.

**A suggestive approach**

The planning process at the district level envisages a great deal of back and forth linkages between the state and district authorities as well as consultation with the representatives of the people, the concerned institutions and knowledgeable individuals. It can necessarily be organized within the policy frame of the state and as such the politico-administrative leadership at the state level has to take the policy initiatives in this regard. It is, in fact, a two-way process, viz., policy frame and guidance from the State level, and actual process of planning for the formulation of district plans at the district level. The suggested approach can be discussed under the two heads: (a) Policy frame and perspective for district development, and (b) the proposed planning process for the formulation of district plan which is also depicted through a chart. It may be mentioned here that the policy frame, coupled with perspective for district development, is the prerequisite for initiating the planning process at this level, and serves as a brain wave in the entire system of planning.[43]

## POLICY FRAME AND PERSPECTIVE FOR DISTRICT DEVELOPMENT

Policy initiatives of the state Government within the national priorities will consist of: (a) trend analysis of the state economy especially performance of major sectors of production, overall development objectives and policies for development with special reference to beneficiary-oriented programmes, (b) assessment of present position of development in each district and prospects of development based on local resources, (c) perspective of development of a district vis-a-vis other districts and the state as a whole, (d) identification of district sector schemes, (e) criteria for the distribution of resources between the state and district sector schemes and among the districts, (f) communication of financial ceilings to districts, (g) decentralization of administrative and financial powers at the district level, and (h) strengthening of district planning cells. These are external factors and not a part of the district planning process but these intimately influence the planning process at the district level.

### Proposed planning process

Practically, the process of planning for the formulation of the district five-year and annual plans will be the same because these documents will require the same set of policy frame, and also pass through the same stages to become the part of the State Five Year Plan, which, in turn, will also become an integral part of the national plan. Consequently, the suggested alternative approach of planning process both for the district five year and annual plans is discussed simultaneously in three stages.

In the first stage, the District Planning Officer is required to communicate the financial ceilings, guidelines and instructions of the Planning Department to the implementing officers for the formulation of their sectoral proposals for inclusion in the district plan. The next step in this stage will be the quick review of the on-going schemes and projects (both plan and non-plan), problems and potentials of development by the implementing officers. After this, the implementing officers will identify and prepare schemes and projects indicating therein their justifications, objectives, physical and financial targets, requirement of loans, locations of schemes and projects, coverage of beneficiaries, implementing schedules, and requirement of manpower.[44]

After the preliminary work of the individual implementing officers, the district plan enters the second important stage in which the schemes and projects need to be examined by the following working groups:

(a) Agriculture and allied services, including cooperation and irrigation

(b) Small and cottage industries

(c) Social services

(d) Transport and communication

(e) Housing and urban development

(f) Coordination group.

The first five working groups[45] are required to examine the preliminary proposals of each implementing officer and suggest schemes for the respective sectors after examining various aspects, such as the level of development reached, feasibility of further development and optimum utilization of the available resources as well as keeping in view the guidelines and priorities laid down by the Government. Each group will prepare its report giving narrative write-up indicating therein financial and physical targets. While preparing the proposals for the respective sectors, the concerned working group will include such programmes as are useful and necessary to raise the standard of living of weaker sections and particularly of those living below the poverty line.

The next step will be presentation of group reports to the coordination group.[46] This group will examine as to whether the proposals of the implementing officers are in consonance with the policies and priorities of the Government and the schemes for the weaker sections of society, especially living below the poverty line, have been adequately provided for by the respective working groups, and if necessary, add such effective schemes in the plan that are conducive to these target groups. This process is likely to help resolve the inter-departmental differences through discussions. The quality of the proposals will also improve the quality of the district plan through interdepartmental technical deliberations of the working groups.

After discussion in the coordination group, the draft district plan will be prepared by the District Planning Officer under the overall supervision of the Deputy Commissioner or Collector or Member-Secretary for consideration and approval of the DPDC. After its approval by the DPDC, the finalization of the draft plan indicating therein various programmes and schemes with physical and financial targets will be done by the District Planning Officer under the overall supervision of the Collector in the light of the decisions of the Council for submission to the Planning Department, with copies to the concerned Directorates and Administrative Secretaries.

The third stage will consist of: (a) approval of the draft district plan in the state level meeting of the concerned officers, presided over by the Planning Minister, with the Executive Committee and Special Executive Committee of the DPDC, (b) integration of the district plan with the state plan for approval of the Planning Commission and the State Legislature; (c) preparation of detailed statements of outlays provided for district level schemes by the Planning Department for circulation to the Member-Secretaries of the DPDCs and the concerned Administrative Departments; and, (d) communication of sanctions by the Administrative Secretaries directly to the implementing officers with an intimation to the concerned Directorates.

With the above planning process, an integrated district development plan, indicating various schemes and projects will emerge, and will require mobilization of resources for financing the schemes and projects through budgetary grants and institutional resources that are being dealt with in the chapters that follow.

## REFERENCES

1. "Planning process" may be described as series of actions or unified system of actions or steps or stages which are essential for the formulation of a plan on a systematic basis.
2. United Nation Centre for Regional Development, Nagoya, Japan, has conducted regional exercises in Philipines (1974), Indonesia (1975), Pakistan (1976), and Thailand (1976) and identified seven steps in the process of planning, These are; (a) diagnosis, (b) macro-framework building, (c) sectoral planning, (d) inter-sectoral coordination, (e) plan finalization, (f) action plan formulatian and (g) planning for implementation (United Nations Centre for Regional Development, Method of Planning for Comprehensive Regional Development, Consolidation of UNCRD'S Experiences, Nagoya, 1977, p. 16).

   In another study on local and intermediate level development, the local level planning process has been summarized in four inter-related stages as: (a) local level socio-economic diagnosis, (b) formulation of local development goals and objectives, (c) planning and programming of local level development, and (d) implementation and evaluation (An Introduction to Local and Intermediate Level Development: UNCRD, Nagoya, Japan, p-31.)
3. See Y.Venugopal Reddy: Multi-Level Planning witb special reference to the District Planning—Some issues, Seminar on District Planning, June 3, June 10, 1973, Lal Bahadur Shastri Academy of Administration, Mussoorie, p. 13.
4. Anand Sarup, The Process of District Planning—An Overview, Seminar on District Planning, June 3, June 10, 1973, *Lal Bahadur Shastri Academy of Administration,* Mussoorie, p. 2-3.
5. Planning Commission: Guidelines for the Formulation of District Plans (Mimeo), Sept., 1969.
6. There are 26 guidepoints relating to land resources and utilization, communication system, marketing facilities, storage and processing facilities, banking and credit facilities, canal irrigation system, power distribution, educational facilities, medical and public health, drinking water facilities, veterinary facilities, agriculture, animal husbandry and dairying, large scale industries, modern small scale industries, handicrafts and village industries, backward communities, Panchayati Raj bodies, local self Government, and employment. The guidepoints mentioned above are merely indicative and it is assumed that these would be carefully examined at the district level and such modifications and improvements as may be warranted by the local situation would be incorporated in them. Refer Guidelines For the Formulation of District Plans (Mimeo) issued by the Planning Commission, New Delhi in Sept., 1969, p. 16.
7. Generally, this exercise is restricted to plan schemes only, and

the non-plan schemes which are not only important to the area and the people but also wide-spread, are left out from such a scrutiny. Non-plan schems are those schemes which in due course of time are transferred from the state exchequer on regular basis. The amount of expenditure incurred on these schemes is more than the plan schemes and could be profitably utilized for the development of the district.

8. Govt. of India, Planning Commission, Guidelines for the Formulation of District Plans, (Mimeo), p. 16.
9. Ibid., p. 16.
10. Ibid., pp. 18-19.
11. Ibid., p. 21.
12. Ibid., p. 23.
13. Ibid., pp. 23-24.
14. Ibid., p. 25.
15. Ibid.
16. Ibid., pp. 26-27.
17. Ibid., p. 28.
18. Ibid.
19. In the Second Five Years Plan: Punjab State: District Karnal (1956-61), plan expenditure was merely divided between the State schemes and local schemes at the state level, and the large number of schemes shown as local schemes in the above document did not emanate from the district level planning process. Actually, planning was done only at the state level, and the districtwise break-up of expendititure on local schmes proposed to be implemented in Karnal district from 1956-61 was drawn up by the Planning Department at the State level (Second Five Year Plan, Punjab State: District Karnal—1956-61, Chandigarh, 1958.).
20. Government of Haryana, Guidelines For the Formulation of District Plans, Chandigarh, 1972.
21. Guidelines for the formulation of District Plan (1974-79) was sent by the Planning Department to the Deputy Commissioner, Karnal, in 1972.
22. The first draft of the district plan was sent by the D.P.O. Karnal to the Planning Departmcnt for perusal and comments on 24.2.1974.
23. DPO (Ka)-76/62, dated 6.5.1976.
24. Based on my personal interviews with the Ex-Deputy Plan Adviser who remained incharge of the District Planning Cell at the state level from 1972 to 1976, and other officers at the headquarter as well as in the field.
25. The post of the District Planning Officer, Karnal was never filled up. This post was either held by the A.G.A. to Deputy Commissioner or the District Statistical Officer of Karnal, in addition to his normal duties.
26. In a state, budget duly approved by the Vidhan Sabha is the only

source which authorizes the incurring of expenditure on plan and non-plan schemes. Planning Department and Finance Department in Haryana did not arrive at any mechanism to dovetail the district plans in the state plan through a budgetary process. Therefore, the proposals contained in the district plan of Karnal district did not become the integral part of the state budget.

27. The Chief Minister of Maharashtra made a brief statement to this effect in both the Houses of the State Legislature in August, 1969, Later in November Session of the same year, the Chief Minister spelt out various steps that were proposed to be taken for the formulation of the perspective district plans.
28. Government of Maharashtra, Planning Department, Indicative Framework of Proposed Perspective For District Development (District Planning Series No. 1), 1973, p. 3.
29. K.V. Sundaram, District Planning: The Case Study of Maharashtra, *Indian Journal of Public Administration,* New Delhi, Jan-March, 1979, pp. 64-65.
30. Ibid.
31. The Fifth Five Year Plan (1974-79) was approved by the District Planning Board, Thane in its meeting on 27th August, 1973.
32. In Thane district, annual plan comprises Tribal Areas Sub-Plan and General Plan (Non-TASP).
33. Circular No. ADP-1074/P-I (A), dated 25-1-1974, Planning Department, Government of Maharashtra, Bombay. Such circulars are issued every year by the Planning Department to the Member-Secretaries of the DPDCs and all other officers concerned with District Planning.
34. This information is condensed from the circulars issued by the Planning Department, Government of Maharashtra, Bombay, from August 1976 to June 1983, and other record available as also from the records of the District Planning Officer, Thane.
35. Refer circular No. DPC-1078/FRG (B), dated 29-8-1977, Planning Department, Government of Maharashtra. Bombay.
36. The financial ceilings as indicated in this table are condensed from the guidelines issued by the Planning Department as well as from the office record of the DPO, Thane.
37. Guidelines for the formulation of district plans issued in July, 1974, by the Planning Department, Punjab, provides for setting up of Working Groups on: (a) Agriculture and Allied Subjects. (b) Industry, Power and Rural Electrification, (c) Transport Communication, and Social Services, and (d) Housing and Urban Development to examine the proposals prepared by the district level officers.

    Similarly, in Gujarat, five Working Groups such as (a) Agricultural and Allied Services including Cooperation and Irrigation, (b) Small and Cottage Industries, (c) Social Services, (d) Development of Basic Infrastructure such as Rural Electrification, Storage,

Roads, and (e) Coordination Group are set up to analyse the progress achieved in different sectors, identify the lags, make assessment of the local material and human resources and prepare schemes useful for the development in the district in respective sectors. The first 4 groups suggest schemes for the respective sectors after examining various aspects like the level of development reached, feasibility of further development and optimum utilization of available resources. Each Group prepares its report giving narrative write up and statistical data, indicating financial and physical targets, while preparing the proposals for the respective sector of development. The concerned Working Group is required to give priority to such programmes as are useful and necessary to raise the standard of living of weaker sections and more particularly those living below the poverty line. The Coordination Group examines as to whether this aspect has been adequately taken into account by the respective Working Groups and if necessary can add in consultation with the respective Group, such effective schemes in the draft district plans as are conducive to fulfil the desired aim.

38. The perusal of the record reveals that only one such meeting was held in March, 1981 to approve the annual plan of Thane for 1981-82 during the last three years, and such meetings to consider and approve the district annual Plans for the years 1982-83 and 1983-84 could not be held due to change in Ministry or some other problems. As the senior officers of the Planning Department are intimately associated with the planning process at the district level, no difficulty is being faced in integrating the district annual plans with the state plan even without holding of state level meetings.
39. DO. No. PC(P) 27/1/81-MLP, dated 2-6-1982 from Shri Manmohan Singh, Member Secretary, Planning Commission, New Delhi to Shri P.P. Caprihan, Chief Secretary, Haryana, Chandigarh.
40. Based on interviews with the district and state level officers.
41. An attempt was made to formulate the Fifth Five Year Plan of Thane and the draft Plan was also sent to the Government for approval but the State Government could not finalize it due to uncertain resource position.
42. Planning is a process which is initiated by the Government to achieve the pre-determined goals such as maximization of production, and providing of justice to the weaker sections of society. In a parliamentary form of Government, political leadership in the centre as well as in the states emerged out of the mandate obtained from the people through the elections which are held after regular intervals. The political leadership that emerges so is expected to honour its commitments by demonstrating its capacity to take even the hard decisions to solve the problems of the people who have given their mandate to it. The very concept of decentralized planning at the district or lower level involves various policy decisions such as

delineation of state and district level schemes, allocation of financial resources to the district, delegation of financial and administrative powers to the district authorities and creation of a viable planning machinery for the formulation of district plans. Above all, it involves shedding of powers by the state levels in favour of the district level which is the most difficult decision to take and can be taken only if the apex political leadership has the political will and commitment in this regard.

43. Policy may be defined as the official guidelines or a set of guidelines for the intentions, goals and actions of an organization in accomplishing specified objectives. Ivan S. Banki, Dictionary of Administration and Management, System Research Institute, Los Angeles, California, 1981, p. 543.
44. Lot of information, data and statistics are required for the formulation of sectoral proposals. The implementing officers are required to update the information and data at the time of formulation of their proposals.
45. Each working group will consist of all the district level officers who have already submitted their sectoral proposals. The meetings of these groups will be presided over by the Deputy Commissioner or Collector/Additional Deputy Commissioner or Chief Executive Officer of the Zila Parishad. Each working group may coopt other officials and non-officials who may prove useful.
46. The Coordination Group may consist of: (a) Collector, (b) Additional D.C. or the Chief Executive Officer of the Zila Parishad, (c) President of the Zila Parishad, (d) Group leaders of the working groups, (e) senior representative of the lead-bank, (f) representative of the Planning Department, and (g) 2 or 3 representatives of the people.

# 5

## RESOURCE PLANNING
## Allocation of Grants

RESOURCE[1] planning through Government grants as well as institutional finance is the life line of decentralized planning at the district level and as such this aspect deserves recognition and appreciation by the authorities. No amount of district planning will succeed without realizing its importance at the time of framing the policy and programmes in this regard. Resource is always a constraint in planning at the national and state levels, and it is not an exception in case of district planning. Therefore, in all attempts in district planning, resource planning has to be given the highest priority. In the absence of resource planning and allocation, every officer at the district level will add up as many schemes in his proposals as he can possibly think of. Not only this, the people's representatives in the district as well as the pressure groups led by powerful elite would further aggravate the position by getting added more and more schemes in the district plan, thereby making it a mere catalogue of felt needs which when added up will go far beyond the available resources. A realistic district plan must, therefore, be a happy synthesis of what is possible. Therefore, realistic allocation of government funds to each district on the basis of certain acceptable formula[2] is of immense importance for the formulation of the implementable district development plan, and this step will provide a firm foundation for building up the "district planning system." In view of the importance of resources for the success of the district plan, financial allocation through the budgetary mechanism and institutional finance mobilization through credit planning are considered as the "lungs of the body of the district plan." Since planning is basically an exercise to make the best use of the scarce resources to achieve the predetermined objectives within a given time frame, all planning efforts, whether at macro or micro level, involve resource allocations. Even the social or voluntary organization aiming at social improvement of a particular section of the community requires resources to carry out its mission. Thus, finance is, really, an integral part of the district plan and the Government is expected to evolve an appropriate budgetary mechanism with regard to the allocation of funds for the financing of district plans, as also to attract the institutional finance abundantly available in the district itself.

The state Government is required to indicate the frame of financial allocations for each sector. Resources available to the district should be augmented and made available well in time to enable the planning cell to set priorities both for the whole plan period and also for each year. Allocation for the district should be based on the plan and not on the political pulls and pressures.[3] This, therefore, suggests that a policy decision has to be taken to evolve a sound formula for the devolution of resources between the state and district level schemes as well as amongst the districts.

District Planning is one important level in the complex of multi-level planning integrating therein the following types of projects, for which both the Government funds and credits will be required:

(a) district level projects and schemes,
(b) block level projects and schemes, and
(c) specific village projects and schemes.

The district plan, thus, covers the total gamut of investment and not merely Government outlays on creation of production assets, facilities, infrastructure or social services for the common benefit.[4] The district plan, therefore, should not merely stop at commercially viable projects. It should also include built-in provisions for preventing growth of disparities due to unequal distribution of benefits from development.

The commercial banks and the central cooperative banks

are important instruments of financing district plans. They finance the plan activities which produce the maximum impact in terms of output and employment, and the Government outlay will be on missing links or facilitating links, either showing no directly attributable flow of income as in health or education facilities, or providing facility on a compulsory basis.[5] In view of the above, a district plan must clearly recognise the distinction between budgetary resources and institutional resources. While budgetary resources are no doubt important and present an important constraint in district planning, availability of resources from financial institutions is no longer a constraint in the sense that funds can be found and made available provided sound viable bankable projects and investment schemes are identified. In other words, district authorities can seek greater support from financial institutions by preparing district credit plans and by encouraging the formulation of schemes that are viable and presenting them in a form that would be acceptable to the financial institutions. In fact, institutional finance cannot only supplement plan resources directly but can reduce budgetary pressure indirectly.[6] To the extent institutional funds are available for financing certain viable schemes, plan funds can be utilized for financing the schemes and programmes for which institutional funds are not available.

The district development plan normally consists of four categories of schemes for which financial resources have to be indicated:

A. (a) schemes to be executed by the people themselves, either through their own resources or through institutional or Government assistance of loans or grants; (b) schemes to be executed by cooperative and corporate sectors; (c) schemes to be executed by the local bodies like village panchayats, Panchyat Samitis, Zila Parishads, municipal corporations, municipalities, notified areas and town areas; (d) schemes to be executed by Government departments as a part of the state plan; (e) centrally sponsored schemes; and (f) schemes of the central sectors.

B. schemes planned at the state level but located in a district;

C. inter-district state schemes; and

D. central projects and schemes located in a district.[7]

The main categories of resources would be (a) budgetary grants, (b) institutional finance, and (c) self finance, and these resources alongwith their sub-categories are indicated in the chart.

Major categories of resources which could possibly be included in the district plan are discussed as under:—

**Centrally sponsored programmes**

There is a large number of centrally sponsored projects and programmes such as IRDP, DPAP, CADA, FFDA, DDP, etc. in the agriculture and rural development sectors, and other schemes relating to housing and urban development, education, welfare of backward classes, social welfare, village and small industries, health and transport which are being implemented at the district level. As a result of the decision taken by the National Development Council, the Government of India has revised the list of Centrally Sponsored Schemes for which 100 per cent assistance was being made available to the state Government until 1978-79. According to this decision, these schemes have now been made shareable for which provision in the state plan will have to be made at 50 per cent of the total provision.[8] All the Centrally Sponsored Schemes categorized as district level schemes need to be provided for in the district plan.

**District sector plan resources**

Plan schemes generally consist of state sector schemes and district sector schemes. A very important source of financing the district sector schemes can be the share of the district out of the district sector allocation of the state plan. This involves division of state plan resources into state and district sector schemes, as also their reallocation amongst the districts on the basis of a rational formula or criteria.

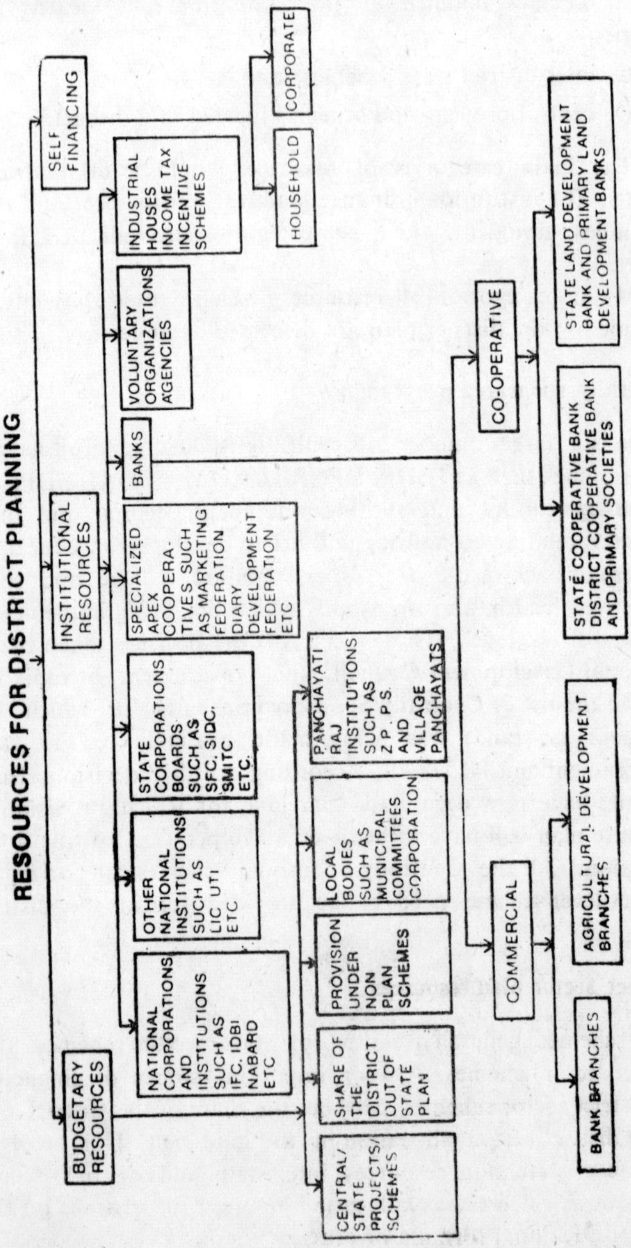
RESOURCES FOR DISTRICT PLANNING
BUDGETARY RESOURCES
INSTITUTIONAL RESOURCES
SELF FINANCING
HOUSEHOLD
CORPORATE
NATIONAL CORPORATIONS AND INSTITUTIONS SUCH AS IFC, IDBI NABARD ETC
OTHER NATIONAL INSTITUTIONS SUCH AS LIC UTI ETC
STATE CORPORATIONS BOARDS SUCH AS SFC, SIDC, SMITC ETC.
SPECIALIZED APEX COOPERATIVES SUCH AS MARKETING FEDERATION DIARY DEVELOPMENT FEDERATION ETC
BANKS
VOLUNTARY ORGANIZATIONS AGENCIES
INDUSTRIAL HOUSES INCOME TAX INCENTIVE SCHEMES
CENTRAL/ STATE PROJECTS/ SCHEMES
SHARE OF THE DISTRICT OUT OF STATE PLAN
PROVISION UNDER NON PLAN SCHEMES
LOCAL BODIES SUCH AS MUNICIPAL COMMITTEES CORPORATION
PANCHAYATI RAJ INSTITUTIONS SUCH AS Z.P. P.S. AND VILLAGE PANCHAYATS
COMMERCIAL
CO-OPERATIVE
BANK BRANCHES
AGRICULTURAL DEVELOPMENT BRANCHES
STATE COOPERATIVE BANK DISTRICT COOPERATIVE BANK AND PRIMARY SOCIETIES
STATE LAND DEVELOPMENT BANK AND PRIMARY LAND DEVELOPMENT BANKS

**Local bodies resources**

Local bodies comprising the Municipal Corporations, the Municipal Committees and PRIs are also important institutions engaged in various developmental activities within the district and have their own resources which come to them through local taxes. They also receive grants and share in some taxes from the state. However, their resources are tied either to finance some particular schemes to provide some basic amenities to the people, or to meet the salaries of the staff. Moreover, the resources raised by them through tax and other sources are not enough for undertaking planned development.

In Karnal, the municipal committees are superceded, and their administration is carried out by the administrators appointed by the Government. Their resources are not enough even to provide the basic amenities such as maintenance of city roads, water supply, santitation, and other basic amenities. Similarly, the Zila Parishad, Karnal, has since been abolished, and the Panchayat Samitis are not in existence and their affairs are managed by the BDPOs who are made their administrators in addition to their normal duties. Only village panchayats in Karnal are functioning. The resources of these bodies are so scanty that they can hardly undertake any development work.[9]

In Thane, the position of the Panchayati Raj institutions is better than that in Karnal but their income from own resources is not enough to undertake new development works in the district. Income and expenditure of Zila Parishad, Thane from its own resources is given in Table 5.1

It is clear from this that the financial position of the Zila Parishad, Thane, is not sound and can hardly undertake any additional development programme.

There are 7 Municipal Councils and one Municipal Corporation[10] in Thane district and their income is not enough to provide basic amenities such as maintenance of water supply, city roads and sanitation and these bodies can hardly take up any additional development schemes in their areas.

TABLE 5.1 : **Income and expenditure of Zila Parishad Thane (own resources) from 1977-78 to 1983-84**

*Rs. in lakhs*

| Item. | Years 1977-78 | 1978-79 | 1979-80 | 1980-81 | 1981-82 | 1982-83 | 1983-84 (Proposed) |
|---|---|---|---|---|---|---|---|
| Income | 60.54 | 87.66 | 76.84 | 79.24 | 73.96 | 66.17 | 70.58 |
| Expenditure | 59.95 | 59.10 | 52.74 | 63.93 | 54.58 | 65.33 | 69.27 |

*Source* : Office of the Chief Executive Officer, Zila Parishad, Thane.

It is thus evident that the local bodies in Karnal and Thane do not have sufficient income to meet the growing development needs. They clamour for grants from the Government even to provide the basic amenities.

In the above situation, the resource mobilization for district plans through budgetary grants and credit which together constitute an "integrated investment plan" for the district is a very important aspect of district planning, and as such both of these major sources are being discussed at length under the following two heads:

(a) Budgetary resources, and

(b) Institutional finance.

## Budgetary Resources

The resource allocation through the budgetary mechanism is the pre-condition for the initiation of the process of district planning, and that too has to be made on some rational criteria,[11] or formula. Most of the schemes at present are being implemented at the district level but the financing is generally not done on rational basis. In many cases, the selection of schemes and projects as well as their financing is done on the basis of "political pulls and pressures" as a result of which the scarce resources are either frittered away or utilized in non-priority schemes. It is somewhat unfortunate that under the present planning process while there is criterion called the 'Gadgil Formula'[12] for devolving funds from the centre to the states as plan assistance but there is no corresponding formula for distributing plan funds from the state to the districts.[13] This is a serious limitation as a result of which district planning did not emerge as a system, except in the states of Maharashtra, Gujarat and Karnataka. For making district planning a success, it is absolutely necessary to develop or adopt a similar formula for the allocation of funds for the state and district sector schemes as also amongst the districts. In view of the prevailing apathetic situation for the distribution of funds, even the idea of setting up a "State Finance Commission" to recommend the distribution of state plan resources between the state and district sector schemes has been mooted.[14] As far as the transfer of funds for the planned development of the district is concerned, two vital issues, viz. (a) rational criteria for the distribution of state plan resources between the state and district sector schemes, and (b) formula for further allocation of district allocable funds amongst the districts, emerge that require appreciation and definite solution through the positive intervention of the politico-administrative leadership at the state level. Now, it may be seen as to what is the position obtaining in the study districts with regard to distribution and allocation of funds.

## EXPERIENCE IN THANE AND KARNAL

Funds are allotted to Thane district, as also to other districts in Maharashtra, for planned development through the mechanism of financial ceilings communicated by the Planning Department every year and this has brought realism and respectability to the very concept of district planning. It is, therefore, proposed to bring out the salient features of the financial arrangement by highlighting the pragmatic policies and procedures that have really helped developing a sound financial system for financing the district plan schemes in Maharashtra with special reference to Thane.[15]

In Maharashtra, one of the important measures taken by the state Government prior to the introduction of district planning in the state in 1974-75 was to indicate the allocation of funds for district level schemes and then suitably re-allocate them to various districts on some rational basis. In order to do this, the state Government took into consideration the policy of balanced development of the districts and the need to accelerate the process in the relatively underdeveloped districts and adopted a scale of weightages with reference to the total population of the district, the urban population, the population of Scheduled Castes and Scheduled Tribes, the relative backwardness in the fields of agriculture, industry and communications, and special problems and needs of development of the coastal districts, drought prone and forest areas. The Formula adopted for this purpose is somewhat similar to the Gadgil Formula adopted by the Planning Commission for the devolution of plan assistance from the Centre to the states.[16]

Devolution of resources in favour of the district plan is a very ticklish issue and it has to emanate from the political will having commitment and respect for the decentralized planning process. The Government of Maharashtra constituted a high powered committee known as the Planning Sub-Committee of the Cabinet under the Chairmanship of the Chief Minister which decides the size of the State Five Year Plan, distribution of funds between the state and district sector schemes, and their further allocations among the districts. The Planning Sub-Committe of the Cabinet held several meetings during the period from 23.4.73 to 7.6.73 in connection with the formulation of the Fifth Five Year Plan, distribution of funds between the state and district sector schemes, and then their suitable allocation among the districts on the basis of some criteria or formula.

Originally, the Planning Sub-Committee decided in 1973 that out of the total plan outlays, 60 per cent should be treated as district level and 40 per cent as state level. This was done on the basis of classification of schemes between the state and district sector schemes then made. The major irrigation projects which were classified as district level were reclassified as state level mainly having regard to their importance to the economy of the State as a whole. The Planning Sub-Committee,[17] therefore, decided that the total outlays for the Fifth Plan should be equally divided instead of in the ratio of 60 : 40. Further to it, higher outlays were to be provided for power generation and transmission during the course of formulation of the Fifth Five Year Plan. It was also considered necessary to step up the outlays for several other state level programmes. In view of the above, it was suggested by the Planning Department that the relative outlays for state and district level schemes may be determined pragmatically on the basis of progress of expenditure on district plans.

On the basis of the progress of expenditure on district plans during 1974-75 and 1975-76 and the allocation made for the district plan in 1976-77 as compared to the total expenditure or approved outlays during these years, the allocation for district level schemes worked out to an average of 42.3 per cent. The Planning Committee, therefore, decided that the allocations to the districts for their annual plans during 1977-78 and 1978-79 should be calculated on the basis of 42.5 per cent. Thus, district allocations from 1974-75 to 1978-79 were about 42.3 per cent to 42.5 per cent. During 1980-81, 1981-82 and 1982-83, the allocation pattern ranged from 40 per cent to 42 per cent of the total plan outlays. It can thus be observed that about 40 per cent of the total annual plan outlays was allocated for the district level schemes and can be the share of the district plans in the state.[18] Once the size of the annual plan is decided, about 40 per cent allocations are set aside for district level schemes. It may also be mentioned here that out of this district outlays, the amount required for district level schemes which are to be planned and funded from the state pool is deducted[19] and the remaining is distributed amongst various districts according to the criteria or formula (Appendix II) approved by the Planning Sub-Committee.

As a sequel to the policy of district planning and balanced development of all districts, the state Government adopted a scale of weightages for determining the allocation to different districts for their annual plans. The formula[20] provides for allocation of outlays as under: (a) total population (60 per cent), (b) backward class population (5 per cent), (c) urban population (5 per cent), (d) backwardness in agriculture (5 per cent). (e) backwardness in irrigation (4 per cent), (f) backwardness in communication (5 per cent), (g) backwardness in industry (5 per cent), (h) special problems of drought prone areas (3 per cent), (i) problems of the people in the coastal areas (1.5 per cent), (j) problems of the forest areas (1.5 per cent), and (k) reserved at the state level for solving special problems (5 per cent). The above formula is also shown by a graphic chart on the next page. As soon as the district sector outlays are finalized, the allocation of funds to Thane, as also to other districts in Maharashtra, is worked out and made on the basis of the above mentioned formula.

It is now proposed to discuss the actual position as to the allocation of outlays to district sector schemes in Maharashtra with special reference to Thane district. The size of the state plan has grown sizeably during the period from 1980-81 to 1983-84 and it would be useful to analyse the share of district sector schemes in the state plan. The position of share of district in the total state annual plan is shown in Table 5.2.

TABLE 5.2: **Total state plan outlays and the share of the district sector schemes including the state pool**

*Rs. in crores*

| Year | Total state plan outlay | District sector outlays | Percentage to total |
|---|---|---|---|
| 1980-81 | 907.00 | 318.00 | 35.06 |
| 1981-82 | 1110.00 | 429.00 | 38.65 |
| 1982-83 | 1322.00 | 547.51 | 41.42 |
| 1983-84 | 1500.00 | 646.00 | 43.07 |

Table 5.2 reveals that the size of the State Plan had gone up from Rs. 907 crores in 1980-81 to Rs. 1500 crores in 1983-84 and the share of district sector outlays including state pool ranged between 35 per cent to 43 per cent of the total state plan outlays during the same period. In absolute figures, the district sector outlay went up from Rs. 318 crores during 1980-81 to Rs. 646

FORMULA FOR THE DISTRIBUTION OF FUNDS AMONG THE DISTRICTS IN MAHARASHTRA

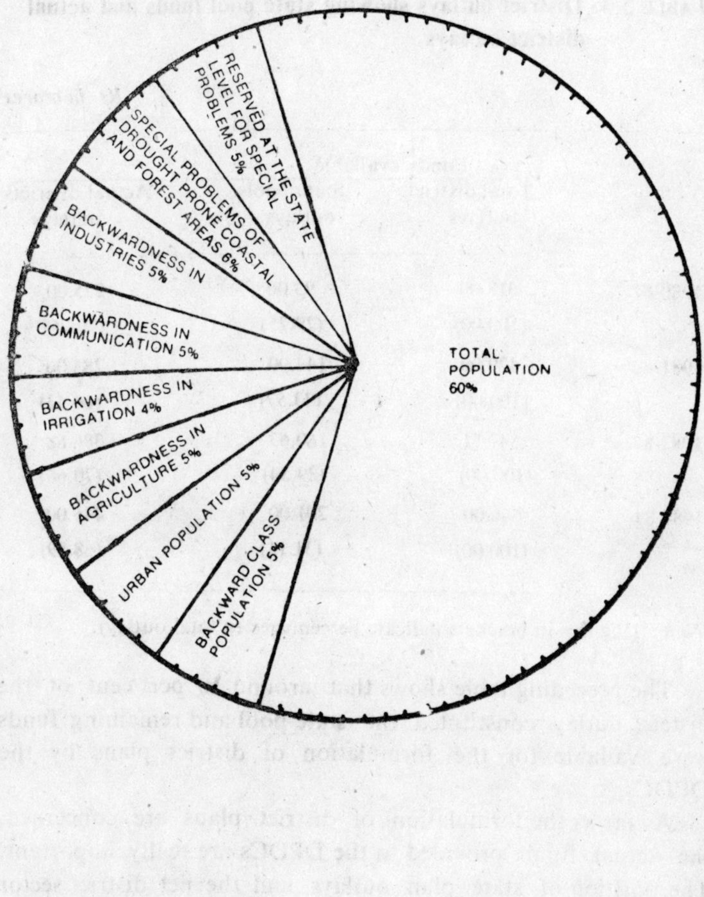

crores during 1983-84 showing an upward trend in district sector outlays.

State pool is a new device that has come to stay in financing the district level schemes formulated by the directorates. It would now be interesting to see the amount earmarked for state pool schemes and the actual allocations made by the Government for the formulation of district plans by the DPDCs in the state. The requisite figures are given in Table 5.3.

TABLE 5.3: **District outlays showing state pool funds and actual district outlays**

*Rs. in crores*

| Year | Funds available | | Actual districts outlays |
|---|---|---|---|
| | Total district outlays | State pool outlays | |
| 1980-81 | 318.00 | 93.00 | 225.00 |
| | (100.00) | (29.25) | (70.75) |
| 1981-82 | 429.00 | 144.00 | 285.00 |
| | (100.00) | (33.57) | (66.43) |
| 1982-83 | 547.51 | 160.63 | 386.88 |
| | (100.00) | (29.34) | (70.66) |
| 1983-84 | 646.00 | 201.00 | 445.00 |
| | (100.00) | (31.11) | (68.89) |

*Note*: (Figures in brackets indicate percentages to total outlay).

The preceding table shows that around 30 per cent of the district outlay constituted the state pool and remaining funds were available for the formulation of district plans by the DPDCs.

As far as the formulation of district plans are concerned, the actual funds provided to the DPDCs are really important. The position of state plan outlays and the net district sector outlays[22] made available to the DPDCs for the formulation of districts plans from 1978-79 to 1983-84 are given Table in 5.4.

## PROPOSED PROCESS OF FORMULATION OF DISTRICT DEVELOPMENT PLAN

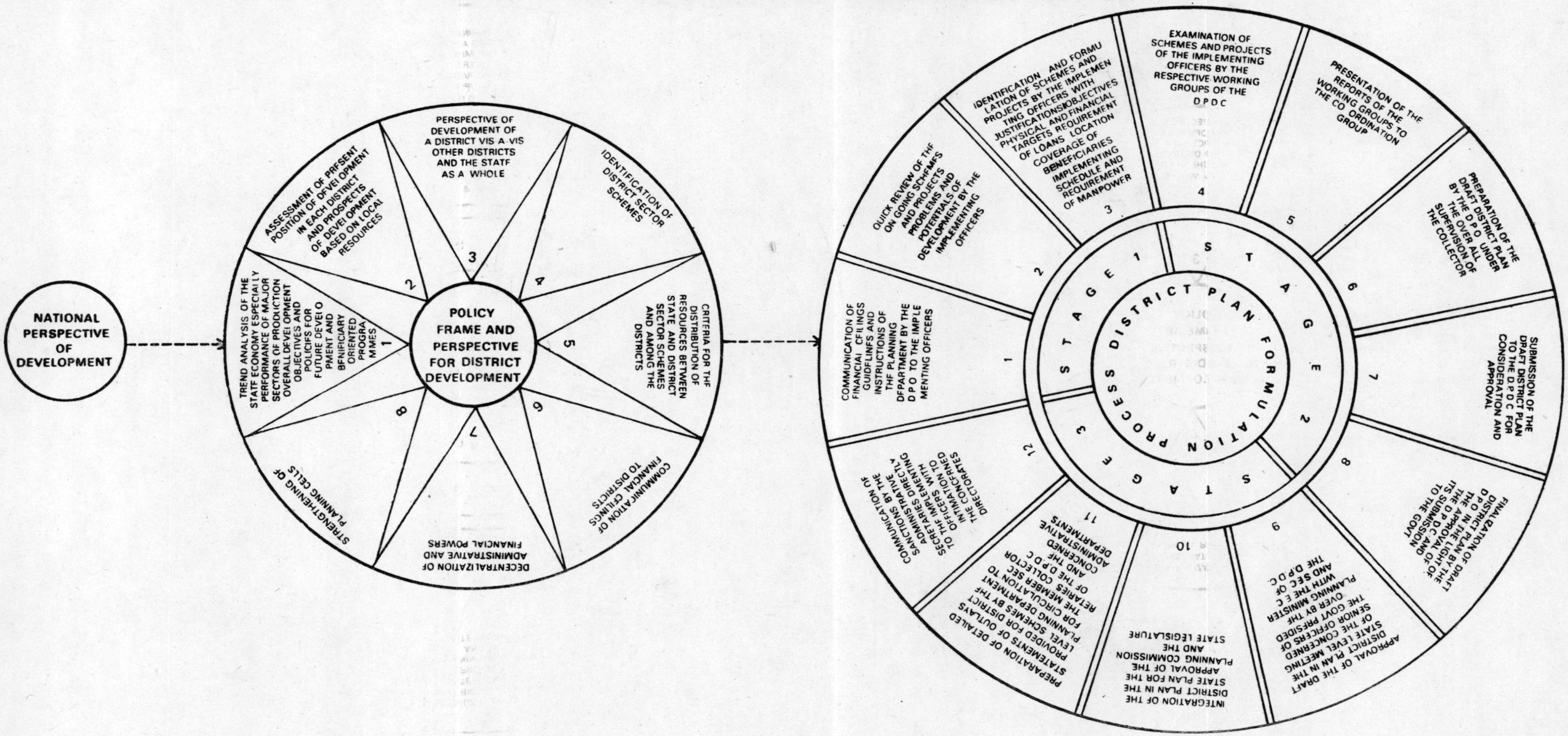


*Facing Page 74*

**TABLE 5.4: Total state plan outlays and net district sector outlays**

*Rs. in crores*

| Year | Total state plan outlays | Net district sector outlays | Percentage share of district outlays to state outlays |
|---|---|---|---|
| 1978-79 | 700.00 | 200.00 | 28.57 |
| 1979-80 | 780.00 | 233.14 | 29.89 |
| 1980-81 | 907.00 | 225.00 | 24.81 |
| 1981-82 | 1110.00 | 285.00 | 25.68 |
| 1982-83 | 1322.00 | 386.88 | 29.26 |
| 1983-84 | 1500.00 | 445.00 | 29.67 |

It is clear from the above table that while the size of State Plan had substantially increased by 114.3 per cent from Rs. 700 crores in 1978-79 to 1500.00 crores in 1983-84, the size of the district sector outlays went up by 122.5 per cent during this period. It is also clear from the above table that the net size of the district sector outlays ranged between 24.81 per cent to 29.89 per cent. In absolute terms, the allocation of resources registered an increase of 122.5 per cent from Rs. 200 crores during 1978-79 to Rs. 445.00 crores during 1983-84. The allocation of financial resources showed an upward trend during all these years except for the year 1980-81. The trend analysis of the above table clearly reveals that the share of the district sector plan has been less than 30 per cent of the total state plan.

The financial allocations earmarked in the state pool at the state level for the financing of the district level schemes are quite substantial, and accordingly diminished the resource base for district planning. In 1979-80, outlays for the district sector schemes were fixed at Rs. 280 crores, out of which Rs. 200 crores were kept for the formulation of district plans by the DPDCs and Rs. 80 crores were earmarked for the state pool for the formulation and financing of district level schemes by the directorates. Similarly, a sum of Rs. 93 crores was earmarked in the state pool for the year 1980-81 and Rs. 144 crores in 1981-82. During 1982-83, out of the total district plan allocation of Rs. 547.52 crores, state pool amounts to Rs. 160.63 crores, i.e. about 29.33 per cent of the entitlement of district level schemes. In the year 1983-84, state pool outlays went as high as Rs. 201 crores out of the total district outlay of Rs. 646 crores, thus reducing the actual share of the district outlays to 68.89 per cent of the total district outlays. As a result of this factor, the amount available for distribution between different districts on the basis of the formula had been substantially reduced. In fact, the share of the district sector schemes was actually less than 30 per cent of the total state plan.[23]

The main reasons for taking up these schemes for financing from the state level pool are: (a) the DPDCs are reluctant to provide sufficient funds for these schemes in their district annual plans, (b) World Bank Projects which are required to be provided necessary funds tend to be neglected by the DPDCs, (c) there are certain schemes which are partially centrally sponsored for which it is necessary to provide funds to avail of the Government of India's assistance, (d) there are also such schemes which require substantial provisions to be made, viz., financing of cooperative spinning mills, medium irrigation projects costing Rs. 5 crores and above, dairy development projects, etc., and the DPDCs find it burdensome to provide sufficient funds for these schemes within their outlays, (e) sufficient funds are not provided by the DPDCs for district level programmes such as rural water supply, Minimum Needs Programme, etc., and (f) there are also pressures from administrative departments to take up more programmes for funding at the state level.

Within the prescribed financial ceilings, Thane district always got its resource share regularly since 1974-75. The financial allocation made in favour of this district from 1978-79 to 1983-84 for the formulation of district plan are shown in Table 5.5.

These figures show that financial ceilings made in favour of this district remained stable at about 5 per cent of the total district outlays during the period from 1978-79 to 1983-84. In terms of absolute figures, the allocation for Thane went up from

Rs. 9.63 crores during 1978-79 to Rs. 22.61 crores during 1983-84, registering an increase of 134.79 per cent.

TABLE 5.5: **Financial ceiling for Thane**

*Rs. in crores*

| Year | Total financial ceiling for the district plans for the state | Financial ceiling of Thane district | Percentage of Thane outlay to total state outlay |
|---|---|---|---|
| 1978-79 | 200.00 | 9.63 | 4.82 |
| 1979-80 | 233.14 | 12.99 | 5.57 |
| 1980-81 | 225.00 | 11.65 | 5.18 |
| 1981-82 | 285.00 | 14.35 | 5.04 |
| 1982-83 | 386.88 | 15.79 | 4.08 |
| 1983-84 | 445.00 | 22.61 | 5.08 |

Thane district has a sizeable Tribal population and adequate funds are also earmarked separately for the TASP and Non-TASP. The DPDC Thane, after deliberations, formulates the annual plan and transmits the same to the Planning Department for approval and integration in the State Plan. The recommendations made by the DPDC. Thane in this regard from 1978-79 to 1983-84 are shown in Table 5.6.

TABLE 5·6: **Recommendations of the DPDC. Thane**

*Rs. in crores*

| Year | Outlays recommended by the DPDC | | |
|---|---|---|---|
| | Non-TASP | TASP | Total |
| 1978-79 | 1.97 (20.46) | 7.66 (79.54) | 9.63 (100) |
| 1979-80 | 4.57 (35.18) | 8.42 (64.82) | 12.99 (100) |
| 1980-81 | 5.15 (36.84) | 8.83 (63.16) | 13.98 (100) |
| 1981-82 | 5.96 (40.52) | 8.75 (59.48) | 14.71 (100) |
| 1982-83 | 6.40 (39.70) | 9.72 (60.30) | 16.12 (100) |
| 1983-84 | 9.16 (40.51) | 13.45 (59.49) | 22.61 (100) |

*Note*: (Figures in brackets indicate percentages of the shares of Non TASP and TASP in Thane district to total district outlays.)

It can be observed from the above table that the DPDC, Thane recommended separate allocations for the Non-TASP and TASP every year keeping in view the guidelines and priorities laid down by the Government. The allocations as recommended by the DPDC, Thane under TASP ranged between 59 per cent to 80 per cent and under the Non-TASP between 20 per cent to 41 per cent.

District Annual Plan, Thane as proposed by the DPDC, is finalized at the state level and finally integrated in the state plan. The total outlay approved by the Government from 1978-79 to 1982-83 is indicated in Table 5.7

TABLE 5.7 **Total plan outlays approved by the state Government in favour of Thane**

*Rs. in crores*

| Year | Outlays approved for Thane | | |
|---|---|---|---|
| | Non-TASP | TASP | Total |
| 1978-79 | 4.24 (34.61) | 8.01 (65.39) | 12.25 (100) |
| 1979-80 | 6.69 (46.11) | 7.82 (53.89) | 14.51 (100) |
| 1980-81 | 5.74 (37.54) | 9.55 (62.46) | 15.29 (100) |
| 1981-82 | 6.00 (37.06) | 10.19 (62.94) | 16.19 (100) |
| 1982-83 | 7.41 (41.12) | 10.61 (58.88) | 18.02 (100) |

*Note*: (Figures in brackets show the percentages of Non TASP and TASP outlay to total outlay in district Thane approved by the Government.)

It is observed from table 5.7 that the total outlays approved by the Government for Thane district showed a steady upward trend. The financial sanctions increased from Rs. 12.25 crores during 1978-79 to Rs. 18.02 crores during 1982-83, registering an increase of 47.10 per cent over 1978-79. The approved outlays under the Non-TASP and TASP also went up considerably, the former from Rs. 4.24 crores to Rs. 7.41 crores, and the latter from Rs. 8.01 crores to Rs. 10.61 crores.

Now, it is possible to have a consecutive glance of the district sector outlays for the state, and financial ceilings for

Thane, outlays recommended by the DPDC, Thane, and the outlays finally approved by the Government to see the size and pattern of approval of the District Annual Plan. The data under each item is tabulated from 1978-79 to 1982-83 in Table 5.8.

TABLE 5.8: **District sector outlays for the state, share of Thane, recommendations of DPDC, Thane, and outlays approved by the Government**

*Rs. in crores*

| Year | Ceiling for district outlays for the state | Financial ceiling for the Thane district | Outlays recommended by DPDC, Thane | Outlays approved for Thane by the Government |
|---|---|---|---|---|
| 1978-79 | 200.00 | 9.63 | 9.63 | 12.25 |
| 1979-80 | 233.14 | 12.99 | 12.99 | 14.51 |
| 1980-81 | 225.00 | 11.65 | 13.98 | 15.29 |
| 1981-82 | 285.00 | 14.35 | 14.71 | 16.19 |
| 1982-83 | 386.88 | 15.79 | 16.12 | 18.02 |

The above table reveals that the actual outlays approved by the Government for Thane exceeded those recommended by the DPDC every year. The outlays approved by the Government were also invariably higher than the initial ceiling fixed for the district by the Planning Department.

The system of financial delegation as evolved above has serious limitations and constraints which are (a) that there is no rational formula for the distribution of the state Plan outlays between the state and district sector schemes, (b) that the state pool funds have substantially reduced the actual outlays for the district sector schemes, and (c) that almost all the funds are spent on the on-going schemes and there is little scope for financing the new schemes and activities.[24]

In Karnal, no attempt has been made to adopt or evolve any formula for the transfer of the plan resources from the state to the district level. The sectors such as agriculture, animal husbandry, cooperation, health, and education included in the district plan were mostly those for which districtwise breakup of investment had been possible.[25] Total estimated expenditure of the District Plan of Karnal was shown as Rs. 114.10 crores, out of which Rs. 49.07 crores were proposed to be spent from Government grants on the proposed divisible schemes during the Fifth Plan[26] and the remaining amount was proposed to be raised from the financial institutions, and all this has been proposed at the district level without any indicative financial frame from the state Government. Resources for the district sector schemes could not actually be built in the Fifth Five Year Plan of Karnal district due to lack of: (a) a rational mechanism for the distribution of plan funds between the state and district sector schemes and their further rational allocations to the districts, and (b) communication of financial ceilings to the districts.[27]

## OVERVIEW

Resource planning is an integrated part of the overall planning process and as such it deserves appreciation by the authorities at the state and district levels. In Haryana, the concerned authority has not been able to evolve any scheme of delegation of financial powers in favour of the district level, and as such the district planning did not reach a take-off stage in Karnal. Therefore, the district plan, at best, could be termed as a mere shopping list or a catalogue of demands.

The experience of Maharashtra reveals that the financial devolution has two main aspects, that is, (a) determination of allocable funds between the state and district sector schemes, and (b) distribution of allocable district plan funds amongst the districts. As far as the first aspect is concerned, the quantum of allocable funds is decided by Planning Sub-Committee of the Cabinet on the recommendations of the Planning Department. Broadly, the district plan share is determined on the basis of past progress of expenditure incurred on the district plan schemes. The district share has been reduced from 60 per cent in 1973 to less than 30 per cent over a period of 10 years due to reclassification of some of the district level schemes into state sector schemes, as also because of a novel device of "state pool fund" engineered at the state level to further squeeze the funding of the district sector schemes. The protagonists of district planning, therefore, suggest the setting up of a Commission for the allocation of funds to the state and district sector schemes. Perhaps, this object can be achieved through the realistic re-classification of state and district sector schemes, and pooling together all the funds of the reclassified district sector schemes under the "district plan share". Once the district plan share is determined, the next step will be to devise ways and means to reallocate these funds amongst the districts for planned development without any political considerations.

Maharashtra has really achieved a success in evolving a formula for the reallocation of grants to its districts, according to which weightage in the allocation of funds is given to various factors like population, backwardness in (a) agriculture, (b) irrigation, (c) communication, and (d) industries; and special problems such as drought prone areas, and coastal areas. Besides, 5 per cent of the funds are kept at the state level as equalization fund for meeting the special problems. Funds are allocated to Thane according to this formula without any political consideration. Generally, the funds finally approved by the Government for Thane exceeded the financial ceilings indicated by the Planning Department.

It may also be pointed out that almost all the funds are spent on the on-going district level schemes and there is little scope for financing the new schemes considered useful in the light of the local potentials and needs. In view of the above, it will be desirable and also pragmatic to earmark 75 per cent of the total district plan outlays for the normal district sector schemes and the remaining 25 per cent of the district plan outlays may be earmarked as discretionary (20%) and incentive (5%) outlays to be placed at the disposal of the DPDCs to formulate schemes of local importance. The DPDCs may finance the discretionary schemes on 100 per cent basis from the discretionary portion of the district plan outlays while the incentive outlays may be provided on the basis of matching contribution of 50 per cent or 25 per cent depending upon the pattern prescribed for the district. These outlays placed at the disposal of the DPDCs, will develop considerable enthusiasm among the people at the district level. The impact of these schemes will reach the village level and the people will get a feeling of participation in the planning process and that they can propose and get schemes of their choice implemented.

Despite certain shortcomings, it is creditable that a sound financial system has been evolved for the allocation of funds for the formulation of district annual plans and procedures in this regard have also been well developed over the years. The micro-financial ceiling technique, as a starting point, is a unique innovation evolved over a period for the formulation of the district plans which ultimately become the integral part of the macro financial frame of the state plan. This has not only made the district planning exercise realistic but also operational. This also helps integrating the district plan with the budgetary process, as a result of which the district plan ceases to be a 'shopping list' or a 'mere catalogue of demands.

After independence, the activities of the Government have increased manifold but the resources have not kept pace with the fast increasing financial commitments. It is, therefore, essential to mobilize resources of all the banks and other institutions for financing the programmes and schemes included in the district plans. Commercial banks after nationalisation have done commendable work in branch expansion and they are now required to be involved in credit planning for the balanced development of the district economies with 'special treatment' for those who are living below the poverty line. In view of the above, the role of the financial institutions consisting of commercial and cooperative banks in the socio-economic development of the districts is being presented in the succeeding chapter.

## REFRENCES

1. There are three main categories of resources, viz., budgetary resources (Government grants as provided in the budget) institutional

resources (loans from the Banks and other institutions) and self-finance. State and district planners are required to make conjunctive efforts to arrange adequate resources for the implementation of the programmes included in the district plan.

2. States of Maharashtra, Gujarat, and Karnataka have evolved a formula for the distribution of funds amongst the districts. This has made the planning exercises realistic in these states.
3. R.P. Misra, Planning From the District Level (Mimeo), Seminar on District Planning, Lal Bahadur Shastri Academy of Administration, Mussoorie, June 3-10, 1973, p. 3.
4. B.N. Ghaira, Financing of the District Plans (Mimeo), Seminar on District Planning, Lal Bahadur Shastri Academy of Administration, Mussoorie, June 3-10, 1973, p. 2. Also refer District Planning: Special Issue (Spring 1975), *Journal of The Lal Bahadur Shastri National Academy of Administration*, Mussoorie, p. 98.
5. Ibid.
6. R.A. Sugavanam, Institutional Finance for Agriculture in the context of District Planning, District Planning in Rajasthan, the H.C.M. State Institute of Public Administration, Jaipur, 1977, pp. 106-107.
7. Tribhuvan Prasad, Concepts, Significance, and Limitations of District Planning (Mimeo), Seminar on District Planning, June, 3-10, 1973, Lal Bahadur Shastri Academy of Administration, Mussoorie, p. 3-4.
8. Refer Circular No. DPC-1080, dated the 5th October, 1979, Planning Department, Government of Maharashtra, Bombay, p. 6.
9. Based on interviews with the officers of the concerned department at the headquarters as well as in the field.
10. Recently, the Municipal Council, Thane, has been made a Corporation.
11. Refer A.S. Dhesi and N.S. Bhullar, Resources for District Plans, (with special reference to Punjab), Vol. II, October 1979, *A Journal of the Department of Political Science*, Guru Nanak Dev University, Amritsar, p. 121.
12. There existed no definite formula before the inception of Fourth Five Year Plan for the purpose of allocating plan assistance among the federating states. The assistance was, therefore, distributed on adhoc basis, and in most of cases on political considerations. The absence of the objectives arrangement for this purpose caused discontenment among several states. They, therefore, demanded scientific method that would take into account the factors that effect the relative financing capacity of the states, and would, thus. accordingly provide for the reasonable equalisation of revenue capacity. In 1968, a formula was developed and a general consensus was subsequently reached in the meeting of NDC to adopt the same. This formula is also popularly known as Gadgil formula.

Uuder this formula, the factors and weights attached thereto for determining the states share in terms of aggregate allocable central assistance are; (a) population (60 per cent), (b) per capita income (below the national average) (10 per cent), (c) tax efforts (10 per cent), (d) special problems (10 per cent), and (e) major irrigation and power projects (10 per cent). The original formula was applied in the Fourth and Fifth Plan. For the Sixth Plan, it has been slightly modified. Now, the last factor, that is, the assistance linked with the major irrigation and power projects is eliminated and the weight of 10 per cent which was originally assigned to this factor is merged with the backwardness factor.

13. See Draft Guidelines for local Level Planning For Blocks In Karnataka: United Nations ESCAP Project, National Workshop On Local Level Planning Bangkok, 22-23, Sept., 1980, p. 15.
14. A.S. Dhesi and N.S. Bhullar, op. cit.
15. Based on the information and data collected from the office of the DPO Thane, District Statistical Officer, Thane, Government Resolutions, Government Circulars, State Plan documents, and District Plans, as also on the personal interviews with the officers of the Planning Department at the State and district levels.
16. In the States of Gujarat, Karnataka, and U.P., such formulae has also been adopted for the allocation of funds amongst districts and weightages are given for the allocation of funds to the district on the basis of population, relative backwardness in agriculure, industry, etc.
17. The Planning Sub-Committee of the Cabinet considered various alternate proposals of the Planning Department for the distribution and allocation of funds in its meetings held on 23.4.1973, 3.5.1973, 16.5.1973, 23.5.1973, 2.6.1973 and 7.6.1973, and approved a formula for the allocatien of funds among the districts in the State.
18. Refer Planning Department, Government of Maharashtra, Bombay, Background note, pp. 2-3. Also refer Planning Commission (MLP Division: State Paper on District Planning in Maharashtra, Status Paper No. 3, p. 2.
19. Ibid.
20. Similar formulae have also been evolved in the States of Gujarat. Karnataka and U.P. for the allocation of funds amongst different districts.
21. This figure includes the amount earmarked for the state pool schemes.
22. These figures showing the district sector outlays have been worked out from the circular letters issued by the Planning Department as well as from the records of the DPO, Thane.
22. Refer Table 5.3.
24. Based on interviews with the district level officers.

25. Refer Development Plan of Karnal District (Fifth Plan and Prespective) Planning Department, Haryana, Chandigarh, p. 2. For details, refer Chapter IV.
26. Ibid., p. 2-3
27. Based on interviews with the officers who were responsible for the formulation of district plan Karnal.

# 6

# RESOURCE PLANNING
## Institutional Finance

INSTITUTIONAL finance is another important source available for financing the district plans. Planners at the state or district level merely confine the planning exercizes to Government grants and generally do not make any attempt to tap the institutional finance abundantly available through the banking network in the districts. The commercial banks, before nationalization, used to extend financial assistance only to a few big industrial houses, and were chary of going to the poor, especially in the rural areas. After nationalization, they have started playing significant role in the socio-economic development of the district economy through the instrumentality of the lead bank scheme. It is, therefore, proposed to discuss the role of the aforementioned scheme in financing the district plan.

Since 1969, the commercial and cooperative banks have opened their branches intensively and extensively both in the urban and rural areas. The commercial banks which were earlier taking interest only in "mandi financing" have also started financing the priority sector, and as such there is no reason as to why they should not be made to play more active and purposeful role in extending financial assistance to the hitherto neglected sectors of the district economy, with emphasis in favour of those living below the poverty line, thereby making them partners in socio-economic reconstruction of the economy.

The commercial banks, especially after nationalization in 1969 are taking keen interest in extending financial assistance for various projects of national or state or district importance. It may be pointed out that significant resources are available with these financial institutions in the district but have so far escaped the attention of the planners in as much as they fell outside the pale of planned funds. These funds are either being frittered away or deployed in relatively non-essential areas.[1] Therefore, enormous resources can be identified and mobilized outside the plan funds and as such the choice devolving upon the district planning body is not so tortuous for mobilizing funds for the district plans.

After the nationalization of commercial banks, various innovations in extending financial assistance to priority sectors such as agriculture, small scale industries, cottage and rural industries, artisans and weavers, self-employed and professionals, transport operators, etc. were introduced by the Reserve Bank of India during the Seventies. One of the most innovative schemes is the "Lead Bank Scheme"[2] which originated from the "Area Approach" to the banking development recommended by the Gadgil Study Group of the National Credit Council. This view was endorsed in the Bankers Committee headed by Shri F.K.F. Nariman, which recommended that specific districts should be allotted to certain banks to play the lead role for banking development. Based on the recommendations of the Gadgil Study Group[3] and the Nariman Committee, the Reserve Bank of India evolved the Lead Bank Scheme in December, 1969 and allotted the districts specifically to the commercial banks.[4] By now, all the 411 districts in the country have been allocated by the Reserve Bank of India to the Commercial Banks for this purpose. The Lead Bank Scheme may be divided into two stages, that is, (a) conducting of socio-economic survey to designate growth centres for branch expansion programme, and (b) formulation of district credit plan. The socio-economic survey conducted by the Lead Banks in the designated district was impressionistic for the development of banking in the district while the district credit plan is an attempt to assess credit needs of the district within the existing framework of infrastructure and banking facilities under the Lead Bank Scheme. The lead bank has been entrusted with the main responsibility to: (a) survey the resources and potential for the development of banking in the district, (b) survey the number of individual and commercial units and other establishments and farms which depend primarily on money-lenders, (c) examine the facilities of marketing of agricultural produce, and storage and warehousing space, (d) survey facilities for stocking fertilizers and other agricultural inputs and also survey facilities for repairing and servicing equipment, (e) train staff who is responsible for disbursing loans and supervising the end-use of credit, (f) assist primary lending agencies, (g) maintain contact with Government and quasi-Government agencies, and (h) identify institutional bottlenecks and credit-gaps and take the initiative in an endeavour to fill them and thus involve itself in the process of economic advancement of the concerned district.[5]

In the first phase of the scheme, the lead banks identified a large number of growth centres where the bank branches could be opened, and these centres were allotted to the commercial banks for opening branches and the number of rural branches increased manifold.[6] In the second phase which commenced in 1976, the role of the banks became development-oriented and credit was considered as a part of the overall process of planned development. In this phase, the lead banks formulated the District Credit Plans for implementation by all the banks in the district including the Central Cooperative Bank and their branches to achieve the objectives of the national plan, viz. (a) removal of unemployment and under-employment, and (b) appreciable rise in the standard of living of the poor section of the population. Now, the third round of the District Credit Plans (DCPs) has also been formulated and is being implemented in the country as per guidelines issued by the Reserve Bank of India in February 1982.[37] Lead Bank Scheme is an innovation in the banking system and a promise for the balanced development of the district economy. It is, therefore, proposed to make an indepth study of its various aspects such as formulation of DCPs, AAPs, availability of institutional finance, achievements thereof, integration of DCPs with the development plans, working of the DCC, and the DLRM, problems and difficulties being faced by the lead bank while implementing the DCPs in the study districts.

## PERFORMANCE OF THE LEAD BANK SCHEME IN KARNAL AND THANE[8]

### Karnal

The Punjab National Bank (PNB) was established in 1895 with its head office at Lahore. After Independence, its head office was shifted from Lahore to New Delhi. Its first branch was opened in Karnal town in May, 1935, and the second in Panipat, another important town of Karnal district, in March, 1937. Thereafter, the other banks also opened their branches in this district. The Punjab National Bank was designated as lead bank for Karnal in the year 1969 by the Reserve Bank of India. As on December 1982, the number of branches of the banks (commercial and cooperatives) had gone as high as 130. By 12th May, 1983, Punjab National Bank had a network of 19 branches in the district. Average population served by per bank branch was 12,800 which compared favourably with the national average of 17,000.

Before nationalization, the PNB and other commercial banks provided loans to the big borrowers and the main emphasis was on making profits and attracting deposits. After nationalization, their main thrust shifted from profitability and profits to provide finances to the neglected sectors as per guidelines of the Government of India, as also of the Reserve Bank of India. In this background, these banks started reorientation of their role from "mandi financing" to priority sectors such as agriculture and allied activities, rural and cottage industries, and SSI units, as also to provide productive loans to the target groups such as Scheduled Castes, small farmers, marginal farmers, landless labourers and rural artisans.

The main objective of the lead bank scheme is to ensure adequate supply of credit for the economic development of the district.[9] In order to achieve the above object, the Punjab National Bank prepared the first district credit plan of Karnal district in October, 1977, and various projects and schemes of all the major sectors of the economy, viz., agriculture and allied activities, industry and services had been covered in it. The first district credit plan proposed to advance loans of Rs. 26 crores in three years (1978-80) to be taken care of by all the financial agencies in the district. In this, efforts have been made to provide for the credit need of the development schemes and projects in the district.[10] The first round of DCP in Karnal terminated on 31st December, 1979. The achievement of the first DCP was Rs. 50.60 crores against the targets of Rs. 26 crores. In the second round, progress of the lead bank scheme was phenomenal as compared to the first round of the DCP In absolute figures, the achievement was Rs. 137.01 crores from January 1980 to December 1982 against a target of Rs 50.82 crores. Now the third round of DCP (1983-85) is in operation. The total financial assistance proposed to be achieved during this period works out to be Rs. 65.35 crores. The sectorwise targets are indicated in Table 6.1.

TABLE 6.1: **Targets of financial assistance under third round of DCP, Karnal**

*Rs. in crores*

| Name of the activity | Amount | Percentage to total |
|---|---|---|
| Crop loan | 22.56 | 34.52 |
| Agriculture district | 18.69 | 28.60 |
| Allied activities | 3.38 | 5.17 |
| Rural and cottage industries | 0.43 | 0.66 |
| Other SSI | 15.94 | 24.39 |
| Transport | 2.85 | 4.36 |
| Other services | 1.50 | 2.30 |
| Total | 65.35 | 100.00 |

In the above proposed financial outlays, the share of the small and marginal farmers and landless agricultural labourers is assessed at Rs. 16.43 crores which is 36.82 per cent of Rs. 44.63 crores for the agriculture sector. The share of SSI upto Rs. 25,000 works out to be Rs. 6.87 crores which constitutes 41.97 per cent of Rs. 16.37 crores. Advances under DRI are proposed to be Rs. 2.32 crores which comes to 3.55 per cent of the total outlay. Out of the proposed DRI outlays, the share of the Scheduled Castes in the DRI works out to be Rs. 1.49 crores which is 64.35 per cent of the total outlay proposed under the DRI. The share of the Scheduled Castes is Rs. 3.06 crores which comes to 4.69 per cent of the total proposed allocation. It is also estimated that about 10,621 persons will be provided employment during the third round of the DCP.

In the second round of the DCPs, the RBI directed the lead banks to formulate the Annual Action Plan (AAP) to inject a greater sense of reality in the implementation of the DCP. This exercise is quite useful and the responsibility of the participating banks is pin-pointed and targets known to them. The targets are rephased and the non-implementable schemes are replaced by the new bankable schemes. Since then, the AAP, is formulated every year.

Banking system in Karnal is well established over the last many years and has done excellent work since 1969. Looking at the achievement of the commercial banks in Karnal, the total advances made by them were Rs. 19.43 crores as on 31.12.76 and the credit-deposit ratio stood as 52.25. Priority sector advances were Rs. 14.91 crores which constituted 77 per cent of the total advances as on 31.12.76. Similarly, the total advances made by the cooperative banks were of the order of Rs. 7.34 crores as on 30.6.76 by the close of the cooperative year. Progress achieved subsequent to it is quite interesting as well as encouraging. Comparative data indicating the number of commercial and cooperative banks, deposits, advances, CD ratio, priority sector advances, percentage of PS advances to total, DRI advances, percentage of DRI advances to total, and 20 PEP advances, for the year 1980 to 1982 are given in Table 6.2.

Table 6.2 reveals that the number of branches of the commercial banks had increased from 92 in 1980 to 109 in 1982 and the advances made by these banks from Rs. 64.95 crores in 1980 to Rs. 93.98 crores in 1982 registering an increase of 45 per cent over 1980. Out of these advances, the share of priority sectors advances was 85 per cent in 1980, 83 per cent in 1981 and 86 per cent in 1982. The CD ratio during this period ranged between 76 per cent to 85 per cent which shows that the banks had not diverted much of finances from this district to other areas. The advances under DRI had also increased but stood at less than 1 per cent of the total advances.

TABLE 6.2: **Comparative figures showing total branches, and progress of the commercial and cooperative banks in Karnal**

*Rs. in crores*

| Item | Commercial banks | | | Cooperative banks | | |
|---|---|---|---|---|---|---|
| | 1980 | 1981 | 1982 | 1980 | 1981 | 1982 |
| Total number of branches of the banks | 92 | 103 | 109 | 18 | 21 | 21 |
| Deposits | 85.93 | 102.35 | 122.40 | 5.63 | 5.59 | 7.24 |
| Advances | 64.95 | 86.86 | 93.98 | 14.24 | 19.93 | 21.88 |
| CD ratio | 75.59 | 84.86 | 76.78 | 253.06 | 356.69 | 302.26 |
| PS advances | 55.29 | 72.25 | 80.88 | 11.39 | 13.89 | 19.74 |
| Percentage of PS advances to total | 85.11 | 83.18 | 86.06 | 80.00 | 69.70 | 90.21 |
| DRI advances | 0.69 | 1.03 | 1.12 | — | — | — |
| Percentages of DRI advances to total | 0.81 | 0.96 | 0.97 | — | — | — |
| 20 PEP advances | 0.83 | 4.58 | 6.54 | — | 1.91 | 2.84 |
| Under IRDP (Fresh financing) | — | 1.61 | 1.06 | — | — | — |

From the preceding table, it is also clear that the cooperative banks had advanced Rs. 14.24 crores in 1980, Rs. 19.93 crores in 1981 and Rs. 21.88 crores in 1982, registering an increase of 53.65 per cent in 1982 over 1980, and percentage advances to priority sectors were 80 per cent in 1980, 69.70 per cent in 1981, and 90.21 per cent in 1982. The credit deposit ratio of the cooperative banks ranged between 253 per cent to 357 per cent during this period.

It is quite clear from the above that the progress achieved in credit promotion in Karnal under the lead bank scheme during the period from 1980 to 1982 is quite striking and the same is presented through Table 6.3.

**TABLE 6.3: Progress achieved in credit promotion in Karnal**

*Rs. in crores*

| Year (January to December) | Commercial banks | Cooperative banks | Total |
|---|---|---|---|
| 1980 | 64.95 | 14.24 | 79.19 |
| 1981 | 86.86 | 19.93 | 106.79 |
| 1982 | 93.98 | 21.88 | 115.86 |

Table 6.3 reveals that the total advances made by the commercial as well as cooperative banks in the district rose from Rs. 79.19 crores in 1980 to Rs. 106.79 crores in 1981 and further to Rs. 115.86 crores in 1982. The pereentage increase was 35 per cent during 1981 over 1980 and 46 per cent in 1982 over 1980.

In order to ensure coordination at various levels between the participating institutions and the Government agencies in Karnal, two committees, viz., the District Consultative Committee (DCC) and the District Level Review Meeting (DLRM) are constituted under the Chairmanship of the Deputy Commissioner, Karnal. The DCC[11] meets once in a quarter to monitor the progress of DCP as well as to sort out various problems in the speedy flow of credit. The meeting of the DLRM[12] is held in the third quarter of the year for two days to review the functioning of the DCCs in this meeting, the progress of the DCP and AAP is also reviewed, and problems discussed in details. Group disscussions are also organised on different subjects and the Group Leader records the major decisions of the respective Group, and presents the same to the DLRM next day for deliberation and approval. The main functions of the DLRM are to: (a) review the implementation of the DCP (b) group discussion on DCP and AAP and (c) decide strategy for implementation of the DCP and AAP.

DCC is the chief Coordinating committee between the banks and the Government agencies functioning in the district. The main functions of the District Consultative Committee are to: (a) allocate credit plan among the financial institutions, (b) monitor the implementation of the credit plan, (c) sort out problems being faced by the banks and the officials agencies, (d) allocate identified growth centres among different banks, (e) step up the flow of credit to priority sectors and neglected sections, (f) serve as a joint forum for disscussing the development needs of the districts,[13] (g) review the progress in the formulation of district credit plan, (h) review the overdue position and recovery performance (i) village adoption scheme, and (j) approval of the district credit plan and annual action plan.[14]

There is also a third committee known as the Standing Committee[15] of the DCC constituted under the chairmanship of the Deputy Commissioner, Karnal. The meeting of this Committee is held every month. The main functions of this Committee are to review the progress of implementation of the Annual Action Plan, and the problems connected therewith.

The main problems that are being faced by the lead bank in financing the DCP and AAP are: (a) lack of integration of DCP and AAP with the district plan, (b) shortage of trained staff, (c) inadequate availability of inputs like seeds, milch animals, etc., (d) lack of cooperation from the non-lead banks in financing the DCP and AAPs, (e) inadequate technical staff to scrutinise the loan application, (f) inadequate staff for recoveries, and (g) lack of powers to the district coordinators to coordinate the loaning programmes of their bank branches.[16]

After discussing the performance and the problems of the Lead Bank Scheme in Karnal, it is now proposed to discuss at length the working of this in Thane.

*Thane*

Bank of Maharashtra has been designated in 1969 as the Lead Bank of Thane district by the Reserve Bank of India. The Lead Bank Scheme has been launched in Thane as a part of the overall policy frame of the RBI as a measure to reduce imbalances in the provisions of banking facilities, as also to ensure a larger flow of credit to agriculture and other neglected sector of the economy in the district.

As far as the role of the Lead Bank in the overall development is concerned, it may be observed, that it does not have the monopoly of banking business in the lead district, nor is the district development the sole responsibility of the lead bank. The lead bank is the leader of the consortium of banks in the district. After identifying the areas requiring branch expansion as well as the areas suffering from credit gaps for the overall development of the area, it has to invoke the cooperation of other banks including cooperative banks and development agencies operating in the district.

There are 204 branches of the commercial banks operating in this district by the end of November 1982. The Bank of Maharashtra is having 47 branches in the district. Out of 204 branches of the commercial banks, 93 branches are in the rural areas, 62 in semi-urban and 49 in urban areas. In addition to this, there are 43 branches of the Thane District Central Cooperative Bank and 11 branches of the Maharashtra State Land Development Bank. As per new guidelines of the RBI for opening new branches per 17,000 population, this district is having adequate banking facilities. However, most of the banches are situated in towns and at the district headqarters, resulting bulk of the rural part inadequately covered. Recently, the RBI has given lincenses to the banks to open 13 new branches, most of which will be in the rural areas. After opening these branches, almost the entire rural area will be effectively covered under banking facilities.

The first District Credit Plan for Thane was formulated for the period from April 1978-March 1979. This plan was based on potential available in the district and schemes identified by various Government agencies and banks. Subsequently, allocations of the institutional finance were made to each branch of banks operating in the district. The plan was extended upto December 1979 as per guidelines of the RBI and the fresh allocations upto December 1979 were made under the Supplementary Plan. The sectorwise outlays of the plan are shown in Table 6.4.

It was the first exercise of this kind and ambitious targets were set out in the plan. As far as the implementation of the above credit plan is concerned, it was half-hearted and nowhere near the target. As a result of this, the review of the financial achievement of this credit plan was also attempted haphazardly in the District Credit Plan for Thane (1980-82).[17] For want of information from a number of institutions, uptodate progress pertaining to the implementation of DCP could not be collected[18]. However, the review is attempted on the basis of information received from some of the participating institutions as also through personal discussions with the branch managers of various banks and officials of various developmental agencies participating in the implementation of the district credit plan. The performance of some of the important schemes and projects such as (a) Dapchari dairy project, (b) wood based industrial complex, (c) digging and energization of wells, and catchment wells under the non-SFDA programme, (d) agricultural inputs, mechanization and infrastructure development, (f) schemes covered under the Integrated Tribal Development Project, (g) financing of powerloom weavers, (h) temporary shopping centres and slum clearance, and (i) crop loan was much below the targets[19]. However, the progress of advancement of loans under the SFDA schemes was satisfactory despite the problem of recovery. The main reasons for the poor performance in credit mobilization for most of the schemes were: (a) poor recoveries of the loans already advanced, (b) non-sponsoring of loan cases by the Governmental agencies, (c) lack of perspective borrowers to avail of financial assistance due to poor publicity about the schemes by the banks and departments, and (d) ineligibility of borrowers due to default.[20]

TABLE 6.4 **Sectorwise targets of the DCP. Thane in the first round from April 1978 to December 1979**

*Rs. in crores*

| Sector | 1978-79 | 1979 Supplementary Plan |
|---|---|---|
| Agriculture | 7.60 | 2.43 |
| Industry | 7.57 | 1.50 |
| Service | 4.16 | 1.50 |
| Total: | 19.33 | 5.43 |

It may, however, be pointed out that the performance of banks in making SSI. advances was very encouraging in relation to the tragets set in the first credit plan. Similarly, the progress under service sector advances was in tune with the targets fixed in the plan.

Therefore, the achievement of the first district credit plan in respect of the agricultural schemes was dismal whereas it was satisfactory in SSI and service sectors from April 1978 to December 1979.

After this, the second round of DCP (1980-82) was formulated and the targets of the banks are shown in Table 6.5 as under:[21]

**TABLE 6.5: Allocation of targets for the year 1980, 1981 and 1982 in Thane**

*Rs. in crores*

| Year | Agriculture | Industries | Services | Total |
|---|---|---|---|---|
| 1980 | 2.53<br>(22.45) | 4.46<br>(39.57) | 4.28<br>(37.98) | 11.27<br>(100.00) |
| 1981 | 3.76<br>(27.11) | 4.95<br>(35.69) | 5.16<br>(37.20) | 13.87<br>(100.00) |
| 1982 | 5.40<br>(36.05) | 5.38<br>(35.91) | 4.20<br>(28.04) | 14.98<br>(100.00) |

The above table shows that allocation for agriculture and allied activities increased and that for industries and services declined during the period from 1980 to 1982. In case of agriculture, the allocation of funds increased from 22.45 per cent during 1980 to 36.05 per cent during 1982. The allocation for industries declined from 39.57 per cent to 35.91 per cent and for services from 37.98 per cent to 28.04 per cent during the above period. The overall allocation was still the highest for industries, followed by services and agriculture. Achievement under the DCP for the years 1980 to 1982 in respect of Thane district are given in Table 6.6.

It is clear that the banks had advanced a loan of Rs. 18.05 crores registering an increase of 60.16 per cent over the original target for 1980 whereas they advanced Rs. 21.64 crores during 1981 registering an increase of 56.02 per cent over the original targetted outlay. Achievement during 1982 went down substantially despite the availability of funds with the banks. The advancement under the agriculture sector increased significantly in 1981 as compared to 1980 but it shrunk too much in 1982.

TABLE 6.6: **Share allotted and performance of the DCP for the years 1980 to 1982**

*Rs. in crores*

| Year | Agriculture | | Industries | | Services | | Total | |
|---|---|---|---|---|---|---|---|---|
| | Allocation | Achievement | Allocation | Achievement | Allocation | Achievement | Allocation | Achievement |
| 1980 | 2.53 | 2.66 (5.14) | 4.46 | 10.07 (125.78) | 4.28 | 5.32 (24.29) | 11.27 | 18.05 (60.16) |
| 1981 | 3.76 | 5.73 (52.39) | 4.95 | 8.24 (66.46) | 5.16 | 7.67 (48.64) | 13.87 | 21.64 (56.02) |
| 1982 | 5.40 | 2.6 (—51.67) | 5.38 | 5.50 (2.23) | 4.20 | 4.75 (13.10) | 14.98 | 12.86 (—14.15) |

(Figures in brackets show percentage excess/shortfall in achievement/allocation).

As far as the availability of resources for financing various schemes is concerned, the commercial banks in Thane are placed in a very comfortable position. In 1979, the credit deposit ratio was 36 per cent. Yearwise figures of deposits and the advances of scheduled commercial banks in the district from 1969 to 1982 are given in Table 6.7.[3]

From Table 6.7, it is clear that the actual deposits of commercial banks increased phenomenally from Rs. 27.10 crores in 1969 to Rs. 202 crores in 1979 whereas the actual advances increased from Rs. 10.97 crores to Rs. 73.00 crores during the same period. The deposits during the year 1980, 1981, and 1982 are estimated on the basis of previous trends, growth of economic activities, branch expansion programme, anticipated monetary and fiscal measures of the Government.[24] The resource position of the commercial banks in Thane district is quite comfortable. The development departments and agencies in this district can mobilize more credit for the socio-economic upliftment of the people especially those living on or below the poverty line.

**TABLE 6.7: CD ratio of commercial banks in Thane district**

*Rs. in crores*

| Year | Deposits. | % growth. | Advances. | % growth | C.D. ratio in percent. |
|---|---|---|---|---|---|
| 1969 | 27.10 | — | 10.97 | — | 40.48 |
| 1970 | 32.87 | 21.29 | 14.92 | 36.01 | 45.39 |
| 1971 | 40.67 | 23.73 | 16.23 | 8.78 | 39.91 |
| 1972 | 45.53 | 11.95 | 19.49 | 20.09 | 42.81 |
| 1973 | 61.14 | 34.29 | 26.16 | 34.22 | 42.79 |
| 1974 | 70.62 | 15.51 | 31.26 | 19.50 | 44.27 |
| 1975 | 83.08 | 17.64 | 35.70 | 14.20 | 42.97 |
| 1976 | 109.52 | 31.82 | 42.99 | 20.42 | 39.25 |
| 1977 | 132.87 | 21.32 | 49.23 | 14.52 | 37.05 |
| 1978 | 169.13 | 27.29 | 60.77 | 23.44 | 35.93 |
| 1979 | 202.00 | 19.43 | 73.00 | 20.13 | 36.14 |
| 1980 | 232.00 | 14.85 | 87.00 | 19.18 | 37.50 |
| 1981 | 265.00 | 14.22 | 105.00 | 20.69 | 39.62 |
| 1982 | 305.00 | 15.09 | 122.00 | 16.19 | 40.00 |

In order to achieve coordination between the banks on the one hand, and the Government departments on the other, three committees namely (a) District Consultative Committee (DCC), (b) District Level Review Meeting (DLRM), and (c) the Standing Committee of the DCC are functioning in Thane. The DCC[25] includes banks operating in the district, Government departments and agencies at the district level, Regional Rural Banks, Primary Land Development Banks, and Central Cooperative Bank, and its meeting are held quarterly under the Chairmanship of the Collector, Thane. It is an important forum for banks, and other agencies to discuss subjects of common interest and understand each other's view point and solve the problems faced by the participating agencies in the implementation of development programmes. The important objectives of the DCC are to: (a) serve as a clearing house for solving problems of the bankers in the district, (b) coordinate the functions of credit and development agencies in the district for implementing development programmes, (c) formulate bankable schemes for implementation by the financial institutions in the district, (d) monitoing the progress of schemes in the district, and (e) evolve a system for exchange of information between credit and development agencies.

The main problems generally dealt with in the D.C.C. are: (a) delay in getting the "no dues" certificates, (b) availability of inputs, (c) marketing of crops, (d) multiple financing, (e) lack of service facilities, (f) lack of extension services such as veterinary services, (g) identification of borrowers at the block and village levels, (h) delay in sanctioning proposals coming within the discretionary powers of branch managers, (i) lack of coordination between banks and Government agencies, (j) non-availability of raw materials, (k) lack of follow-up and recovery problems, (l) disbursement of subsidy, (m) non-submission of data for monitoring, (n) allotment of areas and schemes, (o) share allocation and acceptance, (p) finalization of credit plan and Annual Action Plan, and (q) recovery of loans under Maharashtra Provision of Facilities for Agricultural Credit by Banks Act, 1974.

There is also a Standing Committee of the DCC constituted in 1969. The meeting of this committee is held every month mainly to monitor the implementation of District Credit Plans and Annual Action Plan. It is generally presided over by the Regional Manager or the Lead Bank Officer, Bank of Maharashtra, Thane.

The important functions of this committee are to: (a) review the progress of implementation of various Government sponsored programmes such as disposal of pending loan cases under IRDP, bio-gas scheme, Tribal Sub-Plan, horticulture programmes, etc., (b) review the progress of implementation of Annual Action Plan, (c) discuss allocations under District Credit Plan, Annual Action Plan and other Government sponsored programmes, and (d) help discussions on the formulation of new schemes formulated by the Government from time to time and its allocation amongst various banks for financing the same.

Main problems and issues discussed in the meeting of the Standing Committee are: (a) disposal of pending cases under various Government sponsored programmes, (b) cooperation between Government authorities and banks in successful implementation of government sponsored programmes and Annual Action Plan, (c) assistance and help from Government for recovery, pre-sanction visits etc. by providing vehicles and personnel, (d) lack of submission of returns to the lead bank by banks, (e) refinance facilities from NABARD, (f) allotment of villages to banks for financing under Government sponsored programmes, and (g) lack of veterinary doctors in connection with cattle insurance and veterinary care.

The District Level Review Meeting[27] (DLRM) is held for two days in the third quarter of every year under the Chairmanship of the Collector to: (a) review the implementation of District Credit Plan, (b) arrange group discussions on District Credit Plan and Annual Action Plan, and (c) decide strategy for implementation of DCP and AAP.

The District Level Review Meeting was held on 29th and 30th November 1982, in Hotel Golden Palace, Ravino Kapoor Compound, Thane. In this meeting, review of implementation of District Credit Plan 1980-82 and Annual Action Plan 1982 was made. While reviewing the progress, it was found that majority of the banks had achieved their targets under industries and services sectors but lagged behind in agricultural sector. It was also observed by the Chief Executive Officer, Zila Parishad that most of the banks had not achieved the targets under the IRDP which is really an anti-poverty programme of national importance. After brief discussion, the following four groups were constituted:

(a) Agriculture and allied activities.

(b) Industries and service sectors.

(c) IRDP.

(d) General aspects of lead bank scheme and achievement and difficulties experienced.

The suggestions and decisions of each Group were recorded by the Group Leader and presented to the DLRM on the next day for consideration.

The agriculture and allied activities group recommended that (a) recovery campaign in every half year should be launched in coordination with the DRDA and Government agencies,(b) cases of wells and pumpsets pending for power connection be referred to the concerned BDO, Tehsildar and Collector for further follow up; (c) various Government sponsored programmes like recent crash programme of horticulture be spread over reasonably in time and preliminary proposals be sent well in advance to financial institutions so as to avoid last minute rush for achieving given goals; (d) banks be encouraged to finance for setting up of private nurseries for supplying seedlings and saplings. For promoting such nurseries, Horticulture Department should certify such seedlings and give bulk order for supply to beneficiaries; (e) mortality upto 20 per cent of original programme (plants) be replaced free of cost in subsequent years; (f) for the successful implementation of the small lift irrigation scheme, permission to lift water from notified rivers should be given at least for 12 to 15 years instead of one year; (g) training programme for Gram Sevak and Village Development Officer should be organized by the banks; (h) Maharashtra Provision of Facilities for Agricultural Credit by Banks Act, 1974, had been brought on the statute book since long but there was no awareness among the bankers about its usefulness, and it was, therefore, decided to forward a few test cases to designate officers at Block level for recoveries; (i) there was inordinate delay in supplying the revenue extracts, and the processing of loan applications was delayed. This matter should be brought to the notice of the Collector for issuing necessary instructions to concerned revenue agencies for issuing such extracts in a reasonable period; (j) finance for milch animals under the IRDP for big farmers be concentrated on various existing and proposed milk routes so as to utilize optimum chilling capacity of plants at Saralgaon and Nada; and

(k) pending cases under the IRDP for milch animals be split in the ratio of 80 : 20 for the buffaloes and cows respectively on pilot basis.

Similarly, the following recommendations were made by the group on Industries and Service Sector: (a) the quantum of assistance under the Sick Unit Assistance Scheme of the DIC is very less and the same should be enhanced. The quantum of assistance should be based on total outlay of nursing programme arrived at by the banks with outward limit on assistance from the DIC; (b) the DIC should make thorough scrutiny of proposals before sponsoring the same to the banks, (c) the DIC should hold district and block level examinations of SSI products to promote marketing of these products. A cell for guidance in marketing should also be set up in the district to market their products efficiently; (d) raw material essential for the industries situated in the district be made available by the Government agencies through supply depots established throughout the district in various centres; (e) withdrawal of incentives with effect from 10th January, 1983 to industries established in backward areas would adversely affect the growth of industries in these areas, and as such the incentives already provided should not be withdrawn; (f) setting up of 7 proposed mini industrial estates in the district should be expedited to improve the scope for lending to this sector in these areas; (g) MSFC should popularize their various schemes of financial assistance especially those involving assistance to sectors other than SSI which are comparatively less popular; (h) MSFC should set up branch offices in various places in the district with officers having discretionary powers for sanction of advances; (i) MSFC should make efforts to keep the bankers informed of the salient features of their various schemes through circular letters; and (j) a lead bank bulletin may be circulated among the bankers to keep them aware of the various developments in the banking sector as a whole.

The Group on the IRDP made the recommendations that (a) identification of the eligible beneficiaries should be done carefully. In some cases though the members of the family stay together but shown as separate families. It is suggested that if the particular beneficiary was given eligibility certificate by the BDO, then banker could advance loan and claim subsidy from the DRDA (b) if a branch manager is satisfied that the beneficiary is eligible under the DRI Scheme, a certificate regarding his income signed by the Sarpanch and Gram Sevak be obtained; (c) the loan cases under the IRDP are usually sponsored in large number in the months of January, February and March every year. It is, therefore, suggested that the branchwise target should be fixed and cases should be sponsored accordingly to each branch over a period of 12 months in a phased manner; (d) the DRDA should provide subsidy on Rs. 4,500/- for the purchase of bullock pair and cart; (e) recovery of loan instalments should be linked through the Forest Labour Cooperative Society in respect of bullock carts supplied under IRDP; ( f ) Gram Sevak's help for recovery of loans under IRDP should be extended frequently; (g) list of defaulters should be sent to the BDO with a copy to DRDA for providing help in recovering dues, (h) recovery powers for attachment of assets should be delegated to commercial banks like cooperative banks; ( i ) the Agricultural Assistant to each rural branch and the Agriculture Officer for one thousand agricultural accounts should be provided to the bank branch. The Agricultural Assistant should be recruited from the same district. Special incentives should be given to bank staff in Tribal areas; ( j ) period of law of limitation in respect of Demand Promissary Note should be extended from three years to five years; and (n) the NABARD should extend the refinance facilities under the IRDP to land development banks by relaxing recovery norms of these banks in the district so as to enable them to lend under this programme through their branches in the district.

The suggestions made by the group on 'general aspects to the lead bank scheme and difficulties experienced' are summed up as under:-

**Branch expansion**

Banks generally try to open their branches in the cities which are already overbanked. To overcome this problem, no licences should be given for opening branches at centres which are already overbanked. Banks which have controlling offices in the district should be given preference to open branches.

### District credit plan

Total outlay seems to be adequate as compared to the previous one. Schemewise outlay is also adequate.

### Monitoring and implementation

As the branches are not properly staffed to submit the data as they have to attend to the branch business, the District Coordinator's office may be given additional staff to look after collection and submission of data as regards Lead Bank Scheme.

Some banks have only one or two branches in the district which is or are situated in urban areas. Such branch (es) do (es) not get any applications from the Government agencies although they are eager to advance loans. This unnecessarily creates bad picture. The DRDA, KVIC, and MPBCDC should forward loan applications of eligible persons to them.

### Manpower

Employees posted in rural areas should be given additional incentives and as far as possible local people belonging to the same taluka should be recruited on the lines of those recruited in regional rural banks. Where there are no transport facilities, the staff should be provided with vehicles like bicycle, and motorcycle. Basic infrastructure like post and telegraph offices, and police outpost in rural centres where branches are opened by banks should be created.

### Financing under Government schemes and recovery

The DRDA and KVIC should extend all help to banks for recovery. The Chief Executive Officer of the Zila Parishad proposed to undertake 'recovery drives' in April and October every year.

The roles of the Lead Bank Officer and that of the District Coordinators in the non-lead banks[28] are common features in both districts for the implementation of the lead bank scheme, and as such are discussed as under:-

### Role of Lead Bank Officer

The role of the Lead Bank Officer is to: (a) convene meetings of DCC at regular intervals; (b) prepare and circulate agenda and minutes for the DCC meetings, (c) maintain records of all deliberations in the DCC meetings: (d) ensure the attendance of responsible representatives of the participating institutions whenever there are important items on the agenda; (e) coordinate the efforts of all credit agencies in the district for meeting the credit requirements visualized under the credit plan; (f) develop liaison with the district authorities for synchronizing the efforts of the state Government with those of the credit agencies; (g) prepare notes on issues and problems unresolved at the DCC level for taking up at SLBC and concerned departments of the state Government; (h) bring to the notice of the Regional Manager any shortfalls in the performance of the branches for initiating corrective action; (i) apprise the DCC about the progress of the commercial banks in the implementation of the DCP; and (j) submit periodical returns prescribed under the scheme.

### ROLE OF DISTRICT COORDINATOR

The role of the District Coordinator in the case of non-lead banks in the district is to: (a) attend DCC meetings regularly and participate in the deliberations actively, (b) extend all cooperation to the lead bank in its activities, (c) clearly spell out at the DCC meetings the difficulties experienced in fulfilling credit shares, (d) keep close liaison with the branches operating in the district, (e) take effective steps for fulfilling credit allocations accepted under the credit plan and (f) submit periodical returns prescribed under the scheme.

District Coordinators are assigned this work in addition to their normal heavy duties, as a result of which they are not in a position to fulfil their obligations for the smooth functioning of the lead bank scheme. They are also required to collect and submit to the regional offices lot of data and information regarding the functioning and performance of the Lead Bank Scheme but due to shortage of staff, they are not in a position to do it efficiently. Managers of the banks function absolutely independent of the control of the district coordinators, and as such they fail to control and guide their activities, and the performance of the lead bank scheme is, thus, badly affected[29]

## OVERVIEW

Commercial banks, especially after their nationalization, have been made partners in the socio-economic development of the district as per policy measure.[30] In this situation, it appears necessary to involve them in the process of development of the district economy, in financing the bankable projects and schemes whereas the Government can concentrate on its activities in the fields of services, and development of infrastructural facilities, as also on marketing-cum-processing facilities which are really "facilitating links" in promoting the development.

Lead Bank Scheme is a major innovation in the banking system and seeks to invoke the good offices of all the banks to achieve balanced development of the district economy. It has been launched as a part of the overall policy frame of the Reserve Bank of India, as a measure to (a) reduce imbalances in the provision of banking facilities, (b) ensure a larger flow of credit to agriculture and other neglected sectors, of the economy, and (c) provide "preferential package" to the target groups.

As far as the role of the lead bank in regard to overall development of the district is concerned, it does not have the monopoly of the banking business in the lead district, nor is the district development its sole responsibility in the study districts. It is merely the leader of the consortium of banks and has to invoke the cooperation of the other banks including the cooperative banks, and development agencies operating in the district for the development of the district economy. Under this scheme, the available resources of all the banks are pooled in the District Credit Plan for providing credit facilities for (a) increasing productivity, production and employment opportunity in different sectors, and (b) the weaker sections of society to help them rise above the poverty line.

Under this scheme, the banks have opened their branches extensively especially in the rural areas in Karnal and Thane and process is still continuing. As per policy of the Reserve Bank of India, more and more branches are being opened in the rural areas. It is clear from the above discussion that the financial position of the banks is sound and they can go further in extending financial assistance to the prospective loanees for viable schemes and ventures. Institutional credit is, thus, a very important non-plan additional channel available to the planners for financing the bankable schemes, besides the budgetary grants. It is, in fact, another major source of financing the district plan, thereby reducing the pressure on the budget substantially.

The lead banks in both the districts formulate the District Credit Plans regularly on the basis of guidelines of the Reserve Bank of India, and get them approved from the DCC. They also prepare the Annual Action Plans indicating the credit targets of each bank in the district. District targets are further bifurcated into block plans so as to ensure that each block gets loans according to its potential and need. The plans are constantly reviewed in the meetings of the DCC, DLRM and the Standing Committee of the DCC. These meetings are regularly attended to by the banks and the Government departments, and prove useful channels for ensuring coordination amongst the participating agencies. These banking bodies help sort out problems and difficulties being faced by them. The presence of the district head has lent respectability to these bodies and this enables them greatly to put their heads together to resolve their problems and difficulties coming in the way of formulation, implementation and monitoring of the DCPs and AAPs. The DCC and DLRM are practical devices to achieve coordination for formulation, approval, implementation and review of these plans. Without these devices, perhaps it is unthinkable of heterogeneous elements, comprising all the banks and the departments coming together for this purpose.

As far as the integration of the DCPs and AAPs with the District Plan is concerned, it has not sufficiently caught the imagination of the planners at the district level. In Karnal, the DCP is formulated without any district plan, and as such, there is no integration of the DCP or the AAPs with the district level projects and programmes. In the absence of district development frame, the formulation of the DCP is not realistic inasmuch as it relates to making of provisions for credit for the Government sponsored schemes, especially when the lead bank, while preparing the DCP, cannot have the long-term perspective of development and the likely development of infrastructure on which the success of credit promotion depends. Every year, the Government agencies at the district level transmit to the banks their annual requirements of credit for various schemes and programmes at a belated stage as a result of which it becomes tortuous for the banks to achieve them.

In Thane, the guidelines for the formulation of district plans envisage the credit planning at the district level but in actual practice, both the processes, namely, formulation of district plan and of credit plan have emerged to be two separate systems at the district level, the former does not integrate the latter at any stage of the plan formulation. In fact, the district plan merely contains the schemes and programmes to be financed from the financial ceilings allocated by the Government, and it does not even make a mention of the requirement of loans from the commercial and cooperative banks. Thus, the credit cannot be mobilized for the priority sectors in an integrated manner. However, in the DCP 1983-85 for Thane district, the requirement of loans for Government sponsored schemes and programmes is shown separately which is a very healthy trend.

The non-lead banks have a large number of bank branches in the district. In order to coordinate their activities, one of the managers at the district headquarters is designated as the District Coordinator. It is generally seen that the District Coordinator fails to affect inter branch coordination because of (a) lack of necessary ministerial staff for the collection of data for the lead bank, as also for higher authorities of his own bank, and (b) because of the absolute federal system in the banks in which the managers are independent to conduct and promote the business of their branches, and are not accountable to the District Coordinator. The implementation of the DCPs and AAPs also suffers considerably especially in the areas where the managers do not take any interest in achieving their targets incorporated in these plans.

With the commencement of the lead bank scheme, the work of the banks has also increased manifold and they have opened a large number of small accounts and are expected to open more and more every year. They are short of technical staff to verify and scrutinise the loan cases, and also to complete the bank records which is equally important, if not more. This leads to accumulation of loan cases and the technical staff finds it more convenient to reject than to recommend them for sanctions. This also causes frustration amongst the loanees, and also results in 'no confidence' in the bankingsystem.[31]

The banks, especially the commercial banks, are gradually showing interest to provide loans to the priority sectors particularly agriculture and allied activities, as also to the priority groups living below the poverty line. But the non-recovery of the banks dues has posed a problem especially in Thane district. Although the state Government has passed law on the recommendation of the Talwar Committee to affect recoveries of the bank dues as arrears of land revenue yet its benefit is seldom available to the banks on the ground that the collector is very busy in performing other important duties. In some cases, the banks have no knowledge of this facility and do not refer the cases to the Collectorate for recovery. If this trend continues, the bank dues will sink and recycling of funds will become impossible, and the national priorities will get strangulated.

Despite the above problems, which of course, can be rectified, credit planning through the instrumentality of the lead bank scheme has come to stay and is being done regularly for the overall socio-economic development of the district economies according to the guidelines of the Reserve Bank of India. In these districts, all the banks have been involved in extending financial assistance for the bankable projects, programmes and schemes especially in the priority sector.

The confluence of budgetary grants and institutional finance, integrated in a district plan further supported by the active involvement of personnel of the banks and the district offices, has the potential of increasing production as also of wiping out poverty at the district level. In this entire exercise, the former should exclusively concentrate on providing service, infrastructural facilities, and processing-cum-marketing facilities, as also on the missing links or facilitating links wherever necessary and, the latter should confine its activities to finance the bankable projects and schemes. The district plan should, thus, cover the entire gamut of investment and not merely Government outlays. Assuming that the funds are available, the achievement of national goals by the instrumentalities of the integrated district plans will be a far fetched mission if the district administration is not sufficiently strengthened or revamped. Next chapter is, therefore, devoted to study the district administration with special reference to its role in development.

## REFERENCES

1. Vineet Nayar, Planning For Agriculture at District Level-Karnal: A case study, Seminar on District Planning June 3-10, 1973, Lal Bahadur Shastri Academy of Administration, Mussoorie, p. 2.
2. One of the commercial banks is designated as the lead bank in each district in the country, and it is enjoined upon the lead bank to take up the work of branch expansion systematically to plan for the expansion of branches in the district and also to formulate district credit plan and annual action plans for the allotted district to provide banking facilities to the people. Under this scheme, the lead bank does not have the monopoly in branch expansion or disbursement of loans. In fact, the lead bank is required to formulate the DCP and AAPs in collaboration with the other banks and Government agencies, and the financing of these credit plans are the joint responsibilities of all the commercial and cooperative banks in the district.
3. This Study Group revealed that the commercial banks had not paid sufficient attention to the banking needs of the rural areas in general and backward areas in particular. In 1967, for instance, there were 13 districts in the conntry without any office of a commercial bank and only 5.3 per cent of the agricultural finance and 4.8 percent of the credit need for small scale industries came from the commercial banks. The needs of credit for agriculture, small scale and cottage industries, trade and service sector were neglected. The Gadgil Study Group recommended in its report in 1969 that the nationalized banks should be given specific responsibility for the development of banking in various districts so that these banks could survey the banking potential, establish bank branches, and fill the credit gaps.

4. In order to finance the Primary Agricultural Credit Societies, the Central Cooperative Banks have been established in each district in all the states but none of these banks was designated as the Lead Banks as the RBI wanted to mobilize the resources of the commercial banks for financing the schemes in the priority sectors. However, the Central Cooperative Banks are involved in financing the schemes in the district.
5. P.S. Sood, Development through Lead Bank Schemes, *Indian Banking Today and Tomorrow*, New Delhi, December, 1981, p. 10.
6. No. of branches in the rural areas in the country increased from 1833 in 1969 to 6807 in 1983.
7. Reserve Bank of India: Lead Bank Scheme, District Credit Plans, Guidelines for the Third Round, Bombay, February 1982. These guidelines relate to the preparation of DCPs for 1983-85, and indicate the objectives, directives to be followed, methodology for the preparation of the Third Round of DCPs, plan of work and format of the DCP.
8. Based on information, data and statistic supplied by the Lead Bank Officer, PNB Karnal and Lead Bank Officer, Bank of Maharashtra, Thane.
9. Punjab National Bank: District Credit Plan Karnal (Haryana) October 1977: Concept and Methodology.
10. Punjab National Bank, District Credit Plan Karnal (Haryana October 1977.
11. DCC is the Chief Coordinating Committee between the banks and the development departments in Karnal district. The Deputy Commissioner, Karnal presides over the meeting of the DCC. The other members of the DCC are (a) Managers of all the commercial banks functioning in the district, (b) Manager, Central Cooperative Bank, Karnal, (c) Managers, Primary Land Development Banks functioning in Karnal district, (d) Additional Deputy Commissioner, Karnal (e) Deputy Director Agriculture, Karnal, (f) Deputy Director, Animal Husbandry, Karnal, and (g) District Statistical Officer, Karnal.
12. DLRM consists of all the commercial and cooperative banks operating in the district, representatives of the NABARD and RBI and Government agencies at the district level. The meeting is held under the chairmanship of the Deputy Commissioner, Karnal.
13. Refer R.P. Goyal, Lead Bank Scheme, Commerce (Pamphlet-134), Bombay, 1979, p. 24.
14. Refer S.K. Achar, Lead Bank Scheme: Impact on Modern Banking, The Economic Times: Supplement on Nationalized Banks, p. 1.
15. The Standing Committee consists of District Coordinators, District Central Cooperative Bank, and District Level Officers. In the absence of the Deputy Commissioner, the meeting is held under the chairmanship of the Additional Deputy Commissioner, Karnal.

16. There are a large number of branches of each bank at the district level and each branch manager functions independently in case of his own branch and is not answerable to any one at the district level. This creates a problem of coordination of an acute nature, as a result of which the lead bank and the district coordinators also find it difficult to involve the unwilling branch managers in financing the DCP and AAPs.
17. Refer District Credit Plan 1980-82 for Thane District, Bank of Maharashtra, pp. 11-20.
18. Ibid., p. 11.
19. Ibid., pp. 11-20.
20. Ibid.
21. Refer District Credit Plan 1983-85, Thane District, Bank of Maharashtra, Maharashtra State, p. 10. Also refer Annual Action Plan, 1980, 1981, and 1982, Thane, Bank of Maharashtra.
22. District Credit Plan (1980-82) for Thane District, Bank of Maharashtra, p. 46.
23. Ibid., p. 47.
24. Ibid.
25. District Consulative Committee is constituted in Thane district under the chairmanship of the District Collector. The other members on this Committee are: (a) all the banks operating in the districts, (b) Government development departments and agencies in the district, and (c) representative of the RBI.
26. The Standing Committee of the DCC consists of Lead Bank Representative as Chairman and the other members on this committee are: (a) District Coordinators, (b) Thane District Central Cooperative Bank, Thane, (c) Land Development Bank, Thane, (d) Project Officer, DRDA, Thane, (e) District Planning Officer, Thane, (f) Agricultural Development Officer, Thane, (g) Dairy Development Officer, New Bombay (h) District Deputy Registrar, Cooperative Societies, Thane (i) District Village Industries Officer Khadi and Village Industries Board, Thane, (i) Field Officer, Mahatma Phule Backward Class Development Corporation, Thane, (j) Lead District Officer, RBI, Bombay, (k) Deputy Manager, NABARD, Bombay.
27. The DLRM comprises: the District Collector as its chairman, and the other members on it are: (a) all members of the DCC, (b) Geologist, Ground Water Survey and Development Agencies, Thane, (c) a representative of Maharashtra Agro-Industries Development Corporation (MAIDC), Bombay, (d) District Publicity Officer, Thane, (e) Conservator of Forests, Thane, (f) Factory Inspector, Thane, and (g) Lead Bank.
28. One of the commercial banks has been designated as the Lead Bank for every district by the RBI. All other banks are non-lead banks and one of the managers of these banks is designated as the District

Coordinator who does not have any coordinating authority over the other branch managers who have the same powers.

29. Based on interviews with the officers of the banks in Karnal and Thane districts.

30. In Haryana, universally accepted land tax upto 6.25 acres of land has since been abolished. In Punjab, increase in bus fare became a subject matter of agitation by the opposition and even the Assembly Session was gheraoed by the opposition in 1982-83. In this situation, the Government finds it difficult to raise resources to finance its plans, for which it has to involve the banks in financing the bankable schemes and projects.

31. Based on interviews with the officers of the Bank of Maharashtra, Thane and Punjab National Bank, Karnal as well as officers of the the non-lead banks.

# 7

# INSTITUTIONALIZATION OF DEVELOPMENT ADMINISTRATION

DEVELOPMENT of an economy, as also of the people, cannot be achieved by the state without building up or strengthening its institutions. District Administration is one of the chief institutions in the Indian Administrative System and this unit, being very near to people and their problems, can be made responsible for planning and implementation of the district sector schemes. Institutionalization of the development administration[1] is necessary to achieve developmental goals, particularly the eradication of poverty, unemployment and inequalities in India, and that too, without neglecting or sacrificing the economic growth. The administration in a developed country, where the rate of literacy is very high and the citizenry is quite enlightened, is required to perform certain specific jobs than that in a developing country like India where the masses are poor, illiterate and ignorant, as also, by and large, fatalists. Most of the people in India have low per capita income which is largely spent on food, and as such remain perpetual victims of under-nutrition, and malnutrition; bad housing and over-crowding; bad hygiene and poor medical care. As far as their aptitudes are concerned, these are characterized by lack of training facilities and low level of skills; defective education and mass illiteracy; and false and harmful beliefs. Their attitudes to work and life are also characterized by lack of discipline; caste and religious prejudices; poor ambition, and unwillingness to take risks; and contempt for manual labour especially amongst those who are literate or even semi-literate. These problems get further elongated in a soft state[2], and elude solutions perpetually as the state fails to take hard decisions to transfer assets and technology in favour of the poor. In view of the peculiar circumstances of such a country, the task before the administration is much more difficult than its realization. It is, therefore, necessary to build up viable administrative machinery at the district level for the formulation and implementation of development programmes and schemes.

District administration[3] is the total manifestation of the state authority through which all the activities of the Government get a practical shape at the district level. District, as a unit of administration below the state level, was the nodal point of administration during the British period, and still continues to be so even after Independence. It is largely at the district level that all the agencies of the Government converge and the policies and programmes find a concrete shape.[4] District administration (also) provides the principal points of contact between the citizens and the processes of Government and is truly the cutting edge of the tool of public administration.[5]

During the British period, the district administration was chiefly responsible for law and order, collection of revenues as well as for administering regulatory functions keeping in view the exigencies of the time. In this scheme of things, Collector became the king-pin of the district administration and the sole repository in the district of the executive authority of the Government.[6] The words of the Collector were taken as law, and he became the chief representative of the Government at the district level. Whenever there was any problem of any type, the Government depended upon his report. In short, he became the eyes and ears of the Government. With the advent of Independence, Government was involved more and more in development and welfare activities. The district which had emerged as the basic territorial unit for administration during the colonial days continued to play that role even later with the added emphasis on planning and implementation of welfare and developmental schemes. The Collector, the police, the technical officers on the one hand, and the local Government bodies such as the municipalities and the Panchayati Raj institutions on the other, function as the agencies of the state Government at the district level.[7]

The real problems of the district administration started with changes in its ecology[8] particularly when "development" became the major issue and the structure of district administration underwent a kaleilodoscopic change especially after Independence. There has been a phenomenal increase in the activities of the Government, particularly in the spheres of welfare and development, leading to the proliferation of a number of departments.[9] This has led to the expansion and strengthening of the already existing district level offices such as agriculture, animal husbandry, forest, irrigation, PWD (Buildings and Roads), and Public Health. In addition, there has also been a mushroom growth of various new departments at the district level like planning, panchayats, development, social welfare, welfare of Scheduled Castes and Tribes, labour rehabilitation, sports, and family planning. Besides this, IRDP, CADA, DPAP, DDP, Fish Farmers Development Agency, NREP, etc. with their governing bodies also made their appearance in the already expanding district administration. Not only this, but almost all the departments at the state level, while safeguarding their single line control, also managed to get letters issued from the state Government to constitute various district level committees[10] to be presided over by the Collector or Deputy Commissioner, and this committee system, over the years, has become an integral part of the district administration.

Looking back to 1952, the planners and political leaders presumed that the lack of development was for want of: (a) resources, and (b) transfer of technology. In order to bridge the gap in resources and technology, the Community Development Programme was launched in the country and the Block Development Officers with subject-matter specialists in the fields of agriculture, cooperation, animal husbandry, industry, etc. were located in the rural areas for the first time which really gave birth to "development administration". In order to elicit popular participation, the Panchayati Raj institutions[11] (PRIs) were created in 1959 by the states in the country with varying degree of powers.

Thus, in addition to the bureaucratic apparatus, the Panchayati Raj institutions also came into existence and became a part of the district administration. It was conceived that all development functions at the district level should be made the sole responsibility of these institutions and they should be responsible for the formulation and implementation of district and local plans and implementation of central and state schemes within the district.[12] All district level officers in charge of development departments should be transferred to the Zila Parishad.[13]

Report of the study team of the ARC on district administration observed that the Government has taken a very important step towards democratic decentralization by transferring most of the development work in the rural areas to District Panchayats. There are now two distinct wings of administration in the district, general administration and development work in the state sector under the Collector, and other district officers and rural development under the District Panchayats.[14]

By bringing together the various state departments at the district level under one unified control of the district panchayats, an ideal atmosphere is created for both vertical and horizontal coordination at the district level.[15] Further, with the administrative machinery at his disposal, the District Development Officer can be an excellent institution for development administration in the district provided he is amply empowered and fully charged with the responsibility of execution.[16]

In the federal Constitution, planning is based on a scheme of partnership between the centre and states in which their roles in their respective spheres in planning, development and social welfare activities are well defined. However, below the state level, the Constitution does not define the relationship between the district[17] and the state, though the Constitution in the Directive Principles of the State Policy makes a mention only of village panchayats as a form of local Government. In practice, other tiers of locally elected bodies like Panchayat Samitis and Zila Parishads have been constituted in the states through enactments since 1959 and also vested with powers which vary from state to state depending upon the role visualized for them by the state Governments. The political leadership, however, in most states visualized these instiutions as a potential danger to its own position and did not delegate much of administrative and financial powers in their favour. Even where some such powers were vested, they were not allowed to exercise them.

The functioning of these institutions also reveals that they were mostly fed on grants or doles, and as such they could not discharge the functions and responsibilities for which they were created. An analysis of Panchayati Raj institutions has shown that the decentralization of Government functions and responsibilities associated with Zila Parishads, Panchayat Samitis and Village Panchayats has at best meant only partial association of local representatives with administration and not the setting up of a machinery for planning from below.[19] By and large, there is no meaningful involvement of the citizens and their elected representatives into the administrative system at the district level, except in some states such as Maharashtra and Gujarat. In this way, the gap between public authority as manifested in district bureaucracy and political leadership as representatives of the common masses still persists.[20] Despite various efforts made to strengthen the district administration, it has yet to become a competent tool of development administration.

A sound district administration requires that the involvement of the citizens and the elected representatives should be built into the administrative system. One of the serious problems in local public administration is, therefore, the development of a system capable of integrating both the political and administrative systems.[21] The development administration at the district level must, therefore, ensure the following norms:

(a) It must offer an integration of the political, administrative and local institutions for determining the programme of development for the area (district) and the manner in which it can be implemented, thus enabling direct interaction between citizens, Panchayati Raj bodies, non-official agencies like cooperatives and implementing agencies.

(b) It must bring together all the administrative operations at the area level under effective coordination and controlof a single agency. The system devised must be able to effectively counteract the powerful forces of centralization and fragmental decision-making associated with vertical administrative heirarchies dealing with separate segments of the economy.

(c) It must provide an effective mechanism for formulating a programme of development based on the local resources, needs and expectations of the people.

(d) It must clearly lay down a programme of work for the participating agencies which could be made responsible for the proper execution of their respective assignments.[22]

The above model of district development administration presupposes: (a) an integration of politico-administrative system for determining the programme of development for the district (b) coordinating authority, (c) an effective mechanism for formulating a programme of development based upon the local resources, needs and expectations of the people, and (d) a schedule of work for the implementing agencies with responsibility for proper execution of schemes. Now, it is proposed to discuss the experience of Karnal and Thane vis-a-vis the parameters mentioned above.

## POSITION IN KARNAL

In Karnal,[23] as also in other districts in Haryana, political system comprising Panchayati Raj institutions and local bodies at the district or even at the lower levels, is either very weak or defunct and as such cannot meaningfully participate in the development process. The Zila Parishad, Karnal[24] was conceived merely as an advisory body[25] and its income was Rs. 13.66 lacs, Rs. 14.00 lacs and Rs. 12.00 lacs during the years 1969-70, 1970-71, and 1971-72 respectively. It had since been abolished in 1973 and not revived so far. The Collector was non-voting member of Zila Parishad, with which he was associated in purely advisory capacity. He has the powers to inspect and supervise the work of the other Panchayati Raj institutions. Panchayat Samitis were, by and large, ineffective to undertake any development work in their jurisdiction due to meagre financial resources. For example, the income of Panchayat Samiti, Karnal, was only Rs. 4.16 lacs in 1980-81, Rs. 4.61 lacs in 1981-82 and Rs. 4.61 lacs in 1982-83.

Elections of the Panchayat Samitis were last held in 1972

and these Samitis were constituted for 5 years. On the completion of their term in November, 1977, they ceased to function legally as there was no enabling provision in the Punjab Panchayat Samitis Act, 1961 for their continuation as such. In their place, the Block Development and Panchayat Officers were appointed as administrators to carry out their functions. The entrusting of the work of the Panchayat Samitis to the Block Development and Panchayat Officers did not prove useful due to misuse of funds and grants by many of them.[26] The Government, therefore, constituted a Committee of three officers consisting of: (a) Sub Divisional Officer (Civil) as its Chairman, (b) Additional General Assistant of the district as member, and (c) concerned Block Development and Panchayat Officer as member to administer the affairs of the Panchayat Samitis. As far as the Village Panchayats are concerned, elections are held regularly. Recently, elections to 5625 Gram Panchayats were held from 23rd May to 30th June, 1983, and the village panchayats have been reconstituted. In the absence of shtrong Panchayati Raj institutions, especially at the higher level, the Block Development and Panchayat Officers and the staff meant for these bodies work without any specific duty schedule in the district administration.[27]

The other units of Local Government in Karnal are Municipal Committees and Improvement Trusts.[28] These bodies are also superceded for the last many years and are not revived. Different dates had been fixed up for holding elections to the Municipal Committees but these had been postponed on political considerations.[29] The affairs of these Committees are being managed through the administrators appointed by the Government.

The District Planning Advisory Board[30] is set up under the Chairmanship of the Deputy Commissioner and it is assisted by the District Planning Committee and the District Executive Committee. District Executive Committee[31] is headed by the Deputy Commissioner, Karnal and entrusted with the work of preparation of district plan and to watch its execution in consultation with district level officers of other departments. The District Planning Committee,[32] which is also headed by the Deputy Commissioner, assists the District Planning Advisory

Board in the formulation of short term and perspective plans of the district, and to review the progress as to the implementation of development programmes in the district. However, the meetings of these bodies were rarely held for the purpose for which these were created.[33]

Besides, he is also the Chairman of various development committees of various development departments in the district and sorts out inter-departmental problems.[34] In almost all the development programmes, he is assigned the role of coordination. Whenever the main programmes such as IRDP and FFDP arc conceived, an additional burden falls on the institution of the Deputy Commissioner. Recently, the post of the Additional Deputy Commissioner (Development) has been created to look after the growing development work under the overall supervision of the Deputy Commissioner. Thus, with this, the Deputy Commissioner as an institution is further strengthened though it (institution) has lost quite some of its glory and prestige[35], especially with the increasing application of science and technology in administration.

In Maharashtra, a sincere attempt has been made to institutionalize the development wing of the district administration. The experience of this state makes an interesting study, and as such it is proposed to bring about the salient features of the whole of the system through an in-depth study of the District Planning and Development Council (DPDC), Thane, highlighting (a) the integration of the political, administrative and local institutions for the formulation of the district development plans, (b) mechanism for affecting coordination of all the development operations under the control of a single agency, (c) fixation of programme of work for the participating agencies and accountability of the implementing officer to the system so evolved, and (d) role of the Collector as the coordinator of the development efforts in the district.[36]

## Position in Thane

In the first phase of development administration, Panchayati Raj institutions came into existence in Maharashtra in May, 1962 with the enactment of the Maharashtra Zila Parishads and Panchayat Samitis Act, 1961. In the scheme of decentralization, the Collector is kept out of the Zila Parishad which is the strongest of the three tiers and has a non-official Chairman. It is responsible for the entire field of local activities in rural areas and also exercises certain regulatory and administrative powers. The activities of this body encompass practically all the basic needs of the people in rural areas.[37] The broad features of the Panchayati Raj institutions are summarized below:[38]

(a) A strong body for the administration of development and welfare activities in the rural areas has been formed at the district level.

(b) A very large devolution of the functions and activities of the state Government in the matter of rural development in the district has been made in favour of the Zila Parishad.

(c) Control of the officials working under the Zila Parishad has been completely vested in the Chief Executive Officer who is an officer in the senior scale of the IAS.

(d) The administration of Zila Parishad is carried out by functional committees such as (i) Finance Committee, (ii) Works Committee, (iii) Agriculture Committee, (iv) Social Welfare Committee, (v) Education Committee, (vi) Health Committee, and (vii) Animal Husbandry and Dairy Committee[39] set up at the district level.

As many as 141 schemes relating to agriculture, animal husbandry, forests, removal of untouchability, social welfare, economic development of the backward classes, programmes for the welfare of backward classes, training of backward classes, education, medical, ayurveda, public health, building and communication, public health engineering, industries and cottage industries, cooperation, publicity, community development, social education, and village upliftment have been transferred to Zila Parishad,[40] and these schemes are known as District List Schemes. As regards the state sector in the district, it is now concerned with schemes which have no direct bearing on rural development in the district and such development activities which have not been transferred to Zila Parishad.

The plain reading of Section 100 of the aforementioned Act

reveals that the Zila Parishads in the state are vested with the obligatory functions "to promote planned development of the district by utilizing, to the maximum extent, local resources and for that purpose prepare annual and long term plans."[41] A number of plan, purposive and agency schemes have been transferred by the Government to Zila Parishad for execution or maintenance under Section 100 of the Act.[42] In the execution or maintenance of works or development schemes under this Section, the Zila Parishad acts as agent of the state Government and is paid by the Government such sums (including any extra cost of administration incurred in executing works or schemes) as may be determined by the State Government.

The Zila Parishad was also statutorily enjoined upon to promote planned development in respect of the local sector schemes included in Schedule I, as also under Section 123 of the Act but an experience revealed that it did not take it seriously. The Evaluation Committee on Panchayati Raj, in its report, did not find any particular evidence to show that there was any conscious and systematic planning in local sector.[43] Some of the lacunae in the present local planning, as pointed out by the above Committee, are summarized as under:—

(a) Under Section 100 (4) of the Act, Zila Parishad has to prepare annual and long term plans after taking into account the plans prepared by their Panchayat Samitis. Similarly, under Section 108, Panchayat Samitis also have to prepare overall plans of works and development schemes to be undertaken in block areas for enabling the Zila Parishad to prepare their development plans. The Committee observed that it is indeed a matter of concern that inspite of these enabling provisions for local planning with reference to the relevant specific items, the Panchayati Raj bodies have not attempted any concerted planning for the development of their areas in a scientific and systematic manner after taking into account the potentialities of development and availability of all types of resources. As a matter of fact, the plan process at the Panchayati Raj level has no scientific basis. It is nothing more than a mere distribution of the financial resources from the state to the Zila Parishad and from the Zila Parishad to the Panchayat Samitis.

(b) Consequently, meaningful physical planning in terms of target setting is rarely done. There are quite a few schemes of which figures of achievement of targets are not available and the progress of such schemes is assessed merely on the basis of quantum of financial expenditures.

(c) In making plan allocations to Zila Parishad by the state Government and to the Panchayat Samitis by the Zila Parishad, no specific norms, such as population, backwardness of areas etc. have been prescribed.

(d) The state Government has not so far attempted categorization of schemes and resources for various sectors based on certain "priorities" considerations.

(e) The plan and non-plan resources made available to Zila Parishad by Government are largely tied down to certain schemes, staff, etc. The Zila Parishad's own resources are also not sizeable. Consequently, it has no particular freedom for local planning.

(f) The present system of watching the progress of plan schemes and their problems and difficulties through a system of conferences and committees is defective.

(g) The Planning Officers of Zila Parishad have so far proved ineffective.

(h) The Zila Parishad budget is not an operational budget nor has it been made an instrument of planning. Similarly, reappropriations in budget are sometimes managed to pull benefits to particular areas.

(i) Investment from 'General funds' or from Zila Parishad's own resources is rarely directed towards the backward areas.

(j) Plan funds are predominantly invested in areas of assured rainfall at the expense of dry areas.

In view of the above, the Committee recommended that the Government should attempt an immediate categorization of schemes to be taken up in various sectors, that is, the state sector, the Zila Parishad Sector and Panchayat Samiti Sector. The allocation of resources should be based on certain specific norms, such as population, backwardness of areas, etc. Since Social Welfare is the most neglected and suffering sector,

50 per cent of income from land revenue and "equalization grants" be spent by the Zila Parishad on development of Scheduled Castes and Scheduled Tribes. The Committee also recommended the transfer of a large number of schemes to Zila Parishad and Panchayat Samitis so as to make the decentralized planning meaningful.

The state Government has been taking steps to create, expand, strengthen, and institutionalize the district development administration for planning and implementation of the development activities and programmes only in the rural areas. But this system cannot be legally entrusted with coordination of the activities of other local bodies and organizations which are functioning in the district.[44] The sphere of action of Zila Parishad and Panchayat Samitis was limited to such schemes and programmes which are entrusted to them under the Act. Apart from these, some activities were still retained in the state sector which also had a direct impact on the development of the district as a whole. Besides, programmes of various financial institutions, urban local bodies, statutory corporations and boards constituted by the state Government have to be coordinated with the development programme of rural areas drawn by the Zila Parishad and Panchayat Samitis. Thus, there was no single agency which could be entrusted with the function of bringing about close coordination amongst various agencies responsible for the development of the district. Besides, there are other activities such as slum clearance, town planning, etc. in the urban areas which cannot be passed on to the Panchayati Raj institutions. In view of the above, the District Planning Boards were constituted in Maharashtra in 1972 for providing proper planning machinery at the district level[45] and this step must be regarded as the beginning of the second phase in the institutionalization of development administration for the formulation and review of progress of development plans at the district level.

The preamble to the resolution[46] in this regard issued on 20th October, 1972 runs as under:—

The Government of Maharashtra has decided to adopt the district as the unit for planning and to formulate perspective plans for each district so that imbalances in development as between districts and areas within the same district are steadily removed to the extent possible and all the districts are given an opportunity to attain full development having regard to their potentials, available manpower and other resources. The preparation and implementation of the perspective plans and Five Year Plans within such perspective plans calls for coordinated efforts on the part of various organisations concerned with the development of the district, such as Government departments, local bodies including Zila Parishads, Panchayat Samitis, Village Panchayats, Municipal Councils and financial institutions, like the District Central Cooperative Bank, the District Mortgage Bank,[47] the nationalized banks, and other commercial banks, corporations and boards. At present, there is no agency at the district level to bring about the coordination between all such agencies in the task of formulation and implementation of the perspective and the Five Year Plans for the district. The Planning Commission has also advised that the state Government should strengthen planning machinery at the district level with a view to bring about coordination between the various developmental agencies in the district and for formulating and implementing coordinated plans of development for each district. Thus, in this background, District Planning Boards were created in the state.

The District Planning Board, Thane, was set up on the 20th October, 1972 under the Chairmanship of the designated Minister of the district[48] with the Divisional Commissioner as its Vice-Chairman. It consisted of 11 other members[49] including Planning Officer, Zila Parishad, Thane as its Member-Secretary. The Board was required to meet as often as required but atleast once in every three months. The functions of this Board[50] were to: (a) ensure coordinated action by various implementing agencies including Zila Parishad, (b) give guidelines to various implementing agencies with regard to formulation and implementation of the Prespective and the Five Year Plans of the district, and (c) approve Five Year Plans and Annual Plans of the district subject to the orders of the state Government.

The District Planning Board was assisted by a District Planning Team consisting of the Chief Executive Officer of the Zila Parishad, Deputy Director of Agriculture, Deputy Registrar of Cooperative Societies, the District Statistical Officer, Divisional Forest Officer, and the Industries Officer. The Planning Officer of the Zila Parishad was its Member-Secretary. The District Planning Team was entrusted with the overall review of of all the resources available or being made available to various agencies in the district, and supervise implementation of various plan schemes including central plans and centrally sponsored schemes.[51] On 18th June, 1978, 3 non-official members were nominated on the District Planning Board, Thane and the Chief Executive Officer of the Zila Parishad was made the Member-Secretary of the District Planning Board in place of the Planning Officer.

The constitution of the above District Planning Board was open to the following criticism: (a) that it did not give representation to the elected MLAs and MPs, (b) that persons representing various interests such as trade, industry, commerce, universities, social welfare, etc. are not given representation, and (c) that the board is merely advisory in nature.[52]

In view of the above criticism, the state Government also constituted the District Development Consultative Council Thane by its resolution[53] on 20.6.1973 under the Chairmanship of the designated Minister of the district and the other members on it were: (a) Vice-Chairman and other members of the District Planning Board, (b) all members of the Lok Sabha and Vidhan Sabha elected from the district, (c) all members of the Rajya Sabha and Vidhan Parishad residing in the district, and (d) four representatives to be nominated by the Government to represent the interest of industry, trade and commerce, universities and social welfare institutions in the district.[54]

The Government constituted the District Development Consultative Council, Thane to serve as a forum for ascertaining the views of the people in the matter of development of the district and their felt needs and for periodical review of the district plan. The main functions of the Council were: (a) to advise the District Planning Board in the formulation of the perspective, five year and annual plans; and (b) to associate itself with the review of the district plan from time to time.

The working of these Boards and Councils was reviewed in the year 1974. At that time, it was felt necessary that the elected representatives of the people should be more directly associated in the process of formulation and implementation of plans of the district, and, therefore, the Government constituted a new planning body at the district level known as the District Planning and Development Council, Thane, in the year 1974 under the Chairmanship of the designated Minister of this district with the following as its members: (a) Commissioner of the concerned Division, (b) all members of the Lok Sabha and Vidhan Sabha elected from the District, (c) all members of Rajya Sabha and Vidhan Parishad residing in the district, (d) Collector of the district, (e) President of the Zila Parishad, (f) Mayor of the Municipal Corporation or the President of the largest municipal council in the district, (g) Manager, District Central Cooperative Bank, (h) Director, Maharashtra State Cooperative Land Development Board representing the district on the Board of Directors, (i) Regional Manager of the Lead Bank (Bank of Maharashtra), (j) a representative of the Regional Development Corporation, (Konkan Development Corporation), (k) three non-official members of the former District Planning Board nominated by the Government, (l) Four non-official members of the former District Development Consultative Council nominated by the Government, and (m) Chief Executive Officer, Zila Parishad, Thane as Member-Secretary.

The main functions of the DPDC[55] are to: (a) ensure coordinated action by various implementing agencies at the district level including the Zila Parishad,[56] (b) give guidance to various implementing agencies at the district level in regard to preparation and implementation of the Perspective, Five Year and Annual Plans of the district, (c) approve the Perspective, Five Year and Annual Plans of the district, and (d) review from time to time the implementation of the Five Year, and Annual Plans and make recommendations to the state Government and State Planning Board in that behalf.

The DPDC was required to meet twice or at the most three times in a year, and it was expected to offer guidelines to the implementing agencies in the task of plan formulation and ensure coordinated action by the implementing agencies including the Zila Parishad. The state Government, thus, with error and trial method, evolved a mechanism for the association of local bodies in planning process at the district level. However, to assist the District Planning and Development Council in the day-to-day planning and development activities, a small "Executive Committee" was constituted[57] under the Chairmanship of the designated Minister of the district with 10 other members.[58]

The Executive Committee of the Council was required to meet as often as required but at least once in two months. For the meetings of the Executive Committee, district heads of various departments and, or regional officers were invited to attend the meetings so as to provide continuous dialogue between the departments responsible for various developmental activities in the district and district planning authorities. The Executive Committee was also entrusted with the overall review of all the resources available or being made available to various agencies in the district to ensure their proper allocation in the light of the district priorities and needs, supervise implementation of the plan schemes, including central plan and centrally sponsored schemes. In November, 1974, Government issued instructions that the Chairmen of various Subject Committees of the Zila Parishad may be invited as special invitees, wherever deemed necessary, with the approval of the Chairman of the DPDC for attending the meetings of the DPDC.[59]

A point was also raised as to whether the additional non-official member appointed by the Government vide resolution No. DPC-2173-P-I(A), dated 3rd January, 1974, to represent the interests of Scheduled Castes, Scheduled Tribes, and Adivasis in the former District Planning Board, Thane could still continue to work as non-official member on the DPDC of the district. It was clarified by the Government that the additional non-official member already nominated by the Government on the DPB of Thane would also continue to be the member of the DPDC.[60]

On 23rd August, 1975, the Government changed the Chairman of the DPDC and its Executive Committee.[61] Minister of Finance, Small Savings, Cultural Affairs, Sports, and youth Services thus became Chairman of the DPDC Thane.

In the year 1975, another decision was taken by the Government as to who should preside over the meetings of the DPDCs and its Executive Committees in the absence of the designated

Minister. By a resolution,[62] it was decided that: (a) in the absence of the Chairman, Minister of State who is a member of the DPDC should be designated as the Vice-Chairman and preside over the meeting; (b) when both the Chairman and Vice-Chairman mentioned above, are absent, the Commissioner of the concerned Division should function as the Vice-Chairman; (c) the State Minister other than the Chairman of the DPDC should also be a member of the Executive Committee of the DPDC (d) in the absence of the Chairman of the Executive Committee, the State Minister for the district should preside over the meetings of the Executive Committee;[63] and (e) when Chairman and the State Minister are absent, the Commissioner of the concerned Division should conduct the meeting of the Executive Committee of the DPDC.[64]

DPDC decided in its meeting held on 16th November, 1974 that the Chairman of the Central Cooperative Bank, Thane should be made a member of the Executive Commitee of DPDC instead of the Manager, as the Chairman of the Bank is the competent authority to take important decisions in this Bank. So the case in this regard was referred to Government on 25th November, 1974 by the Member-Secretary but Government did not acceed to this proposal of the DPDC. However, the Government further decided that the Chairman of the District Central Cooperative Bank may be invited to the meeting of the Executive Committee of the DPDC whenever the questions regarding institutional finance from cooperative bank are to be discussed.[65] In 1975, the Government finally decided that the Chairman of the District Central Cooperative Bank should be appointed as a member of the Executive Committee instead of the Manager of the Bank as the Executive Committee of the DPDC has to take very important decisions with regard to financing of several projects.

When the DPDC was set up, the Chief Executive Officer, Zila Parishad, Thane was appointed as its Member-Secretary. However, it was noticed that the Chief Executive Officer was fully busy with various items of work relating to Zila Prishad's own functions. Further, district planning covered not only local sector schemes under the Zila Parishad in the rural areas but also state sector schemes, the schemes implemented by urban local bodies and various institutional agencies over which the Zila Parishad had no control. In view of the above and also considering the role of the Collector as the "Chief administrative head of the district", it was thought that it would be desirable if the Collector was entrusted with the work of district planning. In December, 1975, therefore, it was decided by the Government to appoint the Collector of the district as the Member-Secretary of the DPDC.

In the year 1976, the Government also reviewed the functioning of the Executive Committee of the DPDC so as to make it meaningful.[66] It was felt that, for various reasons, it had not been possible for the Executive Committee of the DPDC to meet at least once in the two months, with the result that the supervision over the implementation of plan programmes in the district suffered. The proposal for reappropriation of savings and excesses during the current financial year was also considered by the Executive Committee late in the year and ad-hoc recommendations were made to the Government in these matters.[67]

The Government considered that timely and more frequent reviews of the implementation of plan programmes by the Executive Committee of the DPDC is necessary in order to: (a) ensure expeditious implementation of the various development programmes, (b) identify precise reasons for slow progress in implementation of certain programmes, such as late sanction of schemes, non-availability of equipment and machinery, delay in land acquisition, inadequacy of staff, etc., and (c) suggest remedial measures for consideration and expeditious orders of the Government so as to remove such administrative bottlenecks in the implementation of the development programmes of the district.[68] With a view to ensure proper implementation of the development programmes and removal of difficulties experienced by the district implementing officers and agencies, the government decided[69] that:

(a) The Collector, the Member-Secretary of the DPDC, should arrange to collect from various implementing officers and agencies, concerned with the district level schemes included in the annual budget, a monthly report on the progress of expenditure and physical achievement of the programmes. This information should be collected by the Collector by the 10th of the month following the month of report and he should arrange to place a consolidated report for the consideration of the Executive Committee of the DPDC.

(b) Executive Committee of the DPDC should meet at least once in a month to execute, inter-alia, the following business[70] to: (i) consider monthly progress report received from various district implementing officers and agencies and indentify reasons for shortfall in expenditure or physical achievement; (ii) suggest measures for expeditious implementation of plan programmes; (iii) consider new scheme or works for inclusion in the annual plan by adjustment within the budgeted outlay of the district in case that is found to be very necessary; (iv) consider excess requirements and savings indicated by the district implementing officers and agencies and propose reappropriation for approval of the Government.

(c) The Collector soon after the meeting of the Executive Committee arranges to forward to the Government in the Planning Department a summary record of the discussions in the meeting of the Executive Committee together with such specific recommendations made by it with a view to remove administrative and other bottlenecks and for expeditious implementation of the development programmes under the District Annual Plan. In case the Chairman and or Vice-Chairman of the DPDC is unable to attend the meeting of the Executive Committee, the members present should nominate one of the members to preside over such meetings.[71]

On 10th April, 1978, the Government decided that Shri P.S. Deshmukh of Shahapur, District Thane, non-official member of the Maharastra State Electricity Board should be invited to attend the meetings of the DPDC Thane as a special invitee.[72]

In 1978, Government changed the designated Minister of the DPDCs and also decided that ministers and state ministers should be appointed as additional members and Vice-Chairmen of the DPDC, its Executive Committee and Special Executive Committee for the Tribal Areas Sub-Plan. Accordingly, the Minister for Revenue, Rehabilitation and Fisheries was made Chairman of the DPDC Thane.[73]

By another resolution, dated 3.7.78, the Government also decided to add the following members in the DPDC[74] (a) one of the Presidents of 'A' class municipal councils in the district, (b) one of the Presidents of 'B' class municipal councils in the district, and (c) one of the Presidents of 'C' class municipal councils in the district. It was further provided in this resolution that the above members should be nominated by the Chairman of the DPDC. Not only this, the Government also decided that the Chairman of the DPDC should nominate one of the four representatives of urban local bodies, i.e. Mayor of the Corporation and one President of "A", "B" and "C" class municipal councils each to be a member of the Executive Committee of the DPDC.[75]

In September, 1978, the Government decided to appoint Minister for Revenue and Rehabilitation as the Chairman of the DPDC Thane and its Executive Committee.[76]

According to resolution dated 1st October, 1974, an Executive Committee of the DPDC was constituted for assisting the DPDC in day-to-day planning and development activities. As per the constitution of the Executive Committee, only two non-officials, out of all the non-official members of the DPDC were to be appointed as members of the Executive Committee. The Government had under consideration the question of associating the elected representatives of the people in the Parliament and State Legislature more closely with the development of the district. The elected representatives of the people had also expressed a desire to associate themselves more closely with day-to-day functioning of the DPDC. In this situation, the Government decided that all the members of the Parliament and State Legislature from the district should invariably be invited to the monthly meetings of the Executive Committee of the DPDC.[77]

Government issued as many as 20 resolutions from first October, 1974 to 20th April, 1978 to modify or expand the composition of the DPDC and its Executive Committee. From the point of view of systematic district planning, Government, later, considered it necessary to issue a consolidated order regarding the constitution of the DPDC and its Executive Committee. Accordingly, in supersession of all orders issued earlier, a consolidated order constituting the DPDC under the Chairmanship of the designated Minister of the district was issued[78] on 21st of June, 1978. According to this order, Divisional Commissioner was appointed its Vice-Chairman and the Collector as its Member-Secretary. A large number of official members were given representation on the DPDC.[79]

As the areas of some of the Lok Sabha Constituencies extended to more than one district, the members of Lok Sabha elected from each such Constituency, were appointed as ex-officio members of the DPDC. Accordingly, members of the Lok Sabha from North Bombay and Daheru Constituencies were appointed as members of the DPDC, Thane.[80] Besides this, Minister for Education, Cultural Affairs, Youth Services and Sports was made Chairman of the DPDC Thane[81] but no Minister was designated as Vice-Chairman of the DPDC Thane. In this consolidated order, functions of the DPDC remained the same as before.

To assist the DPDC in day-to-day planning and development activities, an Executive Committee of Thane was also constituted[82] under the Chairmanship of the Minister. It was also provided in the above resolution that the Executive Committee should discharge all the functions of the DPDC and meet as often as required but at least once a month. In case the Chairman or the Vice-Chairman was unable to attend the meeting on the fixed date, one of the members present may be nominated to discharge the functions of the Chairman. This Committee, however, was quite unwieldy because of a large number of official and non-official members.[83] The Managing Director of the Industrial Development Corporation of Maharashtra was also appointed as the member of the DPDC, Thane by the Government on 25th of October, 1979.

The designated Minister of the DPDC and its Executive Committee was again changed on 30th June, 1980, and Minister of State for Public Works, Transport, Social Welfare and Khar Lands was appointed Chairman of the DPDC and its Executive Committee.[84] Subsequently, the Government appointed Minister of State for Cooperation, Industries, Ports, Food & Civil Supplies, Urban Development and Legislative Affairs, as Chairman of this Council and its Executive Committee and the

Deputy Minister for Finance, Irrigation, Food and Civil Supplies, Energy and Aukaf as Vice-Chairman on 5th February, 1982.[85] In the year 1982, the Government reconstituted the DPDCs, Executive Committees and Special Executive Committees in the State.

## RECONSTITUTED DISTRICT PLANNING AND DEVELOPMENT COUNCIL

The Government of Maharashtra again reconstituted the District Planning and Development Council of Thane on 24.6.1982 under the Chairmanship of the designated Minister of the district, and Deputy Minister for Finance, Irrigation, Food & Civil Supplies, Energy and Aukaf, and the Divisional Commissioner were appointed its Vice-Chairmen. The other members were: (a) all members of the Lok Sabha and Vidhan Sabha elected from the district, (b) all members of the Rajya Sabha and Vidhan Parishad residing in the district, (c) President of the Zila Parishad, (d) one of the Presidents of the 'A' class municipal councils in the district to be nominated by the Chairman of the DPDC, (e) one of the Presidents of 'B' class municipal councils in the district to be nominated by the Chairman of the DPDC, (f) one of the Presidents of 'C' class municipal councils to be nominated by the Chairman, DPDC, (g) Chairman of the District Central Cooperative Bank, (h) Director, Maharashtra State Cooperative Land Development Bank representing the district on the Board of Directors, (i) Regional Manager of the Lead Bank (Bank of Maharashtra), (j) a representative of the Regional Development Corporation (Konkan Development Corporation), (k) 13 non-official members to be nominated by the Government which should include one member belonging to any of the categories of Scheduled Castes, Neo-Budhists, Vimukta Jatis, and Nomadic Tribes in case the population of these categories together is upto 10 per cent of the district population, and 2 such members, if the population exceeds 10 per cent, (1) Metropolitan Commissioner of Bombay, Metropolitan Regional Development Authority, (m) Chairman of the District Committee of the Maharashtra State Khadi & Village Industries Board, (n) Superintendent of the Post Offices in the district, (o) Chief Executive Officer of the Zila Parishad, and (p) Collector, Thane as Member-Secretary of the DPDC.

The Chairmen of the Panchayat Samitis in the district were also invited to attend the meetings of the DPDC as invitees at the time of formulation of the annual plan only so as to ensure their participation in the formulation of the district annual plan.[86]

The DPDC is required to meet twice or at the most thrice in a year and its enlarged functions apart from those mentioned earlier, are to: (a) consider and approve reappropriation of savings and excesses within the approved District Annual Plan, as per the directions given by the Government from time to time; and (b) perform any other functions as may be directed by the Government from time to time.

## RECONSTITUTED EXECUTIVE COMMITTEE

The Executive Committee of the DPDC Thane was also reconstituted on 24.6.1982 on the ground that its "present size was unwieldy."[88] It was felt that by making the Executive Committee more compact, it would be able to conduct its functions in a more business-like manner and this would add to the efficiency of district planning process.[89] The Executive Committee was reconstituted under the Chairmanship of the designated minister and the other members were: (a) Deputy Minister (Vice-Chairman), (b) Divisional Commissioner of the concerned Division (Vice-Chairman), (c) President of Zila Parishad, (d) Two or 1/5th members of the State Legislature (whichever is more) by rotation for one year at a time in such a way that all of them get the opportunity to work on the Executive Committee (the names are to be decided by the Chairman alphabetically every financial year in advance), (e) one of the members of Parliament to be nominated by the Chairman of the DPDC, (f) one representative of the Municipal Corporation and Councils to be nominated by thc Chairman of the DPDC, (g) Collector, (h) Chief Executive Officer, (i) Chairman of the District Central Cooperative Bank, (j) one member representing any of the categories of Scheduled Castes, Neo-Budhists, Vimukta Jatis and Nomadic Tribes in case the population of all these categories is 10 per cent of the total population of the district and 2 members if their population is more than 10 per cent of the total population of the districts, and (k) District Planning Officer (Member-Secretary).[90]

On 16th July, 1982, the above resolution of the Government was revised, and the composition of the Executive Committee of the DPDC was enlarged to include:[91] (a) all the members of the Lok Sabha and Vidhan Sabha elected from the district; and (b) all the members of the Rajya Sabha and Vidhan Parishad residing in the district.

The Executive Committee of the DPDC is required to meet as often as required but at least once in a month. It, being the Committee of the DPDC, is entrusted with all the functions of the DPDC.[92] In addition, it is also required to formulate and review the implementation of the Special Component Plan for Scheduled Castes and Neo-Budhists in every meeting. It is also entrusted with the review of the progress of the IRDP in the district.

It was brought to the notice of the Government that many a time, the officials invited for the meetings of the DPDC and its Executive Committee do not attend these meetings. As a result, the information required in the meetings did not become available and the very purpose of holding such meetings was defeated. Accordingly, the Government directed that the officers or their representatives should attend the meetings regularly.[93]

On 16.10.1982, the Government issued a resolution and appointed new Chairmen and Additional Chairmen of the DPDCs in the State. Accordingly, Minister for Housing, Rehabilitation and Social Welfare became the Chairman of the DPDC and its Executive Committee, and Minister for Revenue, Khar Land and Fisheries became Additional Chairman of the DPDC and its Executive Committee.[94]

## SPECIAL EXECUTIVE COMMITTEE FOR THE TRIBAL AREAS SUB-PLAN

In Thane, Tribal Areas Sub-Plan is also being prepared from the year 1974-75 for which separate funds are earmarked by the

Government. In order to secure the active participation of Adivasi beneficiaries in the formulation and implementation of the Tribal Areas Sub-Plan, as also the "development of Adivasi as a men by opening avenues for inculcating in him the qualities of leadership", the Government appointed a Special Tribal Areas Sub-Plan Executive Committee.[95] of the DPDC, Thane under the Chairmanship of the designated Minister[96] with one of the elected Tribal representatives as its Vice-Chairman. The other members of this committee are:[97] (a) Tribal Commissioner, (b) President, Zila Parishad, (c) all Tribal MPs from the district, (d) all Tribal MLAs from the district, (e) Chairman of the Social Welfare Committee of the Zila Parishad of the district, (f) all Chairmen of the Panchayat Samitis where such Panchayat Samitis fall in the area of operation of the Tribal Sub-Plan, (g) two non-official representatives of the Tribals in the district, (h) District Collector, and (i) Chief Executive Officer of the Zila Parishad (Member-Secretary).

The function of this Committee is to prepare the Tribal Areas Sub-Plan within the financial ceilings allotted for the Tribal Sub-Plan for the district, and this Sub Plan is required to be placed before the DPDC of the district for approval. This Committee was also responsible for overseeing the progress of implementation of the Sub-Plan, and render general guidance to the taluka and growth centre level committees which may be formed from time to time.[98]

In 1977, the Collector of Thane was appointed as Member-Secretary of the Special Executive Committee for Tribal Areas Sub-Plan instead of the Chief Executive Officer, Zila Parishad, Thane. It was also decided that the Chief Executive Officer, Zila Parishad, Thane should continue to be the member of the Special Executive Committee.[99]

## RECONSTITUTED SPECIAL EXECUTIVE COMMITTEE

In supersession of all the resolutions[100] issued so far including those indicated in the preamble, in-so-far as they relate to the constitution of the Special Executive Committees of the DPDC, the Government issued a fresh consolidated resolution[101] regarding the constitution of this cmmittee of the DPDC for securing active participation of the Adivasi beneficiaries in the formulation and implementation of the Tribal Areas Sub-Plan, as also the social and economic development of Adivasis by opening avenues for inculcating in them qualities of leadership.

In these consolidated instructions,[102] the composition of the Special Executive Committee of the DPDC Thane remained the same as before. However, the functions of this committee were elaborated and the same are summarized as under:[103] (a) to formulate the Five Year and Annual Plans for the Tribal Areas within the district, subject to the broad guidelines indicated by the Goverment and the financial ceilings indicated from time to time; (b) to undertake periodical reviews of the implementation of the Tribal Areas Sub-Plan as approved by the Government, identify reasons for shortfall in expenditure and physical achievements and to consider remedial measures for expeditious implementation of the Tribal Areas Sub-Plan; and (c) to consider and recommend to the Government reappropriation and readjustment of funds subject to Government orders in this regard.

The programmes under the Tribal Areas Sub-Plan for Five Year or Annual Plans, approved by the Special Executive Committee are placed before the DPDC for approval.[104]

The Special Executive Committee is required to meet as often as required but at least once in a month. In case the Chairman and or Vice-Chairman of the Special Executive Committee is unable to attend the monthly meetings, the present members can nominate one of the member to preside over such meetings and conduct business laid down in this resolution.[105]

For the expeditious implementation of the programmes, the Collector of the district and the Member-Secretary of the DPDC and the Special Executive Committee for the Tribal Areas Sub-Plan is required to arrange to collect from various implementing officers and agencies concerned with the district level schemes included in the Annual Budget, a monthly progress report on the progress of expenditure and physical achievements on the prescribed proforma which is similar to the one prescribed for the review of monthly progress of General Plan Schemes by this Committee. The Collector is required to collect this information from the concerned officers by 10th of the month following the month of report and arrange to place it before the DPDC or its Special Executive Committee. After the monthly meeting, the Collector consolidates record of discussions of the Special Evecutive Committee and sends the same with the specific recommendations made by the Committee with a view to remove administrative and other bottlenecks and for expeditious implementation of the development programmes under the district's Tribal Areas Sub-Plan.[106]

The main criticism[107] voiced against the working of the planning machinery comprising DPDC, its Executive Committee and Special Executive Committee is that (a) these bodies have been inducted in the district administration to "kill the Panchayati Raj institutions," (b) Zila Parishad is a district level body but entrusted with a few development schemes, (c) Panchayati Raj bodies below the Zila Parishad do not have adequate voice in the district planning process, (d) the Chairman of the Subject Committees of the Zila Parishad are not given adequate representation on the DPDC, (e) district planning cells are very weak and do not provide any assistance to the DPDC in formulation. monitoring and evaluation of the district plans, (f) meetings of the DPDC and Executive Committees are not held regularly, and the durations of these meetings are very short, (g) DPDC is a district assembly merely devoted to deliberations and its decision-making function is not very effective, (b) Executive Committee, as it stands today, is quite "unwieldy" and also meets only on a few occassions in a year, and as such fails to discharge its functions in regard to review, monitoring and evaluation of the schemes included in the district plan, (i) membership of the Executive Committee comprises of MLAs, MPs and other non-officials who are generally engaged in routine criticism of the administration for its omissions and commissions, ( j) the district Minister is a very busy person and has no time to chair the meetings of the DPDC and its Executive Committee. Generally, no meetings are held if the district Minister has no time to preside over such meetings, (k) Collector has no positive role to play in reviewing the schemes especially when the Executive Committee does not meet, (1) since 1982, the district Minister is appointed from outside the district and the meetings of the Executive Committee are not held every month as he has to visit his own constituency, (m) as the planning cells are very weak, and have no technical hands, no evaluation studies are conducted for placing these before DPDC and its Executive Committee, (n) Generally, monitoring is used by the non-official members as an instrument to "overawe" one or two officials by finding faults, and thereafter no review of schemes of other officers is done, (o) there are as many as 226 schemes in the General Plan and 135 in the Tribal Sub-Plan, the Executive Committee and the Special Executive Committee cannot review them meaningfully in one day meetings, (p) the officials feel demoralized as healthy discussion do not take place in these meetings, and (q) the DPDC while approving the district plan, give importance in many cases to unimportant schemes.[108]

The Collector, the Member-Secretary of the DPDC, is assisted by a small District Planning Unit in attending to the work of formulation, monitoring and evaluation of the district plans. The planning unit is under the overall charge of the Collector and consists of a District Planning Officer, two Research Assistants and one Planning Assistant, besides some nominal clerical staff. The planning unit is not only extremely small but also plays a routine role in the process of formulation, implementation, monitoring and evaluation of district plans. Therefore, the functions of the planning unit are at present limited to routine matters like preparing of agenda and minutes for the Executive Committee meetings and of the DPDC and sending returns to the state Governments, and compiling of the annual plan.[109] This unit does not have necessary expertise or technical hands for the formulation of the district plan. However, at the state level, the planning officers in the Planning Department have been assigned a group of districts and they coordinate the work of these districts. They also attend to meetings of the Executive Committees and the Special Executive Committees of the DPDC.

## OVERVIEW

Institutionalization of development administration at the district level is the pre-requisite for the success of all the socio-economic programmes launched by the Government at this level. The experience of Karnal reveals that the bureaucratic wing of district development administration is well-established under the overall supervision of the Deputy Commissioner and it discharges its functions as per priorities laid down by the Government. However, the association of the local leadership in the development process is almost negligible. The story of Panchayati Raj in Karnal district in Haryana has been a story of ups and downs, and its three phases have been those of ascendency, stagnation and decline.[110] Zila Parishad has since been abolished and the Panchayat Samitis have ceased to function after the expiry of their regular terms. As far as the village panchayats are concerned, they are not in a position to affect any development worth the name in the absence of any real devolution of financial powers. These sick bodies get activated only when a dose of financial assistance is provided by the Government. Municipal bodies are no better than these rural institutions. Not only this, even the district planning bodies remained dormant since their inception. Besides this, the proposed District Planning Cell did not take its roots in the district administration. In a nut-shell, these institutions are either non-exist or very weak, and as such incapable of shouldering higher responsibilities. However, the bureaucratic appratus is well-established but it has no popular support. By now, the district administration has become unmanageable because of a number of additional functions. The authority of the Collector is being eroded continuously. Each district head is more responsive to his respective Directorate than to the district authority. This dual control has weakened the capability of the district administration to perform its role effectively in the socio-economic development of the district.

The district administration in Thane, on the other hand, can be divided into two sectors-one concerned with regulatory work and the other with developmental functions. In this model of district administration, schemes relating, to agriculture, animal husbandry, forests, removal of untouchability, economic development of backward classes, education, medical, public health, building communication, public health engineering, industries, and cottage industries, cooperation, community development and village upliftment, have been transferred to the Panchayati Raj institutions which were expected to prepare local plans and implement them in their jurisdiction leaving the Collector for the revenue administration, law and order, food and civil supplies, administration of controls, census, elections, scarcity administration and local calamities, prohibition and excise, small savings, jails and prisons, and employment exchanges. This bifurcates the district administration into regulatory and developmental sectors and also clearly lays down a firm foundation of the development administration[111] at the district level. However, the present analysis clearly brings out that the planning function was not taken up seriously by the Panchayati Raj institutions.

In 1972, the Government constituted the District Planning Boards and District Development Consultative Councils in the State. Accordingly, the District Planning Board, as well as the District Development Consultative Council, Thane, came into existence on 20th October, 1972 and 20th June, 1973, respectively under the Chairmanship of the designated Minister of the district. The main functions of the Board were: (a) to ensure coordinated action by various agencies including Zila Parishad, (b) to give guidelines to various implementing agencies with regard to formulation and implementation of the perspective and Five Year Plans of the District, and (c) to approve 'Five Year Plans and Annual Plans' of the district subject to the approval of the Government.

The District Development Consultative Council served as a forum for determining the views of the people in matter of development of the district. Its main functions were: (a) to advise the District Planning Board in the formulation of the Perspective, Five Year and Annual Plans, and (b) to associate itself with the review of the district plan from time to time.

The working of these Boards and Councils was reviewed by the Government in the year 1974 and both these bodies were replaced by the District Planning and Development Councils in the State in the year 1974, as a result of which, DPDC, Thane came into existence in 1974 under the Chairmanship of the District Minister. To assist the DPDC, in day-to-day planning and development activities, a small "Executive Committee" was also constituted under the Chairmanship of the designated Minister in 1974, and the majority of the members on this Committee were officers. The elected representatives of the people from the district were not given representation on this Committee. The Executive Committee was also entrusted with the review of all the plan schemes being implemented in the district. Since the membership of this Committee is considered as prestigious, the MLAs, MPs and other influential persons demanded their representation on this Committee. In the year 1978, all the Members of the Parliament and Legislatures from the district were put on the Executive Committee of the DPDC so as to associate the elected representatives of the people in the planning process at the district level.

On 24th June 1982, the DPDC, Thane and its Executive Committee were re-constituted under the Chairmanship of the District Minister. In this reconstituted Executive Committee, the participation of MLAs and MPs was again reduced to the bare minimum on the ground that its present size is unwieldy but on 16th July 1982, the Government revised its decision and all the MPs and MLAs from the district were made members of this Committee. The main functions entrusted to the reconstituted DPDC are: (a) to ensure coordinated action by various implementing agencies at the district level including the Zila Parishad, (b) to give guidelines to various implementing agencies at the district level in regard to the preparation of the Perspective, Five Year and Annual Plans of the district, (c) to approve the Perspective, Five Year and Annual Plans of the districts, (d) to review from time to time the implementation of the Five Year and Annual Plans and make recommendations to the Government in that behalf, (e) to consider and approve the re-appropriation of savings and excesses within the approved district annual plans, and (f) to perform any other function as may be directed by the Government from time to time.

As far as the function of the Executive Committee of the DPDC is concerned, it is vested with all the functions of the DPDC. It is also required to review the implementation of Special Component Plan for the Scheduled Castes and

Neo-Budhists, as also the review of the Integrated Rural Development Programme in the district.

For the formulation of the Tribal Area Sub-Plan, Thane, the Government also constituted a special Tribal Sub-Plan Executive Committee comprising of inter-alia other members, all the Tribal MPs and MLAs from the district, Tribal Commissioner, and two non-official representatives of the Tribals in the district, under the Chairmanship of the designated Minister. The main functions of this Committee are to, (a) prepare the Tribal Area Sub-Plan for Thane district within the prescribed financial ceiling, and (b) to review the implementation of the schemes and programmes included in the Sub-Plan.

The planning machinery in this district consists of a skeleton staff and performs only routine functions such as collection of statistics from the district level officers and preparation of agenda items for various meetings. The district planning cell is very weak and does not serve as a strong support to the DPDC in the context of new tasks entrusted to it in matters relating to the formulation of district plans, monitoring and evaluation of the progress of these plans.

In spite of some of the deficiencies, the leadership in Maharashtra has vividly demonstrated its "political will" in evolving, expanding and then institutionalizing development administration in Thane integrating therein the political, administrative and local institutions through the instrumentalities of DPDC and its committees. It has, thus given birth to a new concept of unified authority at the district level capable of formulating, reviewing, monitoring and evaluating the district plans. The diversity of functions at the district level and their manageability render coordination very difficult and this aspect is being examined in the next chapter.

## REFERENCES

1. In the developing economy, it is essential to create new institutions, if necessary, or strengthen or revamp the old ones to achieve the goals of development. A number of institutions and agencies such as Cooperatives, municipal committees, improvement trusts, Zila Parishads, Panchayai Samitis, Village Panchayats, DRDAs and

other development departments have come up at the district level with their programmes and schemes, In order to have proper planning and effective implementation of programmes and schemes, it is necessary to strengthen and institutionalize the development administration at the district level.

2. In order to achieve developmental goals, the state has to devise its policies and programmes with a preferential package in favour of its poor. The soft state generally fails to take suitable measures for the development of the economy and the poor in view of the pressures of the powerful lobbies, vested interests, and the privileged groups. Even if it legislates on some of the important issues such as land reforms, it fails on its enforcement. The other characteristics of the soft state are: (a) unwillingness to use force, (b) concentration on economic programmes, (c) neglect of institutional reforms, and (d) poor tax structure. In this situation, the very idea of transfer of resource technology in favour of the poor fails to materialise.
3. Refer S.S. Khera, District Administration in India. Asia Publishing House, Bombay, 1964, p. 2-5, wherein he has briefly described the contours of district administration. According to him, district administration in India deals with a widely embracive sphere of the total management of public affairs. . . . District Administration is that portion of public administration which functions in the territorial limits of a district. It includes all the agencies of Government, the individual officials and functionaries, public servants, including a public servant who is a Government servant equally one who is not. For the term public servant includes many who are not Government servants as such. It comprehends all institutions for the management of public affairs in the district, all the bodies corporate such the panchayats of different kinds, the gram sabhas, the panchayat samitis, the zila parishads, municipal committees, and local boards of every kind. It includes all advisory bodies associated with the administration.
4. S.K. Sharma, Deputy Commissioner in Punjab, Indian Institute of Public Administration, New Delhi, 1971, p. 1.
5. T.N. Chaturvedi (Ed.), District Administration, Vol. I., Indian Institute of Public Administration, Silver Jubilee, New Delhi, 1980, p. 4.
6. S.K. Sharma, op. cit., New Delhi, 1971, p. 1.
7. Refer S. Jambunathan, Crucial role for the district, Commerce (Annual Number), 1969, Bombay, p. 128.
8. Ishwar Dayal, Kuldeep Mathur and Mohit Bhattacharya, District Administration: A Survey for Reorganization, The Machmillian Company of India Limited, New Delhi 1975, p. 2.
9. S.K. Sharma, Deputy op. cit., New Delhi, 1971, p. 1.

10. Collector is the represcntative of the Government at the district level and as such a much sought after man to preside over various committees being organized by the Government departments, voluntary organizations and other agencies.
11. The term "Panchayati Raj institutions" stands for Gram Panchayats, Panchayat Samitis and Zila Parishads which together could be called a form of a local-self government for managing the affairs of rural areas.
12. Panchayats in District Planning and Administration (Debate) Kurukshetra, February 1968, p. 7.
13. Ibid.
14. Refer Administrative Reforms Commission: Report of the Gujarat Working Group on District Administration, Vol. II (Mimeo), Document No. 1, p. 4.
15. Ibid., p. 7.
16. Ibid., p. 11.
17. District, as the unit of administration, is in existence for more than two centuries but the framers of the Constitution did not assign it any original powers. It, being the delegatese of the State Government, performs only those functions and exercises those powers which are vested in it by the state Government through various Acts, manual, rules and instructions. In view of the above, district is generally treated as a mere implementing agency of the state in the implementation of various programmes and schemes in the district.
18. Based on interviews with President of Zila Parishad. Thane, Chairman of the Subject Committees of Zila Parishad, Thane, and district and state level officers.
19. K.N. Raj, Planning from Below with reference to District Development and State Plans, *Economic and Political Weekly*, Special Number, July, 1971, p. 1611.
20. Shanti Kothari and Rameshray Roy, Relations Between Politicians and Administrators at District Level, Indian Institute of Public Administration, New Delhi, 1981, p. 171.
21. Refer Planning Commission, Report of the Working Group on Block Level Planning: Integrating Development Administration at Area Level, Appendix III, New Delhi, 1978, p. 52.
22. Ibid.
23. Consolidated from the available record and interviews with the district and state level officers.
24. In Haryana, Zila Parishads have been abolished in 1973 and the Collectors are ex-officio appointed as Administrators of the Zila Parishads in the State. Practically, these bodies are now non-exist.
25. Zila Parishads were merely given an advisory role and the powers to plan and implement various programmes and schemes were vested

in the Panchayat Samitis and the Gram Panchayats. The system of Local Government developed in Haryana did not assign development tasks to the Zila Parishads.

26. Based on interviews with the senior officers of the Panchayat Department in Haryana.
27. Ibid.
28. Municipal Committees and Improvement Trusts have been superceded in the entire State and not revived so far.
29. Based on interviews with the local leaders in Karnal, as also with the administrators of the Municipal Committees in the district.
30. The membership of this Board consists of (a) all the members of the District Planning Committee, and (b) representatives of the people like MPs, MLAs, Municipal Commissioners and other knowledgeable persons. Its main function is to advise the district authorities about the socio-economic programmes.
31. The other members are DPO and DSO.
32. All the members of District Executive Committee and all the district level officers of other departments are its members.
33. Based on interviews with district level officers in Karnal.
34. S.K. Sharma, op.cit., Chapter V.
35. S.K. Sharma, Ibid., New Delhi, 1971, p. 290.
36. Condensed from Resolutions issued by the Planning Department, Government of Maharashtra, Bombay from time to time: and also based on interviews with the concerned officers at the district level and the President, Zila Parishad, Thane.
37. A.L. Fletcher, The Collector in the Nineteen Sixties (Special Number) *Indian 7ournal of Public Administration*, New Delhi, p. 373.
38. Administrative Reforms Commission, Report (Volume II) (Mimeo), Study Team On District Administration, December, 1966, Also refer Document No. IV Report of the Maharashtra Working Group on District Administration, pp. 7-8.
39. Refer section 78 of the Maharashtra Zila Parishads and Panchayat Samitis Act, (Maharashtra Act No, V of 1962, 1961, Bombay, p. 6798.
40. Ibid., First and Second Schedule, pp. 6868-6877.
41. Refer Ibid., section 100 (4), p. 6807.
42. Refer Ibid., Section 123 (1), p. 6813.
43. Government of Maharashtra, Rural Development Department, Report of the Evaluation Committee On Panchayati Raj, Bomboy, 1971, p. 84.
44. Panchayati Raj Institutions are the creations of the Government of Maharashtra through an enactment christened as "The Maharashtra Zila Parishads and Panchayat Samitis Act, 1961, and have been assigned functions and responsibilities under the aforementioned

Act in the rural areas, and as such these bodies cannot perform such functions in the urban areas for which municipal committees and corporations exist.

45. Resolution No. PD/SPM-2072/P-I, dated 20th October, 1972, General Administration Department, Government of Maharashtra, Bombay.
46. Ibid., p. 1.
47. Now, the Mortgage Bank is designated as Land Development Bank in Maharashtra.
48. Ibid., p. 1-2.
49. The other members on the District Planning Boards were (a) District Collector, (b) President of Zila Parishad, (c) President of the largest municipal council, (d) Chief Executive Officer of the Zila Parishad, (e) Chairman of District Central Cooperative Bank, (f) Chairman, District Land Mortgage Bank, (g) Regional Manager of the Lead Bank (Bank of Maharashtra), (h) Three non-officials to be nominated by the Government, and (i) Planning Officer, Zila Parishad, Thane.
50. Ibid., p. 2.
51. Ibid., p. 3.
52. Refer K.V. Sundram, District Planning: The case of Maharashtra, *Indian Journal of Public Administration*, Jan-March, 1979, p. 59.
53. Resolution No. DDC-1073/P-1(A), dated 20.6.73, Planning Department, Government of Maharashtra, Bombay.
54. The Government of Maharashtra, nominated 4 non-official members on the District Development Consultative Council for Thane district on 5,12.1973.
55. Ibid., p. 4
56. Before the Constitution of the DPDC, the Zila Parishad was enjoying vast powers in matters relating to planning and implementation of various programmes and schemes in the rural areas. Zila Parishad and Panchayat Samitis were having final say in planning and fixing programmes and schemes in the rural areas. The President of the Zila Parishad, Thane and Chairman of various Committees felt that the DPDC has taken over their functions and the Panchayati Raj Institutions have been made redundant by the DPDC.
57. Resolution No. DPO-1074/P-1, dated 1st October, 1974, Planning Department of Maharashtra, Bombay, p. 4.
58. The other members on the DPDC were: (a) Divisional Commissioner, (b) President of the Zila Parishad, (c) District Collector, (d) The Chief Executive Officer of the Zila Parishad, (e) Two other representatives of the DPDC to be elected by the Council, (f) Manager, District Central Cooperative Bank, (g) Manager, Lead Bank, and (h) Planning Officer as its Member-Secretary.

59. Circular No. DPC-1074/p-1, dated 25th November, 1974, Planning Departmen t of Maharashtra, Bombay.
60. No. DPC-1074/4775/P.1, dated 17.12.74, Planning Department, Government of Maharashtra, Bombay, pp. 1-2.
61. Resolution No. DPC-1025/PRG-DPP, dated 23rd August, 1975. Planning Depar tment, Government of Maharashtra, Bombay. p. 1.
62. Resolution No. DPC-1075/PRG-DPP, dated 18th September, 1975.
63. All the meetings of the DPDC and of the Executive Committee, Thane are held under the Chairmanship of the Minister. The Membe-Secretary fixes the meeting according to the convenience of the Chairman.
64. In Thane district, Commissioner of the Division has not presided any of the meetings of the DPDC and its Executive Committee. Whenever the District Minister is not in a position to attend these meetings, these are postponed. Therefore, the well-intentioned instructions of the Government have become redundant.
65. No. DPC-1074/4847/P-1, dated 18.12.74, Planning Department, Government of Maharashtra, Bombay, p. 1-2.
66. Circular No. DPC.1076/PRG-DPP, dated 11.2.76, Planning Department, Government of Maharashtra, Bombay.
67. Ibid , p. 1.
68. Ibid.
69. Ibid., p. 1-2.
70. Ibid., p. 2.
71. In the absence of the District Magistrate, the meeting is postponed. It is borne out from the record that this procedure for holding meetings has not been made use of even once in Thane district since 1975.
72. No· DPC-1078/meetings/PRG-14, dated 10th April, 1978, Planning Department, Government of Maharashtra, Bombay.
73. Resolution No. DPC-1078/PRG-14, dated 5.5.1978, Planning Department, Government of Maharashtra, Bombay.
74. Resolution No. DPC-1078/PRG-8, dated 3rd July, 1978.
75. Ibid., p. 1-2
76. DPC-1078/PRG-14, dated 8th September,1978, Planning Depertment, Government of Maharashtra, Bombay, p. 1.
77. Resolution No. DPC-1078/PRG-8, dated 13.12.1978.
78. Resolution No. DPC-1079/PRG-8, dated 21.6.1979, Planning Department, Government of Maharashtra, Bombay, pp. 2-3. Only those members who are concerned with DPDC, Thane are shown here.
79. The other members of the DPDC were: (a) all member of Lok Sabha and Vidhan Sabha elected from the district, (b) all members of Rajya Sabha and Vidhan Parishad residing in the district, (c) President, Zila Parishad, (d) Mayor of the Municipal Corporation, if any, (e) one

of the Presidents of the 'A' Class Municipal Councils in the district to be nominated by the Chairman of the DPDC., (f) one of the Presidents of 'B' Class Muncipal Councils in the district to be nominated by the Chairman of the DPDC, (g) one of the Presidents of 'C' Class Municipal Councils in the district to be nominated by the Chairman, DPDC, (h) Chairman, District Central Cooperative Bank, (i) Director, Maharashtra State Cooperative Bank, representing the district on the Board of Directors, (j) a representative of the Regional Development Corporation, (Konkan Development Corporation), (k) Regional Manager of the Lead Bank (Bank of Maharashtra, Thane), (l) Nine non-officials to be nominated by the Government, (m) Metropolitan Commissioner of Bombay Metropolitan Development Authority, (n) Chairman of the District Committee of the Maharashtra State Khadi and Village Industries Board, (o) Superintendent of post Offices, and (p) Chief Executive Officer, Zila Parishad.

80. Ibid., Annexure VI.
81. Refer Ibid., Annexure I.
82. Ibid., p. 5-6.
83. The other members on the Executive Committee of the DPDC. Thane were: (a) Divisional Commissioner (vice-Chairman), (b) President, Zila Parishad, (c) one President of 'A', 'B', and 'C' Class Municipal Councils each, to be nominated by the Chairman of the DPDC (d) Collector of the District, (e) Chief Executive Officer, Zila Parishad, (f) two other representatives of the DPDC to be nominated by consensus, (g) all member of Parliament and the State Legislature from the district, (h) Chairman, Central Cooperative Bank,(i) Manager, Lead Bank (Bank of Maharashtra), and (j) District Planning Officer (Secretary).
84. Resolution No. DPC-1080/D-17, dated 30th June, 1980, Planning Department, Government of Maharashtra, Bombay (Annexure p-2).
85. Resolution No. DPC-1082/CR-7/D-17, dated 5th February, 1982, Planning Department, Government of Maharashtra, Bombay.
86. Ibid, p. 5.
87. Ibid., p. 4.
88. Refer Ibid, Preamble, p. 1.
89. Ibid.
90. Ibid., p. 3.
11. Resolution No. DPC-1082/CR.II/D-17, dated 16.7.1982, Planning Department, Govt. of Maharashtra, Bombay, p.-1.
92. Ibid., p. 4.
93. Circular No. NIS-1082/CR-57/17, dated 1st September, 1982, Planning Department, Government of Maharashtra, Bombay.
94. Resolution No. DPC-1082/CR-7/D-17, dated 16.10.82, Planning Department, Government of Maharashtra, Bombay.

95. This Committee is generally know as "Special Executive Committee" for the formulation and overviewing the progress in implementing the Tribal programmes in the district. In all, 14 such Committees are constituted in Maharashtra for this purpose.
96. Resolution No. TSP-1075/K/PRG-SSP, dated 30th September, 1973, Planning Department. Government of Maharashtra, Bombay.
97. Ibid., pp. 1-2.
98. Ibid., p. 2.
99. Resolution No. TSP-1077-1895/PRG-8, dated 6th October, 1979, Planning Department, Government of Maharashtra, Bombay.
100. Resolutions are: (a) Government Resolution No. TSP-1075/X/PRG-SSP, dated 30.9.1975, (b) Government Resolution No. TSP-1076/9/PRG-I, dated 19.6.76, (c) Government Resolution No. TSP-1076/PRG, dated 19.6.76, (d) Government letter No. TSP/10/PRG-I, dated 23.6.76, (e) Government Resolution No. TSP-1077/1895/PRG-8, dated 6.10.1977, (f) Government Resolution No. TSP-2078/315/PRG-8, dated 5.10.78, and (g) Government Resolution No. TSP-1078/PRG-10, dated 5th September, 1979,
101. Resolution No. TSP-1079/PRG-10, dated October 15,1979 Planning Department, Government of Maharashtra, Bombay.
102. Resolution No. TSP-1079/PAC-10, dated October 15, 1979, Planning Department, Government of Maharashtra, Bombay.
103. Ibid.,
104. Ibid., p. 2.
105. Ibid., p. 3.
106. The Collector is not supposed to make any recommendation to the Government for the expeditious implementations of programme. In case, the committee does not meet, he simply transmits the progress report to the Government.
107. Based on interviews with the President of Zila Parishad, Thane, and district level offlcers in Thane district.
108. For Tnane district, Wandri Medium Irrigation Project is a high priority project, The construction work on this project started in 1979 and was to be completed in 3 years at the total cost of Rs. 3.5 crores but the DPDC Thane did not accord it high priority in making financial allocations. In view of this, it is now likely to be completed in 1984-85 at the revised estimated cost of Rs. 7.00 crores.
109. K.V. Sundaram, District Planning: The case of Maharashtra, p. 15.
110. Refer T.K. Chaturvedi, (Ed.), Panchayati Raj, Indian Institute of Public Administration, New Delhi, 1981. p. 194.
111. Refer George F. Gant: Development Administration: Concept, Goals and Methods: The University of Wisconsin Press, London England, 1979, p. 20 wherein he observed that the term "development administration" came into use in the 1950s to represent those aspects of public administration and those changes in public administration

which are needed to carry out policies, projects and programmes to improve the socio-economic conditions of the people. "Development Administration" is the term used to denote the complex of agencies, management systems, and processes which a Government establishes to achieve its development goals.

# 8

# COLLECTOR AS THE CHIEF COORDINATOR

DISTRICT administration has become a heterogenous unit of management below the state level after independence especially with the strengthening of the existing district departmental offices as well as with the creation of the new ones. Therefore, with the rapid proliferation of governmental activities in the district on account of the economic and social commitment of the state to the society, the function of coordination[1] has asumed a new dimension and greater importance.[2]

The district being the basic unit of administration in India, the Collector or the Deputy Commissioner occupies a unique position in the country's administration. The historical position of this office, its status and prestige in the eyes of the people, the concentration of powers in it and the recognition of the incumbent of this office as head of the district has enabled, and continues to enable the Government to maintain a proper grip on district administration, secure coordination between departments, provide adequate control and safeguards against abuses of authority by local bodies, secure the implementation of development programmes in accordance with its policies and mobilize public opinion and resources in times of need.[3] The Collector, in fact, is not an individual officer but an institution[4] that can help energize the proliferating developmental activities of various departments, local bodies, Panchayati Raj institutions, corporations, boards, financial institutions and voluntary organizations operating in the district. As observed earlier, it is largely at the district level that all the agencies of the Government converge and programmes find a concrete shape,[5] and district administration provides for the principal points of contact between the citizens and processes of the Government,[6] and as such there is an absolute need of a central authority at the district level to arbiter between the sprawling different departments on the one hand and the interest of the common man on the other.

The district administration has now evolved into a fairly clear establishment, conforming to the total purpose and apparatus of the Government in the district. The purpose of the district administration is three-fold, that is, the maintenance of law and order, revenue administration and development activities for the economic and social advancement of the people of the district. In this apparatus of district administration, the central pivot point is the Collector of the district.[7]

The district administration has pased through various phases of history but the continuity it maintained has been remarkable. The ghost of the mutiny of 1857 haunted the British. To ensure peace and order in the district, one man should be held responsible for it and that was the Collector. Thus, the Collectors were 'little Nepoleons' who combined all important functions concerning law and order, revenue and settlement of litigations in their offices.[8] He inspired awe, fear, respect and obedience. Thus the Collector personified the British Raj.[9]

With the horizontal and vertical proliferation of development departments and their activities, especially after Independence, an important issue that has to be answered is as to how to activise the people and harness their enthusiasm and cooperation for achieving development of the district and its communities as the plans cannot be implemented successfully without people's participation. So long as revenue, law and order were the main considerations, he held his complete sway over the district administration but the rise of Panchayati Raj institutions, creation of new departments and extension of their heirarchies down to the village level have affected the role and functions of Collector. The Collector today, has, broadly speaking, much larger responsibilities in fields of development and welfare, alongwith the traditional regulatory powers, but with somewhat lower prestige and status.[10] His undisputed, exclusive position as the agent of the Government in the district has gradually eroded;

he now shares executive authority with other district level officers and Panchayti Raj institutions. Several departmental and procedural predilections are causing problems to the state Government in making him the captain of the team and many suggestions have been put forward.[11] Despite various stresses and strains, the Planning Commission, in its planning documents underlined the need to strengthen the district administration with Collector as its head.[12]

The Balwantrai Mehta Committee Study Team on Community Development and National Extension Service, which in fact gave shape to the concept of Panchayati Raj, also envisaged that at the district level, the Collector or the Deputy Commissioner should be the captain of the team of officers of all the departments and should be made fully responsible for securing the necessary performance and cooperation in the preparation and execution of the district plans for community development.[13] Thus, in order to ensure coordination, the District Magistrate is to be given real authority to coordinate the activities of all technical officers engaged in development work at the district level.[14] Now, it is proposed to have a glance of the role of Collector as the chief coordinator in the study districts.

## DEPUTY COMMISSIONER, KARNAL

Deputy Commissioner, Karnal, being the sole representative of the state Government in the district, occupies a unique position.[15] The general administration of the district is vested in the Deputy Commissioner, who, for administrative purposes, is under the Divisional Commissioner, Ambala. He performs a triple function. As Deputy Commissioner, he is the executive head of the district with multifarious responsibilities relating to development, panchayats, local bodies, and civil administration. As District Magistrate, he is responsible for law and order and heads the police and prosecuting agency. As Collector, he is the Chief Officer of the revenue administration. He is, in short, the head of the district administration, a coordinating officer among various departments and a connecting link between the public and the Government in-so-far as he executes the policies, administers the rules and regulations framed by the Government from time to time and also looks after the welfare, needs and requirement of the people.[16] Because of his past glory, distinguished position, and status in the district, he exercises formal and informal control over everything that happens under the sun in the district. People, out of tradition, consider him as "Maibaap". Looking at the authority and the power exercised by him, some of the people regard him as the "Mini Chief Minister" and as such a centre of power for solving all the local, special and state problems. All the district officers, financial institutions, corporations. boards, local bodies, Panchayati Raj institutions and voluntary organizations look forward to him for advice, guidance, support and authority to resolve their problems on the spot that they encounter in implementing their programmes. Whenever, a new programme is introduced in the district, or high priorities are accorded to the on-going programme, personal involvement of the Deputy Commissioner is much sought after by the Directorates and other development agencies by forming district level committees, or bodies under his Chairmanship to overview the implementation of the programmes and schemes of such departments and agencies.

Before the introduction of the Community Development Programme, the Deputy Commissioner was a very powerful man in the district administration. He was primarily concerned with (a) maintenance of law and order, (b) revenue administration, and (c) regulatory measures with some concern for the development of the district. During this period, all powers including judicial were vested in him as Collector, District Magistrate and Deputy Commissioner. He, being the sole representative of the Government, was personified as the Government at the district level, and his words were taken as law by the people. He was so powerful that some of the people were afraid of him. As far as his involvement in the development was concerned, his functions were very much limited and that too to facilitate the administration of law and order and collection of revenue.

It may be mentioned here that in order to pacify and win over the confidence of the people in the district, the District Board was constituted for carrying out the limited development functions in the district[17] in 1883 and the Deputy Commissioner was its ex-officio Chairman. This Board was entrusted with development functions, such as (a) the construction, repair and maintenance of public roads and other means of communication; (b) the establishment and management of public hospitals, dispensaries, sarais and schools; (c) the training of teachers and the establishment of scholarships; (d) the supply, storage, and preservation from pollution of water for drinking, cooking and bathing purposes; and (e) the planting and preservation of the trees.[18]

The State Government was also competent to transfer certain other functions, such as (a) the establishment of markets, rest houses and other public institutions, (b) the construction and repair of embankments and the supply, storage and control of water for agricultural purposes, (c) the preservation and reclamation of soil, (d) the construction, repair and maintenance of famine preventive works, (e) registration of marriages, births and deaths, (f) fairs, and agricultural shows and industrial exhibitions, (g) establishment and management of pounds, (h) any other local works or measures likely to promote the health, comfort, convenience and interest of the public or the agricultural or industrial prosperity of the country, and (i) any other matter which the State Government may declare fit for this purpose.[19]

The District Board was also authorised to impose any tax with the previous sanction of the State Government and levy of fees for carrying out its activities. The Board was also provided funds for carrying out the transferred activities. All the above revenue receipts were deposited in the "District Fund" which was constituted under the aforementioned Act.[20]

The Deputy Commissioner was vested with power to suspend the execution of any resolution or order or act of the District Board, if in his opinion, the resolution, order or act is in excess of the powers conferred by law, or the execution of the resolution or order, or the doing of the act, is likely to lead to a breach of peace, or to cause injury or annoyance to the public or to any class or, body of persons.[21] Thus, he was armed with extraordinary powers over the Board's working, and this position continued till the introduction of the Community Development Programme.

A new programme known as Community Development Programme was launched in the year 1952. In order to implement this programme, a new administrative set up named as the National Extension Service was constituted at the block level. In this administrative arrangement, the Block Development Officer was the kingpin in block administration under whom the development functionaries of all the development departments, viz., agriculture, animal husbandry, cooperation, industry, education, and panchayats were placed so as to provide integrated services to the common man under one roof. A Project Advisory Committee comprising local representatives and officials was also constituted under the Chairmanship of the Block Development Officer and subsequently its name was changed to Block Development Committee.

In the scheme of development, the Deputy Commissioner was appointed as District Development Officer, and the officers of all the development departments in the district were placed under his administrative control. This had been accepted as a general pattern in most of the states of India but the people's participation was missing. In order to seek people's participation in the implementation of the programme, an Advisory Committee at the district level consisting of representatives of the people, progressive farmers, and the district level officers was constituted under the Chairmanship of the Deputy Commissioner.

During this period, it was still felt that there is no involvement of the people in plan formulation, as also in the programmes being implemented under the Community Development Programme. The Study Team on Community Development and National Extension Service, headed by Shri Balwantrai Mehta, recommended in December, 1957 a three-tier scheme of democratic decentralization at the level of the village, the block and the district. Under this scheme, the popular body at the district level was to have supervisory and coordinating duties, the executive responsibilities being vested with the people's institutions at the block level to elicit people's participation in the formulation of Community Development Programme, as also its execution.

Thus, in the next phase, the Panchayati Raj institutions came into existence to elicit the effective involvement of the people through their elected bodies at the district, block and village levels.[22] Zila Parishad, Karnal, as constituted in February 1964 under the Panjab Panchayat Samitis and Zila Parishads Act, 1961 was merely conceived as an advisory coordinating body. The functions and responsibilities of Zila Parishad were to: (a) advise, supervise and coordinate the functions of the Panchayat Samitis in the district, (b) approve the budget of the Panchayat Samitis, (c) issue directions to the Panchayat Samitis for efficient discharge of their duties,(d) coordinate and consolidate development plans of the Panchayat Samitis, (e) secure the execution of plans, projects or works common to two or more Panchayat Samitis, (f) exercise and perform such other powers and functions entrusted to it by the Government, (g) advise the Government on all matters relating to the development of the district and the maintenance of services in it, and (h) advise Government for the allocation of works to the Panchayat Samitis. It was, however, not entrusted with work relating to planning and execution of the development programmes.

It was actually the Panchayat Samiti at the block level that was entrusted with planning and execution of development schemes and Block Development Officer was appointed as the Executive Officer of the Panchayat Samiti to carry out its resolutions and the Community Development Programme in the block with the assistance of extension functionaries of various development departments. Almost all the functions relating to rural areas in the fields of: (a) agriculture, (b) animal husbandry and fisheries, (c) health and rural sanitation, (d) communication, (e) social education, (f) cooperation, and (g) a number of miscellaneous subjects such as development of cottage and small scale industries, construction, repair and maintenance of schools and removal of dangerous buildings, were entrusted to the Panchayat Samitis.[23] The Government can also entrust certain functions to the Panchayat Samiti which will be required to carry out such functions as an agent of the Government.[24] Besides, the Panchayat Samiti will be the agent of the Government for the formulation and execution of the Community

Development Programme financed out of grants made by the Government to the Panchayat Samiti within its area.[25]

The Deputy Commissioner, was the non-voting member of the Zila Parishad, Karnal. He was empowered to: (a) enter on and inspect any immovable property occupied or vested in Zila Parishad or any work in progress being undertaken by these institutions, (b) by order in writing call and inspect any document, (c) by order in writing require any Zila Parishad to furnish such statements, accounts, reports or copies of documents, and (d) record in writing for consideration of the Zila Parishad any observations. Similar powers have been vested in the Sub-Divisional Officer (Civil) in case of all the Panchayat Samitis in his Sub-Division.

It may be pointed out that although as per provision in the Act, it was the responsibility of the Zila Parishad to coordinate the development activites of the Panchayat Samitis in the district yet the Deputy Commissioner was actively involved with the Community Development Programme under the instructions of the Government,[26] and issued directions to all the departments responsible for the implementation of the programme. To make him fully and actively responsible for development work, he has been entrusted with wide financial and administrative powers in respect of the Community Development Programme. The Block Development Officers have been placed directly under him and as such have to act as his lieutenants for development work. Deputy Commissioner was also entrusted with supervisory and inspecting functions for reviewing the achievements of targets and progress of expenditure. Inter-departmental coordination is also ensured by the Deputy Commissioner, in addition to District Development Committee, through the monthly follow-up meetings attended by the officers alone for discussing the operative programmes.

In the year 1973, the Zila Parishad was abolished[27] and all its powers were vested in the Deputy Commissioner. Panchayat Samitis also became defunct with the expiry of their term in 1977 as there was no enabling provision in the Act of their continuance till their successor bodies are re-elected.[28] Now, the final picture emerges that the Deputy Commissioner, Karnal was vested with supervisory powers over the Panchayati Raj institutions in the district, and after its abolition, his position is further strengthened at the cost of the people's institutions.

The history of development of urban local government institutions in the district covers a period of more than one hundred years. The first step towards the introduction of local government in the district was taken in 1867 by constituting municipalities at Karnal, Panipat and other places. The main functions of the municipal committees are: (a) supply of drinking water,[29] (b) maintain roads and streets,[30] (c) control of dangerous trades,[31] (d) make arrangements for fire fighting,[32] and (e) look after public health and scavenging of town.[33] They also provide street lights, playgrounds, public parks, medical aid and public libraries. These institutions which primarily cared for the civic amenities and planned development have been under the control and supervision of the Deputy Commissioner since their inception. He can inspect any book or document in possession of the Secretary of the municipality and also call for any statement, accounts, reports and copies of documents or proceedings of the committee.[34] He is also authorized to suspend in writing the execution of any resolution or order of the committee if it is in his opinion against the interest of the public or likely to cause waste or damage to municipal funds or property or likely to lead to a breach of peace or encourage lawlessness.[35] Thus, he has an important role even in the field of civic amenities.

The institution of the Deputy Commissioner is wel established and it, by now, represents the total function of thel Government at the district level.[36] Besides the traditional functions, 43 district development offices, 41 boards and corporations functioning in the district, despite tendencies of departmentalism, heavily lean on this institution to sort out their problems, as also inter-departmental difficulties being faced in the implementation of various programmes. Even the banks, as a matter of policy, seek the involvement of the Deputy Commissioner through the mechanism of the District Consultative Committee and DLRM for the formulation of the District Credit Plans, their implementation, review and monitoring. He is also the Chairman, rather the Executive Chairman of the District Rural Development Agency, Karnal, and exercises substantial powers in relation to the working of this Agency.

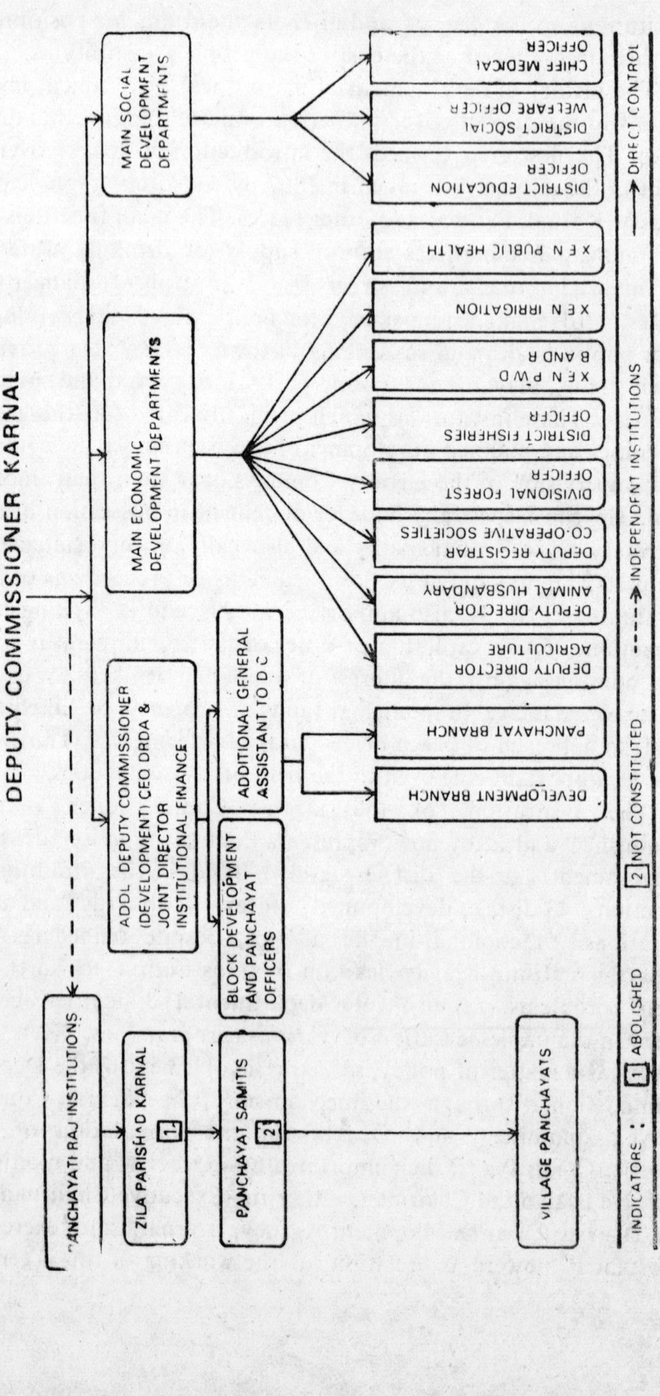
DEPUTY COMMISSIONER KARNAL
PANCHAYATI RAJ INSTITUTIONS
ZILA PARISHAD KARNAL 1
PANCHAYAT SAMITIS 2
VILLAGE PANCHAYATS
ADDL DEPUTY COMMISSIONER (DEVELOPMENT) CEO DRDA & JOINT DIRECTOR INSTITUTIONAL FINANCE
BLOCK DEVELOPMENT AND PANCHAYAT OFFICERS
ADDITIONAL GENERAL ASSISTANT TO D C
DEVELOPMENT BRANCH
PANCHAYAT BRANCH
MAIN ECONOMIC DEVELOPMENT DEPARTMENTS
DEPUTY DIRECTOR AGRICULTURE
DEPUTY DIRECTOR ANIMAL HUSBANDARY
DEPUTY REGISTRAR CO-OPERATIVE SOCIETIES
DIVISIONAL FOREST OFFICER
DISTRICT FISHERIES OFFICER
X E N P W D B AND R
X E N IRRIGATION
X E N PUBLIC HEALTH
MAIN SOCIAL DEVELOPMENT DEPARTMENTS
DISTRICT EDUCATION OFFICER
DISTRICT SOCIAL WELFARE OFFICER
CHIEF MEDICAL OFFICER
INDICATORS : 1 ABOLISHED 2 NOT CONSTITUTED
INDEPENDENT INSTITUTIONS
DIRECT CONTROL

Besides, whenever a new project or programme comes to the district, he is assigned special coordinating role to make it a success. Thus, in almost all the development programmes, he is assigned the pivotal role.

In addition to the proliferation of the offices of the Government, corporations, and boards at the district level, as many as 73 district level committees, councils, and boards have come into existence in Karnal, as also in the other districts in the State. The Deputy Commissiner is the Chairman of all the bodies except the District Public Relations and Grievances Committee and District Level Committee for the implementation of the New 20 Point Programme, of which he is the Vice-Chairman and Member-Secretary respectively. The details of some of the select committees which are constituted by the Government from time to time for ensuring proper coordination and implementation of the development programmes are given below alongwith their functions:—

| *S. No.* | *Name of the committee* | *Functions* |
|---|---|---|
| 1. | District Agriculture Production Committee. | To review the progress relating to agriculture production. |
| 2. | District Officer's Coordination Committee. | For keeping proper liaison between the various officers for proper functioning of the departments. It also sorts out the problems of the development departments in the district. |
| 3. | District Level Committee for the Implementation of the New 20 Point Programme. | To review the progress of 20 point programme and implementation thereof |
| 4. | District Rural Development Agency. | For the formulation and implementation of the integrated rural development programme in the district. |
| 5. | District Dairy Development Committee. | For coordinating the activities of various departments and |

| | | |
|---|---|---|
| | | agencies involved in the implementation of the dairy development programme. |
| 6. | Steering Committee for National Rural Employment Programme | For the implementation of National Rural Employment Programme. |
| 7. | District Manpower Planning and Employment Generation Council. | Planning regarding employment generation. |
| 8. | District Industry Advisory Committee for speedy Industrialisation. | To promote rural industries scheme and extend loan facility to the entrepreneurs. |
| 9. | District Adhoc Committee for the Welfare of SCs and BCs. | To send recommendation to Government for welfare schemes. |
| 10. | District Child Welfare Council. | To coordinate activities and help in the development of child welfare movement. |
| 11. | District Vigilance Committee under Bonded Labour Systems. | To provide for the economic and social rehabilitation of the freed bonded labourers. |
| 12. | District Level Loan Sanctioning Committee for Harijan Kalyan Nigam. | To sanction loans to the Scheduled Castes. |
| 13. | District Planning Advisory Board. | To advise the district authorities about the programmes to be taken up for systematic socio-economic development. |
| 14. | District Planning Committee. | To assist the District Planning Advisory Board in the formulation of short term and perspective plan of the district, and to review the progress in smooth implementation of development programmes. |

The work of the Deputy Commissioner, therefore, increased manifold and this institution was not strengthened till 1981 when the senior scale IAS Officer was appointed as Additional Deputy Commissioner (Development) in the district. The Additional Deputy Commissioner is required to play an effective role in the implementation and coordination of all major development programmes and also to play a pivotal role in policy formulation, monitoring, evaluation and review of planning at the district level under the overall supervision, guidance and control of the Deputy Commissioner.[37] He will also maintain close liaison with the financial institutions operating in the district for the smooth flow of institutional credit.[38] In order to involve him fully in development work, he is not required to be saddled with other routine duties such as revenue, judicial work, law and order, VIP duties or other general administration duties.[39] On 20.4.1982, he was entrusted with the execution, supervision and review of the schemes of the development and panchayat departments.[40]

The above account reveals that the institution of the Deputy Commissioner emerges stronger over the years despite the emergence of new rival rural and urban local bodies such as Panchayati Raj institutions and municipal committees as also the growing rival departmentalism. His role as catalyst is well recognized by all the development departments who generally get him involved in coordinating their programmes through the mechanism of "Committee System".[41] The detailed planning of activites of these departments is not only sectoral but also centralized being done at the state headquarters, thus rendering his coordinating role quite difficult. It is generally pointed out that the approach of various functionaries responsible for development functions at the district level has been such which fails to generate mass response and inspire confidence amongst the people. The structure hardly encourages full delegation and deconcentration of authority.

## COLLECTOR OF THANE

Public Administration in the State in the last century consisted mostly of providing security of person and property and raising the revenue necessary for the purpose.[42] The institution of the Collector had great prestige and power during the British period.[43] The Collector was not merely the representative of the Government but he was for all practical purposes, the Government at the disrict level. Even after Independence, he is the pivot round which the district administration turns.[44] He is not only the head of the revenue department, in so far as the needs and exigencies of the district administration are concerned, he is also expected to superintend the working of the offices of other departments.[45]

Till the establishment of Zila Parishad, Thane in 1962, the Collector used to have certain functions in respect of District Development Board. He was the Chairman of the District Development Board which was set up in 1972 by reconstituting the District Rural Development Board to assist and advise the officials in the implementation of local development programmes. He was involved in the implementation of the Community Development Programme in the district. He also became the Chairman of the Sub-Committee of the District Development Board, known as the District National Extension Service and Community Development Advisory Committee, for advising on questions of policy relating to the implementation of the block development programme.

The role of the Collector with regard to development functions was radically changed with the introduction of Panchayati Raj institutions. The Government of Maharashtra appointed in June 1960 a Committee under the Chairmanship of Shri V.P. Naik, the then Revenue Minister, to examine the problem of democratic decentralization in the context of the conditions prevailing in the state. The Naik Committee recommended that there should be a strong executive body at the district level to be designated as a "District Council". This Committee was of the view that "the Collector is . . . responsible for practically everything that happens or should happen in a district. Burdened with a multiplicity of functions and with physical limitation of time and energy, the Collector is unable to do justice to any of his functions". In the above situation, the Committee did not make the Collector as the Chief Administrator of the proposed District Council. It proposed the appointment of a full time officer in the senior scale of the IAS Cadre to execute the development programmes.

The recommendations of the Naik Committee were accepted by the Government. All the development functions in the fields of (a) agriculture, (b) animal husbandry, (c) forest, (d) social welfare, (e) economic development of backward classes, (f) removal of untouchability, (g) programmes for the welfare of the backward classes, (h) training of backward classes, (i) education, (j) medical, (k) public health, (l) buildings and communications, (m) public health engineering, (n) irrigation, (o) publicity, (p) community development, (q) social education, (r) rural housing, and (s) miscellaneous subjects such as village uplift, building model villages, markets, and dharamshalas,[46] at the district level were entrusted to the Zila Parishad and an officer of the Collector's seniority was also placed at the disposal of the Zila Parishad as its Chief Executive Officer. The Zila Parishad, Thane started functioning in 1962. All the officers, who were earlier responsible to the Collector, are now made responsible to the Chief Executive Officer. The Chief Executive Officer is entitled to attend the meetings of the Zila Parishad or any of its committees. The Collector is, therefore, outside the Zila Parishad and he has not been entrusted any development functions under the Maharashtra Zila Parishads and Panchayat Samitis Act, 1961. Thus, with the commencement of the Panchayati Raj, the Chief Executive Officer, Zila Parishad became the chief coordinator of the development efforts in the district.

With the setting up of the DPB in 1972, the Chief Executive Officer remained the chief coordinator and used to coordinate the development activities of various departments at the district level. When the DPDC was set up in 1974, the Chief Executive Officer of the Zila Parishad was made the Member-Secretary of the DPDC. However, it was noticed subsequently that the Chief Executive Officer, Zila Parishad was fully busy with various items of work relating to Zila Parishad's own functions.[47] Further, district planning covered not only local sector schemes under the Zila Parishad in rural areas but also state sector schemes, the schemes implemented by urban local bodies and various institutional agencies over which the Zila Parishad had no control.[48] In view of this and also considering the role of the Collector as the "chief administrative head of the district", it was thought that, it would be desirable if the Collector was entrusted with the work of district planning. In December, 1975, therefore, it was decided to appoint the Collector of the District as the Member-Secretary of the DPDC. The Collector as the Member-Secretary of the DPDC is assisted by the district planning unit in attending to the work of the formulation, monitoring and evaluation of the district plan. Thus, Collector, again, emerged as the Chief Coordinator of development administration after a period of 12 years.

DPDC has been constituted with the functions of formulation and monitoring of district plans and bringing about coordination between various implementing agencies at the district level. The DPDC mainly operates through its Executive Committee and the Special Executive Committee for the TASP. The Executive Committee is also headed by the District Minister and the Collector is its Member-Secretary. It has all the powers of the DPDC and can discharge all the functions of the DPDC. In addition, it reviews the implementation of the Special Component Plan for the Scheduled Castes and Neo-Budhists in every meeting, as also the implementation of IRDP schemes. In this way, the Collector as the Member-Secretary, assumed an important coordinating role in plan formulation, review of implementation and monitoring of the district plan.

In 1978, the Government constituted a small team comprising: the Collector, the Chief Executive Officer, Zila Parishad, Thane and President, Zila Parishad, Thane and 2-3 non-officials to examine the district plan proposals of the district. The Collector, being the Member-Secretary of the DPDC, is the convener of this team and as such convenes its meetings. This team considers the proposals of each officer, and decides the schemes to be included in the district plans. This team has a decisive voice in the formulation of the district annual plan as the draft plan proposed by it is almost accepted by the DPDC. The Collector, being the convener of this team, plays a major role in formulating the draft plan, and this has further strengthened the institution of the Collector as Chief Coordinator in the formulation of the district annual plan.[49]

For the proper implementation of the developmental schemes and the removal of difficulties experienced by the district implementing officers and agencies, it had been decided by the Government on 11.2.1976[50] that the Collector, as the Member-Secretary should arrange to collect from various implementing officers and agencies concerned with the district level schemes included in the annual budget, a monthly report on the progress of expenditure and physical achievement in the prescribed proforma and place the consolidated report before the Executive Committee of the DPDC to (a) consider the performance of each implementing officer, (b) identify reasons for shortfall in expenditure, as also physical achievements, and (c) suggest measures for expeditious implementation of such programmes where the progress is found to be tardy. The Collector soon after the meeting of the Executive Committee of the DPDC arranges to forward to the Government in the Planning Department, a summary record of the discussions in the Executive Committee and Special Executive Committee together with recommendations made by it with a view to removing administrative and other bottlenecks and for expeditious implementation of the developmental programmes under the district's annual plan.[51]

It may also be pointed out that the Chief Executive Officer is the head of the entire administrative organization of the Zila Parishad, including the organization at the Panchayat Samiti level. He is assisted by 2 Deputy Chief Executive Officers—one Deputy Chief Executive Officer (general administration) and other Deputy Chief Executive Officer (village panchayats). There was a third Deputy Chief Executive Officer (Planning) but from 15th December 1975, planning has gone to the Collector and, therefore, he has been transferred to the Collector. Various other heads of departments who assist the Chief Executive Officer, are : (a) Education Officer, (b) District Health Officer, (c) Agriculture Development Officer, (d) Chief Accounts and Financial Officer, (e) Executive Engineer Works, (f) Executive Engineer Irrigation, (g) Animal Husbandry Officer, and (h) Social Welfare Officer.

The Chief Executive Officer is vested with the executive authority for carrying out the development activities of various departments at the district level.

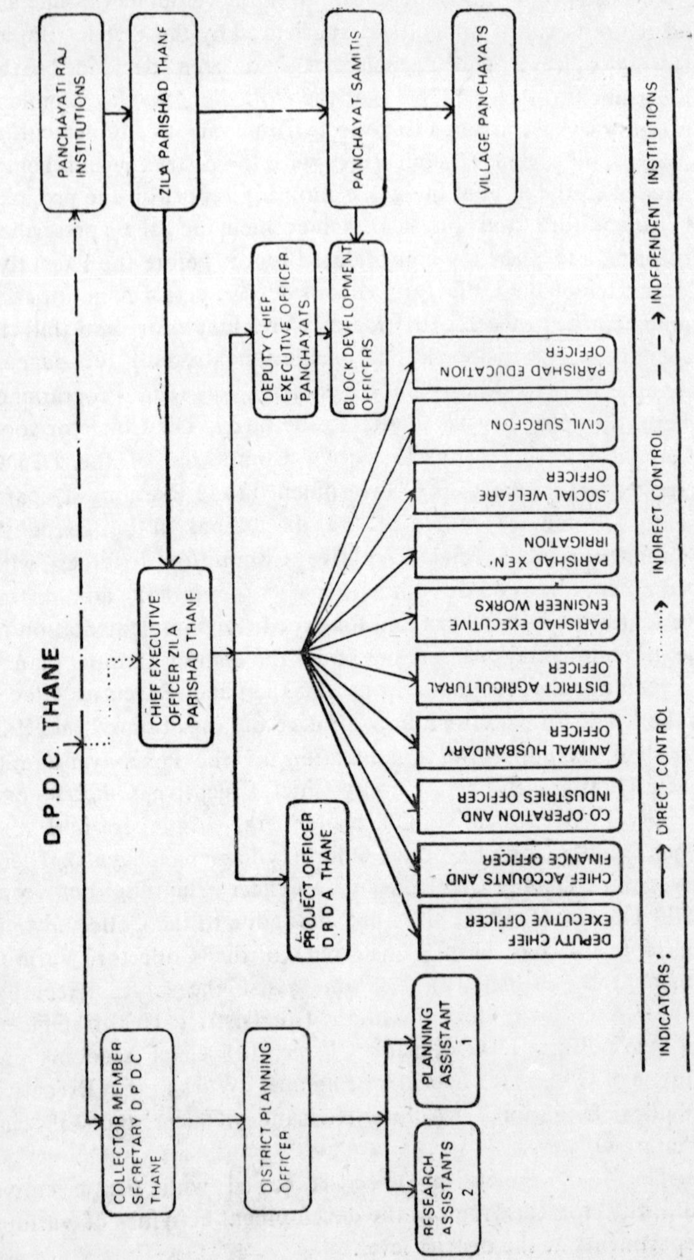
D.P.D.C. THANE
PANCHAYATI RAJ INSTITUTIONS
ZILA PARISHAD THANE
PANCHAYAT SAMITIS
VILLAGE PANCHAYATS
DEPUTY CHIEF EXECUTIVE OFFICER PANCHAYATS
BLOCK DEVELOPMENT OFFICERS
CHIEF EXECUTIVE OFFICER ZILA PARISHAD THANE
PROJECT OFFICER D R D A THANE
PARISHAD EDUCATION OFFICER
CIVIL SURGEON
SOCIAL WELFARE OFFICER
PARISHAD XEN IRRIGATION
PARISHAD EXECUTIVE ENGINEER WORKS
DISTRICT AGRICULTURAL OFFICER
ANIMAL HUSBANDARY OFFICER
CO-OPERATION AND INDUSTRIES OFFICER
CHIEF ACCOUNTS AND FINANCE OFFICER
DEPUTY CHIEF EXECUTIVE OFFICER
COLLECTOR MEMBER SECRETARY D P D C THANE
DISTRICT PLANNING OFFICER
PLANNING ASSISTANT 1
RESEARCH ASSISTANTS 2
INDICATORS:
DIRECT CONTROL
INDIRECT CONTROL
INDEPENDENT INSTITUTIONS

He is a mobilizer, initiator and leader supervising different departments through inspection, day-to-day administration, review of works and control of finances. He also ensures coordination between Block Development Officers at block level and various heads of departments. All the Class I and II Officers working under the Zila Parishad, Thane are responsible only to the Chief Executive Officer. He is authorized to assess and give his opinion confidentially on the work of these officers.[52]

The Zila Parishad functions through the "Committee System" and the Maharashtra Zila Parishads and Panchayat Samitis Act, 1961, provides for the setting up of 8 Sub Committees:[53] viz., (a) Standing Committee, (b) Finance Committee, (c) Works Committee, (d) Agriculture Committee, (e) Health Committee, (f) Education Committee, (g) Social Welfare Committee, and (h) Animal Husbandry and Dairying Committee. The Chief Executive Officer is entitled to attend the meetings of the Zila Parishad or any of its Committees.

SFDA, Thane, provided financial assistance to the small and marginal farmers and landless labourers from 1-9-70 to 30-9-80 and the programme was under implementation in seven blocks only. Subsequently, this programme was redesignated as the Integrated Rural Development Programme and extended to all the thirteen blocks of the district from 2-10-1980 and the Collector was made the Chairman of the Governing Council of the DRDA, Thane. Later on, the Chief Executive Officer, Zila Parishad, Thane, was made the Chairman of this Council on 1.6.1982.[54]

In this capacity he became responsible for coordinating the activities of various development officers in the field of formulation, implementation, review and monitoring of the programmes.

It may be pointed out that in 1975, Collector was made Member-Secretary of the DPDC for looking after the development work. This assignment of additional functions and responsibilities has no doubt increased his work-load and enhanced his prestige and status in the district administration. In order to cope with the increased work-load in respect of his traditional and development responsibilities, the Collector, Thane, took a decision to rationalize the working of various branches directly working under him.[55]

The distribution of subjects between the Collector and Additional Collector has been made and the cases are put up to the respective officer for final decisions according to this delegation.[56] It is quite obvious from this delegation that the Collector has retained all development functions such as (a) formulation of general plan, Tribal Sub-Plan, Special Component Plan, (b) the meetings of the DPDC, its Executive Committee and Special Executive Committee, (c) district and block plans, (d) special schemes, (e) institutional finances, (f) meetings of Taluka and District Coordination and Review Committee, (g) Twenty Point Programme of socio-economic development, and (h) miscellaneous planning matters.[57] In addition, he also deals with important schemes such as (a) Employment Guarantee Schemes and matters connected therewith[58], Sanjay Gandhi Yojna[59], (c) scarcity, rural drinking water supply, and natural calamities[60], (d) Family Welfare Programme[61], (e) matters concerning Industries Department[62], and (f) provision of house sites and huts to the landless and houseless agricultural labourers[63]. In the fields of regulatory and coordination functions, he retains with him (a) revenue administration[64], (b) elections[65], (c) matters relating to municipal administration[66], (d) matters concerning Zila Parishads and Panchayat Samitis Act, 1961, including election[67], (e) Legislative Assembly and Council Questions[68], (f) District Soldiers', Sailors' and Airmen's Board and related matters[69], and (g) district coordination meetings[70] and District Grievances Committee.[71] All other work have been delegated to the Additional Collector.

The above account reveals that the Collector has always been formally or informally assigned an important and effective role in matters relating to law and order, revenue administration as well as development excepting for a period from 1962 to 1975 during which the Chief Executive Officer of the Zila Parishad became the coordinator for development activities. In December 1975, the Collector, being the Chief administrative and the sole representative of the Government at the district level, had been entrusted with the work relating to the coordination of development efforts in the district when he was made the Member-Secretry of DPDC, its Executive Committee and Special Executive Committee. In this capacity, district planning unit headed by the District Planning Officer, Thane, is also placed under his administrative control, and he is charged with the responsibility to assist the DPDC and its committees in the formulation, review of implementation, monitoring and evaluation of the district plans, as also other matters connected therewith. He is also made the convener of the "small team of officers" to examine the plan proposals of various departments in the district, and as such he exercises enormous influence in the formulation of plan proposals being the representative of the Government at the district level. He coordinates the development activities of all the district development departments, agencies, financial institutions, corporations and boards. It is not only through the intstitutions that the development programmes click. Any programme aiming at the socio-economic change through the planning process must take into account the problems and the social conditions existing in the area and with the target group. People, specially in rural areas, require a special approach to their development which is ultimately to be based on a perfect understanding of their sensibilities. This can be better achieved through institutional arrangements in which there is an active participation of people and their representatives.[72]

## OVERVIEW

The issue of coordination of development activities and programmes of various departments, agencies, boards, corporations, banks and other institutions at the district level is an integral part of the effective planning process. Who should be the Chief Coordinator, is a vexed and highly controversial issue. Traditionalists would like to use the institution of Deputy Commissioner or the Collector as the Chief Coordinator but without reinforcing his authority over the district officers. Departmentalists argue that Collector should not meddle in their work at the district level and their inter-departmental problems should be resolved by their state level directorates.

The institution of the Deputy Commissioner, Karnal, is the oldest and is always a strong link in the district administrative heirarchy. He, being captain of the district team, is generally made the coordinator, without taking into consideration as to whether he can possibly perform these functions or not. The net result of this process is that he remains busy, with routine files on his desk, for longer hours. The Collector, as usual, is responsible for the maintenance of law and order, security of the country, revenue collection and enforcement of revenue and land laws. He performs regulatory functions and is also charged with the responsiblity, as the Chief Coordinator, of a wide range of activities and programmes of almost all the state Directorates, departments, organizations, institutions, committees, boards and corporations. In the seventies, "agency system" comprising DRDA, FFDA, etc. also came up, and he was made the Chairman of these agencies.[73] Here again, he is not merely the Chairman for presiding over the meetings of these agencies but a real administrator with power and authority, and is required to spare sufficient time for these assignments of national importance. He is also the Chairman or an office-bearer of more than six dozen of committees formed for the coordination purposes. Additionally, he is the head of the District Red Cross Society, Child Welfare Council and a number of other such welfare bodies. Besides being the ceremonial head and representative of the Government, he is expected to deliver goods in emergent situations, whether national or local. Since Independence, "we have been mercilessly adding more and more new items to the Deputy Commissioner's sagging back and thus the institution of Deputy Commissioner might perish or break"[74] and the introduction of the Agency System in 1970 and proliferation of the district level offices, corporations and boards have added too much to the already heavy kit of the Collector and the much sought after coordination becomes a casualty.

The emergence of the Panchayati Raj did pose problems for the authority, power and status of the Deputy Commisioner, Karnal. However, Panchayati Raj institutions practically petered out of the district development administration, and his overall authority over the development administration remains established.

The above discussions also reveal that the Deputy Commissioner, Karnal, though overburdened with work, does not share his powers, functions and responsibilities with the Additional Deputy Commissioner (Development) by way of delegation order. The Additional Deputy Comissioner (Development) is also assigned non-developmental routine duties by the Deputy Comissioner to assist him.

In Thane district, the Collector is also the pivot on which the district administration revolves. He remains the head of the revenue administration in the district, and is expected to superintend the working of the offices of other departments also. Till the establishment of the Zila Parisahd, the Collector was very powerful, and was assigned the role of Chief Coordinator in all matters relating to the development of the district. However, with the introduction of Panchayati Raj, which is also regarded as a "little short of revolution", the role of the Collector with regard to development functions varied substantially. The Chief Executive Officer of the Zila Parishad became the Chief Coordinator of development activities which, by and large, were statutorily entrusted to the Zila Parishad, and he, since then, has been exercising administrative control over the development staff in the district. The representatives of the people and other local bodies have certainly affected adversely the position of the Collector as Coordinator because of their untiring efforts to find a place of status and position for themselves in the politico-administrative system at the district level. In this situation, he is no longer accepted as the absolute leader of the district heirarchy.

With the setting up of the District Planning Board in Thane, in 1972, Chief Executive Officer was retained as the Chief Coordinator and his position remained so even with the constitution of the DPDC upto December, 1975 when he was shorn of his role as Chief Coordinator without affecting his admistrative control over the district officers. The Collector, being the chief administrative head of the district, was made the Member-Secretary of the DPDC to assist it in formulation, review, monitoring and evaluation of the district plans. This increase in responsibilities resulted in his again becoming a key officer at the district level.

He has started assuming greater involvement in the development process in order to perform his new role effectively and expeditiously. He has transferred a part of his revenue and routine work to the Additional Collector who works under his overall supervision. Strangely enough, this dynamic involvement of the Collector has been affected through an office order which is purely a local arrangement made by the Collector himself. Today, he does not sit on the departmental sideline in Thane, but participates actively and significantly.

Planning for development at the district level presupposes (a) Central authority to coordinate the plan efforts of all the development departments, organisations and institutions, (b) delegation of administrative and financial powers, and (c) effective monitoring and evaluation of development programmes and projects. The Collector, Thane, has not been assigned any specific coordinating role, especially when the Executive Committee and Special Executive Committee fail to meet due to pre-occupations of the Minister with his departmental and ceremonial functions. Moreover, he has no financial and administrative control over the development departments which are, practically, functioning under the Chief Executive Officer of the Zila Parishad, Thane. Thus, his role as the Chief Coordinator is not tenable, especially when the entire development machinery functions under the control of the Panchayati Raj institutions. His position as Chief Coordinator needs to be strengthened which appears to be a far-fetched idea in view of the emergence of strong Panchayati Raj institutions in Thane, and other districts of Maharashtra. The viable alternative to the Collector will be to further involve and strengthen the Zile Parishad by making the President, Zila Parishad as the Senior Vice-Chairman of the DPDC and to restore the position of the Chief Executive Officer, Zila Parishad, as the Member-Secretary of the DPDC which appears to be a natural choice because of his predominance over the district development administration. To make him universally acceptable to all the development departments and other organizations, the post of the Chief Executive Officer needs to be re-designated as the Collector (Development) and Chief Executive Officer, Zila Parishad and this will enable him to effectively coordinate the activities of various development departments, agencies, financial institutions, corporations, boards, and commercial and cooperative banks functioning in the district.

Now, the matter regarding monitoring and evaluation being an integral part of the planning process is taken up in the next chapter.

## REFERENCES

1. Coordination may be described as a process of bringing together the constituent parts of an organisation in harmonious and active inter-relationship so that each part in its turn would perform its assigned functions within the alloted time towards achieving or attaining the anticipated total result of the whole.

2. S.N. Sadasivan, District Level Administration in India. (The Madras Experience) National Seminar on District Administration (February 21-23, 1983), Indian Institute of Public Administration, New Delhi, p. 22.
3. A.L. Fletcher, The Collector in the Nineteen Sixties, *Indian Journal of Public Administration*, Special Number, July-September 1965, New Delhi, p. 368.
4. Refer J.D. Shukla, Uttar Pradesh, op. cit. p. 594.
5. S.K. Sharma, *Deputy Commissioner in Punjab*, Indian Institute of Public Administration, New Delhi, 1971. p. 1.
6. S.S. Khera, *District Administration in India*, Asia Publishing House, Bombay, 1964, p. 255.
7. Ibid., p. 254.
8. C.P. Bhambhri, *Public Administration in India*, Vikas Publishing House Private Limited, Delhi, 1973, p. 162.
9. Ibid.
10. The Collector in the Nineteen Sixties, op. cit. p. (i).
11. Ibid.
12. The First Five Year Plan, New Delhi, p. 130.
13. India, Panchayati Raj at a Glance (as on 31st March, 1964) Ministry of Community Development and Cooperation, New Delhi, pp. 92-93.

14. Sukumar Dam: District Development Administration, *The Modern Review*, May, 1975, p. 343.
15. Based on available records as well as on interview with the concerned officers at the district and state levels.
16. Refer Gazetter of India, Haryana State: Karnal district, 1976, pp. 271-72.
17. District Board, Karnal was set up under the Punjab District Boards Act 1883. The main aim of the Act was to make better provision for local self Government in the district. The Deputy Commissioner, Karnal, remained its Chairman from 1883 to 1949. The first and the last non-official Chairman of the Board was elected during 1946 and continued upto June 1954. After this, the Deputy Commissioner was again made its Chairman. With the enactment of Punjab Panchayat Samitis and Zila Parishads Act, 1961, the District Board was replaced by the Zila Parishad, Karnal in February, 1964.
18. Section 20, Punjab District Boards Act, 1883, p. 159.
19. Ibid., pp. 160-161.
20. Ibid., p. 170.
21. Ibid., p. 176.
22. Refer Panjab Panchayat Samitis and Zila Parishad Act, 1961.
23. Ibid., Section 41, pp. 16-19.
24. Ibid., Section 42, p. 20.
25. Ibid., Section 43, p. 20.
26. Govt. of Panjab, Manual on Community Development 1958, Chandigarh, pp. 24-25.
27. The Zila Parishad in Haryana were abolished in June 1973 under the provisions of the Panjab Samitis and Zila Parishad (Haryana Amendment) Act, 1973, and their duties and functions have been entrusted to the Deputy Commissioner.
28. Election of the Primary members of the Panchayat Samitis has been completed in the State in September/October, 1983 but these bodies are not constituted so far because one member from the market committee is yet to be elected in each Panchayat Samiti. Thereafter, the cooption of the requisite number of Scheduled Castes and women members will be made. When these elections will be completed, only then the election of the Chairman and Vice-Chairman will be held so as to finally constitute the Panchayat Samiti. Thus, it will still take time to constitute these bodies.
29. Refer Haryana Municipal Act, 1973, (as amended upto 31st Jan. 1974), Haryana Government Press, Chandigarh, 1974, Sections 108-113.
30. Ibid., Sections 172-185.
31. Ibid., Section 133.
32. Ibid., Sections 105-107.
33. Ibid., Chapter IX.

34. Ibid., Section 245.
35. Ibid., Section 245.
36. S.K. Sharma: op. cit., p. 192.
37. Refer letter No. I-DSAR-Plg-81, dated 4.5.81 from the Chief Secretary, Haryana to all the Deputy Commissioners in the State, p. 1. The Additional Deputy Commissioner, Karnal (Development) is also ex-officio Chief Executive Officer of the DRDA for looking after the Integrated Rural Development Programme and made responsible for its successful implementation. He has also been entrusted with the monitoring and review of various programmes: (a) Integrated Child Development Scheme, (b) National Rural Employment Programme, (c) Minimum Needs Programme, (d) Twenty Point Economic Programme, (e) Special Component Plan for Scheduled Castes, (f) Manpower, Planning and Employment, and (g) other special programmes under the Sixth Plan.
38. Ibid., p. 2.
39. Ibid.
40. Additional Deputy Commissioner (Development) was not entrusted any work in relation to development and panchayat departments. In order to make him effective, he has been entrusted with the supervision and review of various schemes such as (a) National Rural Employment Programme, (b) matching grants and revenue earning schemes of the panchayats, (c) planning, execution and supervision of the schemes being implemented by the panchayats, (d) proper management of the shamlat lands, (e) inspection of the offices of the Block Development and Panchayat Officers and the Panchayats and cattle fairs within their respective jurisdiction, (f) constrnction of Harijan chaupals and panchayat ghars, (g) supervision of women welfare programmes, and (h) all enquiries against the officials and non-officials, of the development and panchayat departments.
41. Committee System includes all the district level committees, boards and councils set up by the Government of Haryana, generally under the chairmanship of the Deputy Commissiner, from time to time with a view to ensuring coordination and effective implementation of various programmes and schemes being executed by the implementing officers at the district level. In Karnal district, there are as many as 73 such bodies in existence for this purpose.
42. Gazetteer of India, Maharashtra State: Thane District (Revised Edition), Government of Maharashtra, Bombay, 1982, p. 806.
43. Based on interviews with the concerned district and State level officers.
44. Ibid., p. 807.
45. Ibid.
46. Maharashtra Zila Parishads and Panchayat Samitis Act, 1961, Section 100.

47. Resolution No. DPC-1075/PRGI/DP, dated 1.12.1975, Planning Department, Government of Maharashtra, Bombay.
48. Ibid.
39. Based on interviews with the district level officers of Thane.
50. Refer circular No. DPC-1076/PRG-DPP, dated 11.2.1976, Planning Department, Government of Maharashtra, p. 2.
51. The meetings of the Executixe Committee of the DPDC are not held regularly due to preoccupations of the district Minister. In this way, the work relating to the detailed review of the progress of the annual plan suffers.
52. The President of the Zila Parishad, Thane does not initiate or write the confidential Reports of the Chief Executive Officer. However, the President can write to the Government about his work and conduct but generally it is not done. The President can write to the Government to recall the Chief Executive Officer from Zila Parishad.
53. Refer The Maharashtra Zila Parishads and Panchayat Samitis Act, 1961, Section 78.
54. The other members of this Governing Council are Agricultural Development Officer, District Animal Husbandary Officer, Chairman of the District Central Cooperative Bank, District Dairy Development Officer, District Deputy Registrar, Cooperative Societies, Deputy Director, Social Forestry and the Project Officer, DRDA is its Member-Secretary.
55. Refer office order No. PA (C) dated 14th March 1983 issued by the Collector, Thane.
56. Ibid.
57. Ibid.
58. Ibid., pp. 13-14.
59. Ibid., p. 11.
60. Ibid., pp. 8-10.
61. Ibid., p. 7.
62. Ibid., p. 4.
63. Ibid.
64. Ibid., p. 4.
65. Ibid., p. 6.
66. Ibid., p. 7.
67. Ibid., p. 8.
68. Ibid., p. 13.
69. Ibid., p. 9.
70. Ibid., p. 10.
71. Ibid., p. 12.
72. Based on interviews with the district level officers and the President of the Zila Parishad, Thane. Some of the district level officers observed that the DPDC is a district assembly and lays down guidelines for the formulation of district plans, and the main work of

planning is done by the District Planning Officer under the overall supervision and guidance of the Collector. MLAs on this Conncil merely dish out material for raising Assembly questions and do not take much interest in planning work. It is also alleged that the meetings of the Executive Committee are not held regularly as a result of which monitoring of schemes suffers. The meeting of Executive Council and Special Executive Council are of short duration and cannot do justice to all the schemes included in the district budget. These Committees are unwieldy, and MLAs and MPs merely take interest in general problems such as scarcity of water and drought. They hardly do justice to review about 226 schemes included in the Non-TASP and 135 in TASP. In these meetings, about 70 officers and 50 non-officials take part and they cannot have dialogue on all the schemes. It is also said that in the name of popular participation, legislators have become executives. It is also alleged that the Executive Council and Special Executive Council have become multi-headed monitoring body and MLAs and MPs use opportunity to overawe the officers and no guidance is provided to them in these meetings. In fact, they criticize two or three officers only, and the turn of other officers for review does not come.

73. Collector, Thane, is no longer the Chairman of the Governing Council of the DRDA. Thane, Now the Chief Executive Officer, Zila Parishad, Thane is made the Chairman of this Council since 1.6.1982.

74. S.K. Sharma, op. cit., p. 288.

# 9

# MONITORING AND EVALUATION

"MONITORING" and "evaluation" are two important aspects of the comprehensive planning process, and equally useful links in the chain of district planning, and as such deserve recognition with a view to achieving the objectives of planning. Successive Five Year Plans have always stressed the importance of strengthening the implementation machinery so that the projects and programmes included in the plan move according to time schedules and targets achieved. It has also been recognized that implemantation needs to be supported by adequate monitoring and current and post evaluation of major programmes so that lessons of experience enable improvements in the design of programmes themselves.[1] There is further indication from experience that deficiencies in implementation are also due to causal slippages in schedules, cost over-runs and poor performance. Thus, while talking of failures of implementation, one should look upon planning, implementation and evaluation as an integral process, each driving strength from the other (and transmitting its weaknesses all the way through the process).[2] Both these devices are necessary to find out as to whether the plan programmes are really being implemented in the right earnest, and physical and financial targets achieved within the stipulated period, and these would also help the administrators and the planners to take necessary remedial or corrective measures in time. In most of the cases, the district officers receive the progress reports from the field officials and send the same to the concerned Directorates at the state level. Thus, the monitoring is expected to be undertaken by the Directorates at the state level. As far as the evaluation exercises are concerned, these are done by the Economic and Statistical Organization and that too of the selected programmes. Most of the important programmes and projects are never evaluated and the funds are being spent on them year after year without knowing whether these serve the purpose as per mandate from the State Assembly or Parliament. It has been observed by the Planning Commission in the Sixth Five Year Plan that adequate organization and systems at present do not exist for monitoring and evaluation of plan projects and programmes at different levels[3] including the district level. It is, therefore, necessary to develop these systems so as to make them effective instruments to ensure that the benefit of the plan programmes reach the ultimate target groups and areas as well as help re-orientation of the policies and programmes. It should be a continuous process and become an effective aid in sharpening the focus of the planners and administrators to acheive development in the right direction.

## MONITORING

"Monitoring" may be defined as a process of ensuring that performance takes place in conformity with the plan.[4] Succinctly, monitoring may be described as an instant process of receiving or calling for the quarterly, monthly, fortnightly or even weekly or daily reports of the progress of physical and financial targets achieved by the agencies entrusted with the responsibility for the implementation of the schemes, programmes and projects, vis-a-vis their fixed targets.

Broadly, monitoring model may be stated to consist of: (a) monitoring all the items which are to be monitored, (b) breaking up the annual financial and physical programmes into monthly programmes, (c) monitoring periodically (generally monthly) the progress registered against the monthly (or periodically) programme alongwith problems and bottlenecks affecting the progress, and (d) placing the information so monitored before appropriate authority who can take decision and enforce corrective measures to overcome the problems and difficulties. This, therefore, requires a monitoring authority[5] such as the Deputy Commissioner or the Collector or the Chief Executive

Officer or even a committee to monitor the progress of targets. Operationally, the execution of the district plan without proper monitoring of activities may not only lead to poor results but also may result in development completely contrary to the plan. Planning, therefore, requires monitoring mechanism to be postulated and built in the plan[6] of the programme. In case this is done regularly and in time, it will help the monitoring authority to locate the major areas of problems and shortfall in implementation of the plan programmes and rectify the same immediately by advising or even administering warning or caution to the concerned implementing agency to make good the shortfall in achieving its targets.

### EVALUATION

"Evaluation" of the plan programmes is also a part and parcel of the planning process. The term evaluation may be described as an assessment of the progress of the on-going schemes so as to take corrective or remedial measures. This is called as concurrent or internal evaluation since such arrangements are built up in the programme itself. Then there is also post-facto "evaluation" which is restricted to the evaluation of the programme already implemented. This is in the nature of "independent assessment", generally undertaken by an agency not charged with the responsibility of administering the programme.[7] In brief, it may be defined as the retrospective analysis of experience to see if the pre-determined objectives of the programme are achieved and also to determine how and why the objectives were or were not achieved. The evaluation is not concerned with the day-to-day activities of the project or programme. The main aim of the post-facto evaluation is to derive lessons for improvement in the formulation and implementation of programmes. Logically, it would involve the assessment of progress, delineation of areas of success or failure, and identification of the reasons for success or failure.

"Evaluation", thus, is a vital link in the entire chain of planning for development and every programme is finally required to be evaluated with a view to examining whether the objectives have been achieved or not. It will also reflect impact of the programmes in the areas as also on the beneficiaries, as well as about the proper or improper use of budgetary provisions earmarked for the programmes. It also helps reorientation of plan programmes as well as provides experience for better planning in future.

The main objectives of evaluation are to: (a) assess whether the objectives of development programmes are being achieved, (b) find out whether the programmes are reaching the target groups, (c) assess the social and economic impact of programmes in terms of definite indicators of development, (d) discover the missing links and gaps both in planning and implementation stages, and (e) serve as feed-back input which is of crucial importance for mid-course correction in the operational framework so that the desired objectives are achieved.[8]

It may also be pointed out that the evaluation is a discontinuous function whereas monitoring is a continuous function. Monitoring Cell of the implementing organisation is intimately related to day-to-day functioning operations and usually emotionally attached and practically involved in the project, and as such will not be the appropriate cell to conduct post-facto evaluation. It should be the responsibility of Planning Department to evaluate all the projects and programmes so as to derive lessons for future planning on better lines.

Now, it is proposed to examine the actual processes of monitoring and evaluation being followed in the study districts and their effectiveness, especially with reference to agricultural sector.

## Position in Thane

Monitoring is an integral part of the planning process as the success of planning depends not only on proper formulation but also on its implementation with concomitant monitoring at the district level.[9] Concomitant monitoring of the district plan helps to identify difficulties and bottlenecks which can lead to finding solutions to overcome difficulties being faced in plan implementation. The monitoring system has to be evolved to monitor the progress of the district plan for which it is necessary to try several appropriate methods and techniques. These techniques are (a) PERT (Programme, Evaluation and Review Technique), and CPM[10](Critical Path Method), (b) bar charts, (c) programming and scheduling of activities, and (d) monthly progress reports.[11] None of these techniques will be universally applicable to monitor all the programmes and projects, and as such the concerned authorities have to be selective in using these techniques. For instance, PERT and CPM will be of great value to monitor the medium and large size projects such as medium and major irrigation projects, construction and installation of milk plants and hydro-electric projects whereas programmes like IRDP, CADA, DDP and FFDA can be monitored by simple techniques such as charts, scheduling of activities and monthly or quarterly progress reports.

With the introduction of district planning in the state, process of review and monitoring of schemes has also been decentralized, and DPDC, Thane, its Executive Committee and Special Executive Committee have been entrusted with the functions of monitoring and evaluation of the district plans. In addition, these bodies monitor the implementation of the Special Component Plan for the Scheduled Castes and Neo-Budhists in every meeting. The Collector, as the Member-Secretary of the DPDC, is assisted by the district planning unit in attending to this work. Thus, the DPDC Thane, and its committees have been made responsible for the monitoring of the progress of the programmes and schemes.

In the year 1978, the Government reviewed the functioning of the Executive Committee of the DPDC so as to make it meaningful.[12] It was felt that, for various reasons, it had not been possible for the Executive Committee of the DPDC to meet at least once in two months, with the result that the supervision over the implementation of plan programmes in the district had suffered.

Thus, the Government considered that timely and more frequent reviews of the implementation of the plan programmes by the Executive Committee of the DPDC is necessary with a view to: (a) ensure expeditious implementation of various development programmes, (b) indentify precise reasons for slow progress in implementation of certain programmes, such as late sanction of schemes, non-availability of equipment and machinery, delay in land acquisition, and inadequacy of staff and (c) suggest remedial measures for consideration and expeditious orders of the Government so as to remove such administrative bottlenecks in the implementation of the development programmes of the district.[13]

Therefore, the Government decided that with a view to ensure proper implementation of the developmental programmes and removal of difficulties experie nced by the district implementing officers and agencies:[14] (a) the Collector of the district as the Member-Secretary of the DPDC should arrange to collect from various implementing officers and agencies concerned with the district level schemes included in the annual budget, a monthly report on the progress of expenditure and physical achievements in the prescribed proforma. This information should be collected by the Collector from the implementing officers and agencies by the 10th of the month of report and he should arrange to place a consolidated report for the consideration of the Executive Committee of the DPDC, (b) the Executive Committee of the DPDC should meet at least once in a month, say in the third week of the month to execute, inter-alia, the following business:[15]

(i) consideration of the monthly progress reports received from various district implementing officers and agencies;
(ii) identify reasons for shortfall in expenditure as also physical achievements or for lack of progress;
(iii) suggest measures for expeditious implementation of plan programmes and remedial measures required for expeditious implementation of such programmes where progress is found to be tardy;
(iv) consideration of new schemes of works for inclusion in the Annual Plan by adjustment within the budgeted outlay of the district in case that is found to be very necessary; and
(v) consideration of excess requirements and savings indicated by the district implementing officers and agencies and propose re-appropriation for the approval of the Government;

**The proforma prescribed for the submission of the monthly progress report of expenditure and physical achievemlnt:**

District————          Month of report————

| Head/Sub-Head of *development*—Name of the *schemes*—Sub-items of schemes. | Budget provision for the year | Expenditure incurred *Rs. in lacs* | | | *Physical targets/achievements* | | | | | Reasons (in brief) for shotfall in expenditure and *targets*—Difficulties, if any. |
|---|---|---|---|---|---|---|---|---|---|---|
| | | Upto the end of previous months | During the month under report. | Total (4)+ (5). | Item. | Target for the year. | Upto the end of previous months | During the month under report. | By end of the month under report. | |
| 1 | 2 | 3 | 4 | 5 | 6 | 7 | 8 | 9 | 10 | 11 |

(c) The Collector of the district soon after the meeting of the Executive Committee of the DPDC is required to arrange to forward to the Government in the Planning Deprtment, a summary record of the discussions in the meeting of the Executive Committee together with such specific recommendations made by it with a view to remove administrative and other bottlenecks and for expeditious implementation of the development programmes under the District Annual Plan. In case the Chairman or the Vice-Chairman of the DPDC is unable to attend the meeting of the Executive Committee, the members present should nominate one of the members to preside over such a meeting. Similarly, this role is also assigned to the Special Executive Committee.

Thus, the Executive Committee as well as the Special Executive Committee of the DPDC Thane are required to meet every month to monitor the progress achieved as also to remove the difficulties being faced in the implementation of the programmes approved and included in the district plan.[17] In addition, the Special Component Plan is also monitored by these Committees to sort out problems of the implementing officers and issue directions to them to improve the implementation of these schemes. Now, it would be interesting to glance through the proceedings of the DPDC and its committees in so far as they relate to the monitoring of the progress of the plan schemes of Thane during the years 1981-82 and 1982-83.[18] During 1981-82, only three meetings of the DPDC and its Committees were held. The gist of proceedings of these meetings are given below:

Special Executive Committee, in its meeting held on 7.7.1981, directed that (a) Government be moved to raise the limit of expenditure for the construction of primary schools, (b) the allocation approved by the Government for the Wandri Irrigation Project should not be made from the district financial ceiling for 1981-82, (c) Government should make more allocations for irrigation scheme of this district, (d) requirement of land for acquisition for the construction of Ashram Schools (residential schools for the Tribals) should be sent to the Collector, (e) and vacancies of "Primary school teachers", especially in the Tribal areas, should be filled every year well in time by the Education Officer, Zila Parishad, Thane.

DPDC, in its meeting held on 11.8.1981, ordered that (a) the cottage hospital should be located at Shelar instead of at Anjur in Bhiwandi Block, (b) Primary Health Centre be established at Kulgaon in Ulhasnagar Block as already directed, (c) Government may be moved to form one "Sub-Committee" in each DPDC to review the special schemes for Scheduled Castes and Neo-Budhists, (d) number of seats in the existing industrial Training Institutes be increased, (e) Chief Executive officer should take immediate steps to distribute seeds, fertilizers and seedlings within 8 days in the flood affected blocks, and (f) a meeting be held under the Chairmanship of the district Minister to expedite cases of loans for the purchase of milch cattle.

It was decided in the meeting of the Special Executive Committee held on 24.12.1981 that (a) the Vice-Chairman of this Committee should hold a separate meeting of the concerned officers and non-officials to suggest action to improve day-to-day working of the Ashram schools, (b) the surplus land allottees be supplied inputs in time (c) the concerned officers should arrange to obtain the administrative approval for the construction of health centres and cottage hospitals, and (d) the Chairman directed that the complaint regarding charges of higher cost by the District Cooperative Marketing Federation on the purchase of electric pumping sets and oil engines should be looked into and note submitted to him within 15 days.

Similarly, during 1982-83, three meetings of these bodies were held to review and monitor the progress of the implementing officers. In the meeting of the DPDC held on 27.8.82, it directed that (a) names of the locations of two primary health centres to be opened in 1982-83 be put up to the Executive Committee immediately, and (b) immediate arrangements be made to have bore wells in the Tribal residential schools. Similarly, Special Executive Committee decided on 20.11.82 that (a) advance action be taken in time to supply school uniforms and stationery to all the Tribal students, (b) lists of roads in each taluka be supplied to all members immediately, and (c) advance action be taken to fill in the vacancies of teachers by the Chief Executive Offiicer and the Education Officer, and the

Education Officer, Zila Parishad. Likewise, it was decided in the meeting of the Executive Committee held on 20.11.82 that (a) the Executive Engineer (Irrigation) should ensure that all the 38 lift irrigation schemes start functioning (b) Government be moved to sanction one polytechnic, (c) immediate arrangements should be made to electrify the village Kukshet on the Thane-Belapur Road, and (d) Executive Engineer should look into it as to why actual water supply is not made available to the residents of Diva village even though the water supply scheme is completed.

Since the introduction of district planning in Thane, a number of important schemes in the agriculture sector are being implemented under the General Plan and Tribal Areas Sub-Plan. During 1981-82 and 1982-83, review of agriculture schemes was done only in two meetings. In these meetings, agriculture officer was directed that (a) necessary measures should be taken to control the stem-borer in paddy, and (b) proper rates should be provided to the Tribals for their farm produce.

The district planning unit is merely entrusted with the routine work relating to the compilation of progress reports received from the district heads and issue agenda notices for the meetings of the DPDC, its Executive Committee and Special Executive Committee. The DPDC is not assigned with the work of concurrent evaluation of the programmes to assess as to whether the objectives of development programmes are being achieved, as also the missing links and gaps in planning and implementation. Although the Government has entrusted the work of evaluation of programmes to the DPDC,[19] yet practically this work is not done by it or its Committees.

The following criticism is voiced against the role of DPDC, and its Committees as the monitoring authorities: (a) DPDC is a "district assembly" and the MLAs are more interested to find a material for Assembly questions than monitoring of schemes, (b) the meetings of the DPDC, or its Executive Committee and Special Executive Committee are not held regularly[20] and the duration of these meetings is also very short, as a result of which these bodies do not do full justice to monitor the progress of schemes, (c) generally, the MLAs and MPs take more interest in general problems like scarcity of water, and drought, and most of the time is spent on these issues only, (d) these bodies are unwieldy and as such proceedings of the meeting are not business-like, (e) about 70 district officers and 50 non-officials cannot have dialogue on all the 226 schemes of General Plan and about 135 schemes of Tribal Areas Plan, (f) in the name of popular participation in monitoring the schemes, the non-officials try to overawe the officers. (g) no guidance is given in the meetings, and the officers are demoralized completely, (h) the non-officials also visit the sites of the schemes or projects for review purpose, and it entails high cost, (i) monitoring body has become multi-headed and as such does not serve the purpose, and (j) district Minister and the MLAs are very busy during Assembly Sessions[21] and the meetings for monitoring the progress cannot be held as envisaged by the Government, and (k) planning cells are weak to carry out any kind of evaluation of the plan schemes.[22]

**Position in Karnal**

As far as the position of coordination and monitoring of plan schemes in Karnal[23] is concerned, it is done through various district level committees and boards constituted by the Government for this purpose, and these committees are generally set up under the Chairmanship of the Deputy Commissioner, Karnal. The oldest of these committees is the District Agricultural Production Committee which was constituted in 1964 under the Chairmanship of the Deputy Commissioner, Karnal, and all the district officers concerning (a) agriculture, (b) electricity, (c) revenue, (d) irrigation, (e) development, (f) panchayats, (g) cooperation, (h) forest, and (i) animal husbandry are its members. The other important committees constituted for coordinating the activities of development departments are: (a) Officers Board's Coordination Committee, (b) District Adhoc Committee for the Welfare of Scheduled Castes and Backward Classes, (c) District Industries Advisory Committee (d) Steering Committee for the National Rural Employment Programme, and (e) District Level Committee for the implementation of the New 20 Point Programme.[24]

The economy of Karnal is predominantly agricultural in

nature,[25] and a regular review of implementation of various agricultural schemes and activities is being undertaken in the monthly meetings. The gist of proceedings of the meeting in-so-far as it relates to the review of agricultural production programme from August 1982 to March 1983 is given below:[26]

In the meeting held on 13.8.1982, the Deputy Director, Agriculture reported that there was no shortage of seeds and fertilizers during the month of July 1982. 449 new power connections were given and power to tubewells was provided for 12 hours. Similarly, in the monthly meeting held on 10.9.82, it was reported that due to less rainfall, the crops would be damaged if at least 12 hours power supply to the tubewells is not given. In view of the above, the Chairman directed that uninterrupted power be supplied to the tubewells so that the crops could be saved from damage. In the next monthly meeting, the Deputy Director reported that though the crop was saved from damage yet 10 per cent shortage in paddy production was expected. Tubewells have been supplied power for 9 to 10 hours daily. The Executive Engineer, Haryana State Electricity Board (HSEB), Karnal was asked to send daily reports to the Additional Deputy Commissioner about the supply of power to the tubewells.

Similarly, it was reported in the meeting on 10.12.82 that power was being supplied to the tubewells for 8 hours in the night and 5 hours in the morning. It was also reported that there was shortage of pesticides and the District Manager, Haryana State Cooperative Supply and Marketing Federation Limited (HAFED) was asked to solve this problem.

Likewise, it was reported in the monthly meeting held on 14.1.1983 that 9,000 cases for power connection to tubewells were pending with the Executive Engineer, HSEB due to shortage of transformers. On this, the Chairman directed the Executive Engineer to get this issue resolved. It was reported in the meeting held on 15.2.1983 that condition of crop, and the consumption of chemical fertilizers were satisfactory in the district but there was a shortfall in the advancement of crop loans as against the target. The Chairman directed the Central Cooperative Bank, Karnal, to achieve the target fixed for Rabi 1982-83. During January 1983, 111 power connections to the tubewells were provided whereas 2,302 test reports and 9,510 application were pending with the Executive Engineer, HSEB, due to the shortage of transformers. The Chairman asked the Additional General Assistant to arrange a separate meeting with the Executive Engineer so that on the basis of discussions, the Chairman, HSEB, could be contacted for the solution of this problem. Similarly, the next meeting was held on 11.3.1983 and it was reported that only 144 power connections had been provided to the tubewells in February 1983, and 2,490 test reports and 9,544 applications were pending with the Executive Engineer, HSEB, Karnal. It further reported that only 80 transformers were allotted to Karnal district by the HSEB and all the pending test reports would be disposed of within a year. The Superintending Engineer of the Board also informed that the Board would not be able to purchase all the transformers immediately due to financial stringencies.

In April, 1981, Additional Deputy Commissioner (Development) was appointed in Karnal with the expectation that he will play a pivotal role in monitoring, evaluation and review of plan schemes at the district level under the overall supervision, guidance and control of the Deputy Commissioner,[27] and these instructions also stipulated that the Planning Department should issue necessary periodical returns for the monitoring and review of the progress of the schemes. All the development departments were asked to work out the schemewise and districtwise break-up of the "divisible outlays" and supply it to the Deputy Commissioner for facilitating review and monitoring of these schemes and programmes at the district level.[28] The Additional Deputy Commissioner has been entrusted with the work of monitoring, evaluation, and review of the IRDP. In addition, he is also charged with the task of monitoring and reviewing the programmes like (a) National Rural Employment Programme (NREP), (b) Minimum Needs Programme, (c) New 20 Point Economic Programme, (d) Special Component Plan for Scheduled Castes, (e) Manpower, Planning and Employment, and (f) other special programmes under the Sixth Plan.[29]

The New 20 Point Programme is one of the very important programmes being implemented at the district level and the state Government has nominated the Additional Deputy Commissioner as the District Nodal Officer for reporting progress achieved under this programme to the Economic and Statistical Adviser who is appointed as the State Nodal Officer for this purpose. He is required to send the progress report to the Government before the 10th of every month in the prescribed format.[30]

At the state level, a High Powered Committee constituted under the Chairmanship of the Chief Minister reviews the progress of the above programme every alternate month.[31] This Committee has also set up a Sub-Committee to undertake detailed monitoring of the qualitative aspects of implementation by examining the programmes and performance of individual depatments separately. At the State level, a Committee of Secretaries meets every month to review the progress and take effective measures for speedy implementation. The Administrative Secretaries hold monthly meetings of the Heads of Departments under their control and review the progress of programmes.

The meeting of the District Level Committee[32] is held within a week of sending the monthly progress report in which the pace of progress under each item of New 20-Point Programme is reviewed and remedial measures taken promptly whereever progress is found slow. Proceedings of these meetings are sent to the Government immediately thereafter. Besides, a set of proformae has been introduced to collect and monitor the progress report of various schemes and programmes being implemented in the district, and passed on to the Government. The monthly progress reports are collected regarding progress of (a) expenditure and achievement (physical and financial) of the schemes implemented by the DRDA, (b) integrated rural development programme—key indicators, (c) selected indicators under the integrated rural development, (d) no. of identified participants (Scheduled Castes, Scheduled Tribes and others) benefitted during the year upto the end of the month under report for various programmes, (e) number of identified participants (small and marginal farmers, and agricultural labourers, Scheduled castes, scheduled tribes, and others) benefitted during the year upto the end of the month under report under various programmes of the implementing agencies (only the beneficiaries under the completed works to be reported), (f) loans actually advanced during the year upto the end of the month under report through cooperatives and commercial banks to the identified participants and the number of loanees (Scheduled Castes and Scheduled Tribes), and (g) IRDP by various departments and agencies indicating therein annual target, household benefitted and the financial assistance provided, besides (a) districts quarterly report for financial and physical achievements under IRDP., (b) district level annual report for monitoring the beneficiaries under IRDP who crossed the poverty line, (c) quarterly progress report on centrally sponsored schemes of assistance to small and marginal farmers for increasing agricultural production, (d) monthly statement showing the rural youth trained and self employed under the scheme of TRYSEM, (e) monthly progress reports of bio-gas plants and (f) monthly progress report regarding applications forwarded to various banks for getting the loans for the bio-gas plants. The progress reports in all the a bove cases are collected and filled in and sent to the Government where these generally become integral part of the respective moth-eaten files, and corrective or remedial measures are rarely taken.[33]

As far as the evaluation of programmes is concerned, this is being undertaken by the Economic and Statistical Organization and the topics for this purpose are selected by the Government. As many as 80 programmes have been evaluated so far. The findings of these studies are generally taken as an affront by the concerned departments, and as such these study reports have failed to become instruments for the re-orientation of policy and programmes. These studies are mostly related to evaluation of major works and projects at the state level and no specific study has so far been conducted in evaluating the programmes and schemes such as IRDP etc. being implemented in Karnal.[34]

Recently, a cell comprising one Assistant Project Officer (Monitoring), two Investigators and one Statistical Assistant has been created in DRDA. Karnal for monitoring and evaluating the programmes and schemes of the DRDA.[35] Altough it is a novice cell yet it has started doing its work on concurrent evaluation. The DRDA, Karnal, has submitted its report on physical verification of assets on January 6, 1984, to the Government[36] which is tabulated below:

| | |
|---|---|
| a) Total number of assets created upto 31.3.1983 | 9,145 |
| b) Physical verification planned (No. of assets) | 9,145 |
| c) Results received (No. of assets) | 7,612 |
| d) Assets verified physically | 7,413 |
| e) Assets found in possession | 6,764 |
| f) Mortality reported | 150 |
| g) Assets reported misutilized | 499 |
| h) Percentage of (e) to (d) | 91 |
| i) Percentage of (f) to (d) | 2 |
| j) Percentage of (g) to (d) | 7 |

The above report gives an insight into the working of the scheme as also the level of utilization of loans by the beneficiaries who participated in the programme. It also reflects the mortality of the animals purchased with the financial assistance provided by the banks and the DRDA. This type of study can be called as concurrent evaluation, and gives quite useful information as to the total number of assets created, assets in possession of the beneficiaries, misutilization, and mortality, and helps improving the quality of implementation of programmes and schemes being implemented in the district.

## OVERVIEW

Monitoring and evaluation are essential ingredients of the main planning process, and these need to be incorporated in the projects and programmes being implemented at the district level. This will certainly help monitoring in a better way the programmes being launched for implementation at the district level, for which one has also to look for one unifying authority at the district level. Monitoring by remote control from the directorates cannot be as effective as from the district level. It is a continuous process and as such monitoring authority has to monitor the progress of various officers, organizations. institutions, and agencies at the district level. Such an authority is absolutely needed to monitor the performance of the officers involved in the implementation of all projects and programmes which are being implemented, particularly for the poor sections of society. In this way, the monitor will be required to play the role of a guide, a philosopher, and a friend of the implementing officer. Regular and systematic monitoring will help completion of projects and programmes in time, reduce their cost, and also ensure the benefits of these projects and programmes to the target groups as also to the area intended to be benefitted. This would also help identification of bottlenecks in their implementation.

In Thane, the Collector is appointed Member-Secretary of the DPDC or its committees, and acts as a nodal officer for the collection and compilation of progress reports from various Government offices and agencies for placing the same before the DPDC or its committees. He has no authority to issue directions to the implementing officers. It is only the DPDC and its committees which can issue such directions. Achievement of targets of various programmes, such as IRDP, TRYSEM, New 20-Point Programme, and other schemes and activities falling within the ambit of agriculture and allied services, animal husbandry and dairy, industry, especially small scale, rural and cottage industries, small business and trade, transport and self-employment sector, depends on the advancement of loans by the banks. The DPDC and its committees merely reviews the expenditure of Government grants, as a result of which the progress of programmes of the Government in the priority sectors suffers in most of the cases in the district.

The committees of the DDDC, Thane, are too unwieldy to undertake the task of monitoring systematically and effectively. Moreover, because of the preoccupation of the Minister, the meetings of the DPDC or its committees are not held regularly and the Collector finds it difficult to issue any directions to the implementing officers. Perhaps, it will be appropriate to set up a small Monitoring Committee comprising the Collector, Chief Executive Officer, and President of Zila Parishad, Vice-President of the Special Executive Committee, and four non-officials—two each from the DPDC or Executive Committee and Special Executive Committee—to monitor various plan schemes. The reports of the Monitoring Committee may be placed before the DPDC and its committees whenever they meet. This committee should also ensure that the Government sponsored programmes requiring loan components are fully achieved and assets purchased in time. The very association of non-officials will ensure "public scrutiny" in monitoring the beneficiary-oriented and other schemes meaningfully. It will be useful to create a small Monitoring and Evaluation Unit on the pattern of Karnal district for carrying out concurrent evaluation to ensure the proper utilization of Government grants, loans and subsidies.

In Karnal, too many proformae have been introduced for collecting the information regarding the achievement of various development schemes and programmes. The process of coordination, review and montioring of these schemes and programmes is done through various committees set up by the Government from time to time. Meetings of most of these committees are held on a day fixed by the Government and tend to be "monthly melas". It appears necessary to constitute a similar Monitoring Committee as proposed for Thane for the purpose, and should be entrusted with the responsbility for monitoring and overviewing the implementation of the plan schemes. It should meet once a month regularly, and also ensure that the progress of the Government sponsored programmes requiring loan component does not suffer for want of necessary tie-up with the banks. However, the District Council or the Board should continue to discharge its functions in this matter, and the review and monitoring reports of the Monitoring Committee should be placed on its table for consideration and confirmation of the action taken.

The proforma for monitoring the progress of various plan schemes also needs to be simplified in both the districts and the factors obstructing the progress of each scheme need to be recorded against each scheme for taking remedial measures by the implementing officer. For this purpose, a proforma shown on the next page has been devised.

Besides, evaluation studies of important programmes being

## PROFORMA

### Monthly Report of Annual Plan Schemes

Department——————

*Rs. in lakhs*

| Name of scheme. | | Annual Programme. | Achievements *during the month.* Programme Progress | Ach ievements upto *the end of the month.* Programme Progress | (Observations, Remarks, decision to be entered after review and monitoring) |
|---|---|---|---|---|---|
| | PHYS. | | | | |
| | FIN. G.G. | | | | |
| | FIN. B.L. | | | | |
| | PHYS. | | | | |
| | FIN. G.G | | | | |
| | FIN. B.L. | | | | |
| | PHYS. | | | | |
| | FIN. G.G. | | | | |
| | FIN. B.L. | | | | |
| | PHYS. | | | | |
| | FIN. G.G. | | | | |
| | FIN. B.L. | | | | |

PHYS. means **Physical** targets.
FIN. G.G. means Financial Government Grants.
FIN. B.L. means Financial Bank Loans.

implemented in the district should be conducted by the Government to measure their impact on the lives of the target-groups and the area intended to be benefitted. These studies when conducted would also show meaningful insights and enrich the planning process at every level.

## REFERENCES


1. Planning Commission, Sixth-Five Year Plan 1980-85, p. 89.
2. Ibid., p. 99.
3. Planning Commission, Sixth-Five Year Plan, 1980-85, p. 92.
4. Planning and Implementation of Integrated Rural Development Projects: A Manual, National Institute of Rural Development, Hyderabad, 1981, p. 224.
5. Monitors are unwelcome in these days even in the school. This is also true in case of administration. No official would like to be subjected to any warning, caution, etc. In view of this, monitoring will be like a tight rope dancing in which the monitor has to be careful and cautious while performing his task. In Maharashtra, this work is entrusted to the Executive Committee of the DPDC.
6. Refer Planning and Implementation, A Manual, National Institute of Rural Development, Hyderabad, 1981, p. 225.
7. Y. Venugopal Reddy, Multilevel Planning in India, Vikas Publishing House Private Limited, New Delhi, 1979, p. 76.
8. Ibid., p. 237.
9. This is built up on the basis of the available record in the district as well as the material provided by the office of the Agricultural Development Officer, Thane, as also on interviews with the district level officers.
10. PERT AND CPM are highly sophisticated techniques which are generally made use of to monitor the big projects in the public and cooperative sectors to ensure that these projects are completed in time and also start production without any loss of time.
11. Generally, simple methods or techniques such as monthly or fortnightly progress reports are evolved to monitor the progress of programmes and schemes which are being implemented at the district level.
12. Refer Circular No. DPC-1076/PRG-DPP dated 11.2.76, Planning Department, Government of Maharashtra, Bombay.
13. Ibid., p. 1.
14. Ibid,. pp. 1-2.
15. Ibid., p. 2.
16. **Refer Ibid., Annexure.**

17. Formulation of DRDA Schemes in Thane district is not within the purview of the DPDC. The DPDC earmarks funds for this programme as per Government of India guidelines and norms to get central assistence and the planning is done by the DRDA, Thane. However, the monitoring of progress of the DRDA, Thane, is also entrusted to the DPDC, Thane
18. This information has been collected from the office of the District Planning Officer, Thane district.
19. Refer Paper on District Planning in Maharashtra, Status Paper No. 3, Planning Commission (MLP Division), p. 4.
20. The Executive Committee and Special Executive Committee are required to meet at least once a month to review and monitor the progress of the district plan schemes. During 1981-82, only three meetings of these committees were held to review the progress of district plan schemes. In 1982-83, only 2 meetings of these committees were held to review the progress. However, DPDC, Thane met twice every year during 1981-82 and 1982-83 to approve the annual plan and reappropriation. DPDC, the parent body of these committees did not review the progress of the implementing officers even once during this period.
21. Budget Session of the Vidhan Sabha is held in February and March, Monsoon Session in July and August and winter session during November and December every year. District Minister and the MLAs are required to attend these sessions. Practically, it becomes difficult to hold the meetings of these bodies regularly during the sessions.
22. Based on interviews with the district level officers of Thane district.
23. Based on the available record and personal interviews with the district level officers.
24. Monthly meetings of these Committees are held on one day fixed by the Government.
25. After the formation of Haryana state on November 1, 1966, the Intensive Agricultural Development Programme was launched in this district to increase the agricultural production by providing package of inputs such as irrigation facilities, chemical fertilizers, high yielding varieties of seeds, pesticides, crop loan, etc.
26. Based on the proceedings of the monthly meetings held under the chairmanship of the Deputy Commissioner, Karnal.
27. Refer letter No. I-DSAR-Plg-81, dated 27.4.81.
28. Refer letter No. 39/5/81,-Plg., dated 15.6.1981.
29, Refer letter No. I-DSAR-Plg-81, dated 27.4.81 from the Chief Secretary to Government, Haryana, to all the Commissioners of Ambala and Hissar Divisons and all the Deputy Commissioners in the State.
30. Refer letter No. RSA (TP)-10)-83/11468.481, dated 27.5.83 from the

Commissioner and Secretary to Government, Haryana, to all the D.Cs in the State.

31. The High Powered Committee has a non-official as whole-time Deputy Chairman. Besides, it has Ministers, Secretaries, MLAs, prominant social workers and technical experts as its members.
32. This Committee is headed by the Minister-in-charge. Deputy Commissioner and the Heads of District Offices concerned with 20 Point Programme are official members of this committee. MLAs representing the district are non-official members of this Committee.
33. Based on interviews with the district and state level officers.
34. Ibid.
35. These cells are also constituted in other DRDAs in the state.
36. Item No. 22: sent to the Government on 6.1.1984 by the Chief Executive Officer, DRDA, Karnal.

# 10

# SOME CONCLUDING OBSERVATIONS

SYSTEMATIC planning at the national level and to some extent at the state level is undertaken in the light of accepted priorities and desired targets of growth. The remoteness of the planning agencies from areas of implementation; lack of participation of the local people with the development strategy; and the vastness of the geographical coverage seriously affect the matching of financial allocations with the specific needs of various sectors and their potential for regulating the distribution of the gains of development. The integration of sectoral allocations in terms of optimizing production, employment and the incomes becomes difficult when development programmes are viewed from a distance. The unsatisfactory performance of the centralized planning has often been highlighted but, at the same time, complete decentralization has not been universally favoured.

Most of the developing countries, as a part of the developmental effort, lay emphasis on planning at the local level so that there is better mobilization of local resources and effective tackling of local needs. In India, planning from below is chiefly associated with the district development effort because the district continues to be the ultimate viable unit of planning in terms of data collection, planning machinery and infrastructural facilities, marketing and services, as also the availability of officers of various disciplines at the district headquarters. Again, the district has a contingent of district level officers who can provide special assistance needed for drawing up plans with the Panchayati Raj institutions providing the top-level leadership.

In the preceding chapters, an attempt has been made to

explore some select issues of the district level planning, such as (a) Government policy regarding district development planning, and steps taken to implement the same; (b) jurisdiction and scope of the district development planning; (c) planning process and the role of the district planning board or council; (d) allocation of Government funds at the district level and the delegation of administrative and financial powers; (e) integration of credit plans with the district plans; (f) incoporation of anti-poverty programmes for the target-groups in the district plans; (g) strengthening of the planning organization at the district level; (h) popular participation in plan formulation and its programmes; (i) coordination; and, (j) monitoring and evaluation.

An indepth study has been made particularly for (a) providing an understanding of the variety of considerations important to the philosophy and methodology of local level planning; (b) looking into the reasons for the persistence of certain inbuilt problems leading to non-fulfilment of several of the important objectives of district planning; (c) suggesting ways and means to bring about better integration and coordination in planning and implementation of various special development programmes; (d) making suggestions to improve the resource allocation and mobilization, involvement of democratic institutions and development agencies as well as streamlining the administrative procedures involved in implementation; and (e) offering general suggestions to improve the planning process at the district level.

In this study, efforts have also been made to proceed on the hypothesis that better the understanding of the variety of constraints and considerations which go into integration and coordination in planning and implementation of various development schemes at the district level, the greater will be the utility of the schemes in the context of the development effort of the state. Poor conception of various dimensions of district plans results in the failure of the achievement of the various objectives of the development schemes and subsequent loss of resources—both natural and human. Two districts, Karnal in Haryana and Thane in Maharashtra, had been selected for an indepth study. It is based on extensive field work and critical evaluation of the published literature dating back from the dawn of the planning era.

There is hardly any agreement among the planners, academicians, social scientists and others on the concept of development but for the present study, it has been regarded as a multifacet concept encompassing the acceleration of economic growth on the one hand, and elimination or reduction of poverty, inequality and unemployment on the other. Planning may be described as an exercise in which the Government has to choose objectives, arrange resources, spell out policies, strategies and targets, organize a framework for implementing, coordinating, and monitoring the plan. Planning at the district level is being increasingly emphasized for tackling some of the problems of local nature and to make the decentralization realistic.

The involvement of district in planning has to be sought by consistent and steady efforts by the politico-administrative leadership which is expected to bring the results of planning to the doorsteps of the people. For example, in Thane district of Maharashtra, district planning process has been evolved to a considerable extent. First thing that has helped its evolution is the setting up of a high-powered body known as the Planning Sub-Committee of the Cabinet headed by the Chief Minister of Maharashtra. This Committee provides effective and authoritative guidance in the process of formulation of policies and programmes, decides vital issues such as allocation of funds between the state and district sector schemes, approves formula for further distribution of funds amongst the districts and matters relating to classification, and reclassification of district and state-level schemes. There also exists a very strong planning department which implements the decisions of the Planning Sub-Committee and communicates the financial ceilings alongwith the detailed guidelines to the DPDCs for the formulation of the district annual plans. Formulation of district plans is not the privilege of the bureaucracy alone but of the DPDC, on which both officials and non-officials are represented. This body is headed by the designated Minister of the district and charged with the responsibility to formulate district annual plans and monitor their implementation. Therefore, the district planning system has been evolved in Thane district of Maharashtra, because of the "political will and commitment" demonstrated by the Government in constituting the Planning Sub-Committee of the Cabinet and the DPDC under the chairmanship of the designated Minister. These measures have made district planning a "growing concern" in Thane, as also in other districts of Maharashtra.

The experiences of Karnal in Haryana, on the other hand, show that the district development planning remained mostly a concern of the officer of the rank of the Deputy Plan Adviser in the Planning Department at the state level, as a result of which, it did not trickle down to the district level where even the regular District Planning Officer could not be positioned to look after the Plan work. The District Planning Advisory Board, the District Planning Committee and the District Planning Executive Committee rarely met for the purpose for which these were constituted. These planning bodies seem to exist only on paper to report progress in the meetings held with the Planning Commission, as well as in various conferences. Planning in Karnal continues to be more or less centralized at the state headquarters. Decentralization has, therefore, mostly been nonexist or nominal.

In the multi-level planning process, success of district planning would depend upon delegation of powers and authority. The scope of district planning can be delineated on the basis of demand and supply or potentiality approach. The scope of district planning backed by political will and financial ceiling has been clearly demarcated in Thane and other districts in Maharashtra. This step alone has given realism to district planning as a concept and district plans have ceased to be mere shopping lists or catalogues of demands. Thane district has adopted suitable schemes having potential in the district from the list of standardized district level schemes. Keeping in view the list of schemes being included in the district plan of Thane, it is clear that potentiality approach has been adopted, and the schemes which directly benefit the district have been classified as district level schemes. In Karnal, on the other hand, standardization of the district level schemes was not done primarily because of absence of political mechanism for the classification of state and district sector schemes, as a result of which the scope of district planning was what the district level officers thought of, and that too without any backing of financial ceiling. Therefore, district planning process in Karnal is, at best, in an incipient stage and more serious thinking needs to be done.

The Planning Commission designed comprehensive guidelines for the formulation of district plans in September 1969, but it was left to the states to evolve or develop their own planning process and procedures. The thread was not seriously picked up in Haryana with the result that the planning process at the district level did not make much headway. The experience of Karnal reveals that the process of district planning remained a mere paper exercise primarily for want of initiatives at various levels to take hard decisions on certain vital issues, such as criteria for the classification of state and district sector schemes, and formula for the transfer of financial resources in favour of the district. In fact, it suffered, by and large, from the same infirmities as the one recommended by the Planning Commission in its guidelines for the formulation of district plans.

In Thane, the process of district planning was initiated in 1972 with the setting up of the District Planning Board under the chairmanship of the Minister. Subsequently, this Board was replaced by the DPDC for the formulation of (a) Perspective Plan, (b) Five Year Plans, and (c) Annual Plans of the district. Perspective and Five Year Plans, though desirable and useful, are no longer prepared in Thane and other districts of Maharashtra. However, an elaborate process of planning has been evolved only for the formulation of annual plans for the district. The present study shows that the Goverment has clearly demonstrated "political will and commitment" in evolving the process of district annual planning by giving a policy frame without which decentralized planning cannot be operational.

The process of district planning in Thane district, and other districts of Maharashtra, passes through various interrelated stages, such as (a) issuance of guidelines indicating the policies and plan priorities by the Government for the formulation of district annual plans, (b) preparation of sectoral schemes by the implementing officers, (c) examination of the schemes by the small team, (d) discussions with the senior officers of the Planning Department, (e) consolidation of draft plan proposals by the District Planning Officer under the overall supervision of the District Collector, the Member-Secretary of the DPDC, (f) approval of the draft annual plan by the DPDC, (g) submission of the draft district plan to the Planning Department with copies to the Heads of Departments and the Administrative Secretaries, (h) finalization of the draft district plan in the state level meeting headed by the Planning Minister, and finally integration of the district annual plan in the state annual plan. In short, the process of district planning is an article of faith in Thane and other districts in Maharashtra. This success has been mainly due to enlightened political and administrative leadership. After detailed discussions, a model of planning process has been suggested in Chapter IV to take care of the formulation of the integrated district plan. This model requires further testing in the field.

The resource planning through the budgetary mechanism, and institutional finance is a very significant input for decentralized planning. The discussions in Chapters V and VI show that the Government of Haryana has not yet been able to ensure any scientific scheme for transfer of financial resources in favour of the district level. This inadequacy may be one of the reasons for the district plans to remain mere catalogues of demands.

Financial devolution consists of two aspects, determination of allocable funds between the state and district sector schemes and distribution of allocable district plan funds amongst the districts. In Maharashtra, there is no formula for the distribution of plan funds between the state and district sector schemes and the quantum of allocable funds is decided by Planning Sub-Committee of the Cabinet. Broadly, the district share is determined on the basis of past progress of expenditure incurred on districts plan schemes. Reallocation of funds among the district is done quite scientifically on the basis of a formula giving weightages to (a) total population, (b) population of Scheduled Castes and Tribes, (c) urban population, (d) backwardness in agriculture, irrigation, communication and industries, and (e) special problems such as drought prone areas, forests and coastal areas besides retention of 5 per cent unallocated funds at the state level for solving special problems. Due to this formula, there is less of political influence in the allocation of funds among districts. To Thane district, financial allocation is being made according to this formula evolved over the years. The present analysis shows that almost all the funds are spent on the on-going district level schemes and there is hardly any scope for financing the new schemes and activities considered useful for the local needs. It may be desirable to explore the feasibility of earmarking 75 per cent of the total district plan outlay for normal district sector schemes and the remaining 25 per cent of the outlay kept as discretionary and incentive outlay to be placed at the disposal of the DPDCs to formulate schemes of local importance. The DPDCs may be free to finance these schemes on 100 per cent basis from the discretionary portion of the district plan outlay while the incentive outlay may be provided on the basis of matching contribution of 50 per cent or 25 per cent depending upon the pattern prescribed for the district. Again, Tribal Areas-Sub Plan is also an integral part of the district plan and a separate financial ceiling is prescribed by the Planning Department for taking up specific schemes and programmes for the benefit of the weakest sections of the society in Thane and other districts identified for preparing Tribal Sub-Plan. The micro financial ceiling technique evolved over a period for the formulation of the district plans is a unique innovative device which ultimately becomes an integral part of the macro financial frame of the state plan.

The present study shows that banks, especially after their nationalization, have been made partners in the socio-economic development of the district and Lead Bank Scheme is a major innovation in the banking system. Under the Lead Bank Scheme, the banks have opened their branches extensively in the rural areas and the branch expansion process is still continuing, both in Karnal and Thane. However, it may be mentioned that Karnal has more branches in the rural areas as compared to Thane. More branches are required to be opened in Thane district, especially in rural and inaccessible areas to cover Tribal population. District Credit plans are being formulated regularly and implemented in both the districts, but the flow of financial assistance by the banks under the scheme is phenomenal in Karnal whereas it is not satisfactory in Thane district, especially in the agriculture and allied sectors. The financial position of the banks in both the districts is fairly stable and they can do well to provide finances to the priority sectors and target groups according to the priorities laid down by the Government. The analysis also shows that in Karnal the recoveries of loans are satisfactory whereas these are extremely poor in Thane, especially in the agriculture and allied sectors. As a result, the progress of credit expansion has been reduced considerably. The Government facility available for the recovery of bank dues is not made use of by the banks leading to increase in the overdues, especially in Thane and thus reducing the flow of funds in favour of the priority sectors.

The Annual Action Plans are also formulated by the lead banks in both the districts wherein the districtwise and block-wise targets—physical and financial—are also reflected as per directions of the Reserve Bank of India. These plans are regularly reviewed in the meetings of the DCC, DLRM and the Standing Committee of the DCC. All the meetings, by and large, are attended by the banks functioning in the districts and the Government departments for ensuring coordination among them. In both the districts, these bodies help sort out problems and difficulties faced by financial institutions and various development departments and agencies at the district level.

As far as the integration of the District Credit Plan and the Annual Action Plan with the District Plan is concerned, this is unfortunately neither done in Karnal, nor in Thane despite the declared objective of the Government. In fact, the District Credit Plans are formulated by the Lead Banks without any perspective of development of the districts. However, the lead banks in these districts made sincere attempts to formulate the credit plan keeping in view the on-going schemes as well as on the basis of the past performance and a quick estimate of the future requirements of finances for various schemes in these districts. Generally, the credit plans formulated do not reflect the Government priorities and the credit is frittered away to finance the less important schemes and ventures, as a result of which the programmes of national importance like the anti-poverty programmes suffer. It may be desirable to formulate a "Credit Sub-Plan" for the Government sponsored programmes and integrate the same with the District Credit Plan and Annual

Action Plan. This may help better monitoring of the Government sponsored programmes.

The non-lead banks have a large number of branches in the districts studied. In order to coordinate their activities, one of the managers is designated as District Coordinator. It is generally seen that the District Coordinator fails to affect inter-branch coordination, as a result of which the implementation of the credit plan becomes difficult.

With the implementation of the lead bank scheme, the work of the banks has increased manifold and they have opened a large number of small accounts and are still expected to open more and more small accounts every year but they are short of technical staff to verify and scrutinize the loan cases and complete the bank records. This leads to bunching of loan cases and the technical staff finds it more convenient to reject than to recommend these for sanction and disbursement. This also causes frustration amongst the loanees and lack of confidence of public in the banking system.

The confluence of institutional finance and budgetary grants integrated in a district plan together with the whole-hearted support of the staff of the banks and the district offices has the potential to increase production as well as wipe out poverty at the district level and below. In this entire exercise, the former should exclusively support production programmes whereas the latter should wholly concentrate on providing services, infrastructural and processing-cum-marketing facilities as also the missing links or facilitating links through the district administration.

The district administration may be broadly described as a politico-administrative system comprising the Collectorate headed by the Collector as the sole representative of the Government responsible for multi-farious functions. It also encompasses all the institutions for the management of public affairs in the district as well as local bodies—rural and urban. A critical study of the working of district administration in Karnal and Thane shows that there has been sufficient erosion of authority of the Collector and some deterioration in the management of a number of functions, especially in the fields of development and welfare activities.

In Karnal, for example, Panchayati Raj institutions, which are very crucial for the success of development effort are very weak or almost defunct. Zila Parishad abolished in 1973 has not been revived so far. As regards urban local bodies, municipal committees and improvement trusts have been superceded for the last many years and the affairs of these bodies are being managed through the administrators appointed by the Government from time to time. The Deputy Commissioner has been assigned a major role in development whereas the local bodies have hardly any say.

The present study shows that in Thane, an attempt has been made to institutionalize the district development administration comprising local political leadership and bureaucratic apparatus. The Zila Parishad has emerged a very strong body being overall incharge of rural development. The DPDC has been performing a useful role with the help of its Executive Committee and Special Executive Committee. Interviews with the knowledgeable persons show that the working of these committees have not been free from criticism. It is felt that these bodies have been inducted into the district administration to kill the local Government institutions. With the passage of time, the leadership role in development administration has also been shifted from the Chief Executive Officer to the Collector. Even the meetings, especially of the Executive Committee and the Special Executive Committee, are not held regularly to review the implementation of district plan schemes. In Karnal, the district administration does not sufficiently involve local level institutions. The involvement and role of these bodies, on the other hand, is being continuosly eroded in Thane. Comparatively speaking, the present study shows Thane in a happy situation than Karnal. Both the systems, however, require a fresh look.

The Deputy Commissioner, Karnal, continues to be a King-pin for every activity departmental or otherwise in the entire administrative set-up. He, being the captain of the district team, is generally and conveniently made the coordinator of all activities at the district level. Normally, he is responsible for the maintenance of law and order, revenue administration and other regulatory functions and at the same time charged with the responsibility as the chief coordinator of developmental activities. Indepth study of the Thane shows that the entry of the Panchayati Raj institutions and other local bodies such as municipal committees, improvement trusts and representatives of the people have surely affected adversely the position of the Collector as coordinator because the popular leaders untiringly try to find a place of status for themselves at the district level. The introduction of Panchayati Raj institutions has been regarded as little short of revolution, especially when these institutions were created with the expectation to mobilize the people for achieving socio-economic development by evolving peoples plans for the benefit of the people. In this situation, he is no longer accepted as the absolute leader in the district heirarchy. Strangely enough, this study shows that at Karnal, the Deputy Commissioner, though overburdened, does not even share his powers, functions and responsibilities with the Additional Deputy Commissioner (Development) by way of delegation of powers through an executive order. However, the Additional Deputy Commissioner, Karnal who is appointed exclusively for development work, is assigned non-developmental routine duties, contrary to Government instructions, by the Deputy Commissioner to assist him. But in Thane district, till the establishment of the Zila Parishad, the Collector was very powerful and was assigned the role of Chief Coordinator in all matters relating to the development of the district. With the introduction of the Panchayati Raj, the role of the Collector with regard to the development has waned substantially and the Chief Executive Officer of the Zila Parishad becomes the Chief Coordinator of development activities which, by and large, were statutorily entrusted to the Zila Parishad. Since then, he has been exercising administrative control over the development staff in the district. With the setting up of the District Planning Board in 1972, the Chief Executive Officer was made the Chief Coordinator and his position remained so even after the constitution of the DPDC. In December 1975, he was shorn of his role as chief coordinator without affecting his administrative control over the district officers. Instead, the Collector, being the chief administrative head of the district, was made Member-Secretary of the DPDC to assist it in formulation, review, monitoring and evaluation of the district plan.

By virtue of the above delegation, he again emerged as the Chief Coordinator of development administration in the district.

Planning for development at the district level pre-supposes (a) central authority to coordinate the plan efforts of all departments, organisations and institutions, (b) delegation of administrative and financial powers and (c) effective monitoring and evaluation of development programmes and projects. The Collector of Thane has not been assigned any specific role, especially when the Executive Committee and the Special Executive Committee fail to meet due to pre-occupation of the designated Minister in the departmental, ministerial and ceremonial functions. The Collector, unfortunately, does not have financial and administrative control over the development departments which are under the exclusive charge of the Chief Executive Officer. The entire developmental machinery functions under the control of the Panchayati Raj institutions which derive their strength from the statute. These factors significantly curtail Collector's capacity to coordinate, thereby diluting the development administration at the district level. It may be more advisable to strengthen the Zila Parishad by making the President as the senior Vice-Chairman of the DPDC and restoring the position of the Chief Executive Officer as the Member-Secretary.

Monitoring and evaluation are an integral part of the planing process but, unfortunately, serious attention is not devoted to them. This leads to failure in the achievement of targets and providing appropriate timely action. A critical analysis of the implementation problems of development programmes at the district level shows that monitoring is regarded as an insignificant part of the planning process. As a matter of fact, the monitoring authority has to play the role of a guide, a philosopher and a friend of the implementing officers.

In Thane, the District Collector is appointed Member-Secretary of the DPDC and its committees, and as such acts as a nodal officer for the collection and compilation of progress reports from various Government offices and agencies for placing the same before the DPDC or its committees. He has no authority to issue directions on his own to the implementing officers. It is only the DPDC or its committees which can issue such directions.

Commercial and cooperative banks in Thane are advancing loans for various productive and beneficiary-oriented programmes and schemes. In many cases, achievement of targets of various programmes such as IRDP, TRYSEM, New 20-Point Programme, and various other schemes and activities falling within the ambit of agriculture and allied services, animal husbandry and dairy, industry, especially small scale, rural and cottage industries, small business and trade, transport and self-employment sector, depends on the advancement of loans by the banks. The DPDC and its committees confine themselves to review the expenditure of Government grants, as a result of which the progress of priority programmes of the Government suffers in many programmes in the district.

The DPDC and its committees are too unwieldy to undertake the above functions systematically and effectively. Moreover, because of the pre-occupation of the Minister, the meetings of the DPDC or its committees are not held regularly, as a result of which the Collector finds it difficult to issue directions to the implementing officers. Perhaps, it will be appropriate to set up a small Monitoring Committee comprising President, Zila Parishad, Vice-Chairman of the Special Executive Committee and four non-officials, two each from the DPDC and Special Executive Committee, Collector and Chief Executive Officer. The reports of this committee may be placed before the DPDC and its committees whenever they meet. This Monitoring Committee should also ensure that the Government sponsored programmes requiring loan components are fully achieved and assets purchased in time. This arrangement will help public scrutiny in monitoring the district plan schemes, especially the beneficiary-oriented schemes. As far as the concurrent evaluation is concerned, this work should be entrusted to it and its committees. It will be useful to create a small monitoring and evaluation unit on the pattern of Karnal for carrying out concurrent evaluation studies to ensure proper utilization of Government grants, loans and subsidies. In addition, it should be adequately staffed.

In Karnal, too many proformae have been introduced for

collecting the information regarding the achievement of various development schemes and programmes. The process of co-ordination, review and monitoring of these schemes and programmes is done through various committees set up by the Government from time to time. Meetings of most of these committees are held on a day fixed by the Government and tend to be "monthly melas". It appears necessary to constitute a similar Monitoring Committee as proposed for Thane which should be entrusted with the responsibility for monitoring and reviewing the implementation of the plan schemes. It may meet once a month for this purpose, and also ensure that the progress of the Government sponsored programmes requiring loan component does not suffer for want of necessary tie up with the banks. However, the Council or the Board should continue to discharge its functions in this regard and the review and monitoring reports should be placed on its table for consideration and confirmation of the action taken.

As far as the concurrent evaluation of schemes and programmes in Karnal is concerned, the Government has recently set up a Monitoring and Evaluation Cell comprising one Assistant Project Officer (monitoring), two Investigators and one Statistical Assistant to carry out concurrent evaluation of some of the schemes. This is a good step in the right direction and needs strengthening of this unit to ensure proper and effective implementation of various schemes and programmes in the district. It may be difficult to add more staff to this cell due to financial stringencies but it can be strengthened by utilizing the services of the District Statistical Officer and his technical staff. This strengthened unit can do the work of evaluation of various programmes and schemes.

The proforma for monitoring the progress of various district schemes in both these districts also needs to be simplified and the factors obstructing the progress of each scheme recorded for taking remedial measures by the implementing officers.

It is now evident that systematic structural and behavioural changes are essential in order to institutionalize district development planning as a full-fledged and viable system within the framework of multi-level planning. These measures will help in better mobilization and allocation of scarce resources for tackling and containing local problems effectively. Experience of the developing world indicates and the present study supports the findings that, apart from scientific disaggregation of allocation of resources, new patterns and orientation of administrative behaviour have to be developed to make the planning effort more result-oriented. The success of district planning depends, inter-alia, on (a) institutionalizing effective political mechanism at the state level to provide authentic guidance in vital matters relating to district planning, (b) establishing strong Planning Department at the state level, (c) delineating district sector schemes, (d) innovating practical mechanism for the mobilization of institutional finance, (e) vesting of totality of planning functions in a single district planning body, viz., Council or Board, (f) strengthening of planning cells with a team of experts, and (g) delegating administrative and financial powers. Additionally, administrative capability for development is a continuous but steady process and has to be related to the development initiatives envisaged. Sound personnel policies, dynamic organisational structures, growth-oriented strategies and policies emphasising distributive justice are some of the key factors which call for a concerted action. Above everything that has been said above and elsewhere in this study, 'political will' is a necessary prerequisite and a starting point for every development effort and is an invaluable input for innovative and long term planning at the district level. Given the right type of political will supported by the 'bureaucratic will' together with requisite administrative skills, public policies focussing on tackling local problems can become more responsive and action-oriented. The present attempt based on indepth studies and extensive field work touches some of these vital issues and the findings can provide a suitable framework for dialogue and action.

The present indepth study of two districts based on intensive field work clearly brings out that if the understanding of the variety of constraints and considerations, which go into integration and coordination in planning and implementation of various development schemes at the district level, is better, the utility of these schemes will surely increase. It has also been noticed that poor conception of various dimensions of district plan has resulted in the failure of achieving the targets consequently leading to loss of resources—both natural and human. The present analysis, no doubt, relates to the two districts only but the inferences drawn and the data generated can be further cross-checked by taking other districts of the states studied or of different states. An effort has been made to look at the planning system at the district level only without going into the entire planning system as such. The themes discussed in each chapter can be faithfully used to conduct detailed studies—both at the micro and macro levels. A comparative study of attempts at district level planning made in other developing countries of Asia can be of immense help in eradicating poverty and unemployment. No less significant will be the evaluation studies of different development programmes and strategies evolved by various state Governments in India. The study of how people's participation can be ensured at the district level and what role can be assigned to voluntary bodies would go a long way to make the district level planning efficient and effective. Again, the studies relating to how far bureaucracy has been helpful in the developmental process and what role orientations and perceptions can play to make it more responsive to popular demands, are topical. Block level planning is also gaining momentum in the country and it will be worthwhile to pursue this theme to operationalise planning at this level within the frame of district level planning. Depending upon the resources and patience of the researchers, a long term project to look into the entire mechanism of multi-level planning and various linkages can be taken up.

Efforts at streamlining and reorienting machinery for development planning are going on continuously and consistently in the developing countries. As the years pass, its significance and utility is bound to increase. It is, no doubt, at the initial stage today but the future appears to be both promising and rewarding. If this humble effort contributes a little towards better understanding of the development process, the labour put in will have been amply rewarded.

*APPENDIX-I*

## LIST OF IMPORTANT DISTRICT LEVEL SCHEMES (GROUPWISE) IN THANE DISTRICT (MAHARASHTRA)

GROUP-I *Agriculture & Allied Services.*

1. Creation of irrigation facilities for Taluka seed farm.
2. Purchase of plant protection equipment.
3. Plant protection subsidy for pesticides, raticides etc.
4. Opening of retail outlets for stocking of fertilizers.
5. Intensive programme for oilseed production.
6. Subsidy for improved farm implements.
7. Intensive production of pulses crop.
8. Subsidy for inputs.
9. Supply of bullocks and bullock carts to Tribals.
10. Special Component Plan for Scheduled Castes and Neo-Budhists—grant of financial assistance.
11. Divisional and district horticultural offices.
12. Strengthening of nurseries.
13. Rennovation of country mango and ber trees.
14. Capital subsidy for horticulture development for small and marginal farmers for oranges, musambies, kagdilime and guava.
15. Development of cocoa and coffee.
16. Financial assistance to allottees of surplus land.
17. Financial assistance to Tribals for restoration of alienated lands.
18. Financial assistance to Tribal tenant purchasers to pay off purchase price under tenancy laws.
19. Minor irrigation schemes.
20. Minor irrigation (state sector).
21. Bunding and terracing programme.
22. Plantation and afforestation.
23. Ayacut development.
24. Strengthening of the offices of District Animal

Husbandry Officers.

25. Training to farmers.
26. Stipend for training of livestock supervisors.
27. Establishment and construction of buildings for veterinary polyclinics.
28. Providing of medicine to existing veterinary institutions.
29. Establishment and construction of buildings for veterinary dispensaries/ veterinary aid centres.
30. Upgradation of veterinary aid centres.
31. Establishment of mobile epizootic control unit/ veterinary clinics.
32. Subsidy for vaccine to control foot and mouth disease.
33. Establishment of key village centres.
34. Supply of cross-bred bulls, under premium bull scheme.
35. Establishment of district level project cell.
36. Rearing of cross-bred heifers.
37. Poultry programme.
38. Distribution of cockerels.
39. Construction of residential and non-residential buildings at intensive poultry development block.
40. Distribution of chicks to beneficiaries.
41. Organisation of fodder demonstration plots.
42. Publicity and mass propaganda.
43. District set up under Dairy Development Department.
44. Strengthening of co-operative district set up.
45. Managerial subsidy.
46. Capital grants to co-operatives for purchase of milk cans, testing equipments etc.
47. Incentive to small dairy cooperative societies for continuing individual testing during lean season.
48. Training to secretaries of dairy cooperatives.
49. Training programme specially designed for Adivasi and Scheduled Caste farmers and other weaker sections.
50. Supply of dry pregnant buffaloes.
51. Fodder cultivation.
52. Extension of calf rearing unit of Daptchary, Aarey, Palgarh and increasing the govt. herd for supply of cross-bred heifers.
53. Government milk schemes.
54. Establishment of fish seed production farms.

55. Development of fisheries in brackish water.
56. Training of fisher youths.
57. Fish farming in impounded water.
58. Preservation, transport and marketing of fish.
59. Mechanisation of fishing crafts on improvement of fishing boats.
60. Assistance for supply of fishery requirite.
61. Grant of loan to fishermen.
62. Development of fishery cooperatives.
63. Improvement of fishing harbours.
64. Grant of subsidy to fishermen towards payment of insurance premium.
65. Establishment of central nurseries.
66. Community School nurseries.
67. Plantation of forest species for local and commercial uses.
68. Reforestation of degraded forests.
69. Afforestation of denuded forests through poor and unemployed persons.
70. Wild life and nature conservation.
71. Protection of forests.
72. Establishment of firewood and timber depot.
73. Development of minor forests produce.
74. Development of fodder resources.
75. Construction of sheds for labour and field staff.
76. Tusser cultivation.
77. Supply of bullock carts to Adivasis and forest labourers.
78. Felling of trees from malki lands of Scheduled Tribes.
79. Plantation of fruit trees on lands belonging to Scheduled Castes and Scheduled Tribes.
80. Rural fuelwood plantation.
81. A tree for a child.
82. Establishment of central nurseries.
83. Raising of plantation on road-side and canal-side.
84. Maharashtra social forest project plantation.

GROUP-II *Cooperation*

1. Grant of interest subsidy to Scheduled Castes and Neo-Budhists of primary agricultural cooperative societies.
2. Seven years interest-free loan for purchase of shares.
3. Fifteen years interest-free loan for operational expenses.

4. Subsidy towards bad debt reserve.
5. Interest subsidy to Tribals.
6. Financial assistance (loan) for godown amenities.
7. Loan for staff quarters.
8. Assistance for forest labourers.
9. Assistance to cooperative consumer stores in urban areas (primary stores).
10. Primary central cooperative consumer stores seven years interest free loans.
11. Loans to Scheduled Castes/Neo-Budhists for consumption needs.
12. Consumer store for opening branches/shops in Harijan bastis.
13. Distribution of consumers articles in rural areas.
14. Labour contract co-operative societies.

GROUP-III *Water and Power Development*

1. Bhatra (irrigation).
2. Wandri.
3. Rural electrification (plan).
4. Normal development.
5. Electrification of Harijan bastis.
6. System improvement.

GROUP-IV *Industry and Mining*

1. Financial assistance (interest subsidy) to small scale industries.
2. Industrial estates.
3. Development of handicrafts.
4. Seed money assistance to educated unemployed.
5. Training scheme for educated unemployed.
6. Entrepreneurial training programme.
7. District industries centre.
8. Assistance to industrial cooperatives.
9. Assistance to block level village artisans multipurpose cooperative societies (Balutedar).

GROUP-V *Transport and Communication*

1. Dredging of ports.
2. Navigational aids.
3. Inland water transport.
4. Crash programme for basic amenities for small crafts.
5. Anti-sea erosion works.
6. Infrastructure facilities for state transport services.
7. Construction of sakavs in hilly areas.
8. District roads (Non-MNP).
9. District roads under

Minimum Needs Programme.

10. Mininimum Needs Programme—special rural roads programme.

GROUP-VI *Social and Community Services*

1. Opening of Balwaris in primary schools.
2. Appointment of primary teachers for opening of primary schools.
3. Grants to Zila Parishads for appointment of primary school teachers due to revision of norms.
4. Attaching standards V to VII of primary schools to secondary schools.
5. Grants to municipal school boards/municipal councils for expansion of primary education.
6. Non-formal education programme for the age group 9 to 14 (part-time classes).
7. Book banks in primary schools.
8. Special facilities to students belonging to Scheduled Castes/Scheduled Tribes, Vimukt Jatis and Non-Tribes in standards I and II of primary schools (supply of uniforms and writing materials).
9. Grants to Zila Parishad for construction of class rooms for primary school buildings.
10. UNICEF aided programme—supply of Science kit boxes to primary schools.
11. Strengthening of inspection, supervision and monitoring of elementary education.
12. Surprise inspection squads for primary schools.
13. Expansion of school complexes.
14. Awards-ideal primary schools in rural areas.
15. Seminar reading programme for elementary education.
16. Development and expansion of non-government secondary schools-opening of additional divisions.
17. Development of facilities in pre-SSC technical education.
18. Opening of non-government secondary schools.
19. Payment of stipends to Tribal students in standards V to X.
20. Appointment of laboratory assistants in non-Govt. secondary schools.
21. Incentive grants to well

managed selected secondary schools.

22. Book banks in secondary schools.
23. Seminar reading programme for secondary school teachers.
24. District science forums.
25. Strengthening of inspecting machinery for secondary education at district level.
26. Development of higher secondary education (junior colleges)—additional divisions.
27. Training of teachers for implementing NCERT syllabus.
28. Appointment of additional staff in junior colleges of education.
29. Appointment of laboratory assistants in Govt. and non-Govt. junior colleges of education.
30. Training of teachers in work experience.
31. Maintenance grants to non-Govt. colleges.
32. Adult education programme (MNP).
33. Establishment of rural sports centres.
34. Coaching programme and establishment of district coaching centres.
35. Developmen of playgrounds.
36. Development of gymnasia.
37. Stipends to wrestlers.
38. Award of scholarships to budding wrestlers.
39. Strengthening of the district sports offices.
40. Promotion of sports and sports competitions.
41. Organisation of social service camps.
42. Financial assistance to voluntary youth organisations in rural/urban areas.
43. Educational concessions to economically backward class students.
44. Institution of merit scholarships at post-SSC level for economically backward class students.
45. Educational concession to the children of primary school teachers.
46. Grant-in-aid to public/gram panchayat libraries.
47. Vocationalisation of education at plus 2 stage.
48. Civil engineering assistant's course.
49. Enhancement of facilities at Ayurvedic dispensaries in the State.
50. Development and starting of ESIs hospitals.
51. Extension of ESI scheme to new areas.
52. Expansion of facilities in

civil hospitals and dispensaries (non-teaching).

53. Establishment of rural mobile dispensaries.
54. Control of disease like scabbies/diarrhoea and guinea worms in TSP area.
55. Medical education of Ashram school children.
56. Additional incentives for family welfare programme providing PLO etc.
57. National Malaria Control Programme.
58. BCG vaccination and TB control programme.
59. Filaria control programme.
60. TB control programme.
61. Primary Health Centres/sub centres/rural hospitals backing of construction works.
62. Upgradation of primary health units and dispensaries into primary health centres.
63. Upgradation of primary health centres as rural hospitals and providing additional staff as per GOI pattern (MNP).
64. Establishment of primary health centres (MNP).
65. Upgradation of primary health units/dispensaries into subsidiary health centres (MNP).
66. Establishment of sub centres, creation of posts of auxiliary nurse—midwives for every 5,000 population (MNP).
67. Establishment of new cottage hospitals.
68. Improvement of existing cottage hospitals.
69. Municipal water supply and sanitation.
70. Conversion of dry laterines into flush or water borne laterines.
71. Low cost sanitation.
72. Piped water supply (special measures).
73. Wells construction (simple measure).
74. Boring of GSDA.
75. Rural sanitation—roadside gatars.
76. Economically weaker sections housing scheme.
77. Low income group housing scheme.
78. Extension of village Gaothanas and provision of house sites.
79. Tiling of roof huts.
80. Financial assistance to municipal councils.
81. Bombay Metropolitan Region Development Authority Area Development Schemes.
82. Slum improvement programme.
83. Intensive publicity cells

in Tribal areas.
84. Community television sets.
85. Consolidation and making good deficiencies in ITIs.
86. Construction of hostel buildings and staff quarters.
87. Opening and strengthening of ITIs in production of additional seats in existing ITIs.
88. Establishment of advanced vocational training system in ITIs.
89. Introduction of entrepreneurship training programme.
90. Strengthening of administrative set up in Employment Exchanges.
91. Enforcement machinery under the employment exchange compulsory notification of vacancies Act, 1959 and vehicles for employment exchanges.
92. Creation of backward class cell for employment exchanges.
93. Honorarium to educated unemployed for part-time employment.
94. Creation of mobile units at employment exchanges.
95. Employment Guarantee Schemes.
96. Restructuring of the Directorate of Social Welfare.
97. Grant of tuition fees, examination fees to backward class students.
98. Award of scholarships to backward class students in high school.
99. Award of stipends to backward class students in ITIs.
100. Award of post-SSC scholarships.
101. Opening and maintenance of Government hostels for boys and girls.
102. Opening and maintenance of Govt. hostels for backword classes and economically backward classes girls and boys.
103. Construction of buildings for Govt. backward class hostels.
104. Grant-in-aid to aided backward class hostels.
105. Payment of building grants to aided backward class hostels.
106. Grant-in-aid to voluntary agencies for running Ashramshalas for Scheduled Tribes.
107. Ashramshala complexes.
108. Grant-in-aid to Balwaris.
109. Installation of pumping sets for Scheduled Tribes.
110. Supply of oil engines.

111. Financial assistance to cooperative housing societies of backward classes.
112. Financial assistance to individual and group housing for backward classes.
113. Propaganda for removal of untouchability.
114. Improvement of Harijan bastis.
115. Incentive for inter-caste marriage.
116. Sponsorship programme for women and vocational training in different crafts for destitute women.
117. Grant-in-aid to Mahila Mandals for purchase of equipment for starting new production centres.
118. Opening of Government observation homes and approved centres.
119. Payment of grant-in-aid to voluntary agencies for running juvenile guidance centres.
120. Recognition and payment of grant-in-aid to voluntary institutions for physically handicapped.
121. Grant-in-aid to home for aged and infirm.
122. Children in need of care and protection.
123. Setting up of special employment exchanges for physically handicapped persons.
124. Expansion of work under probation of Offenders Act.
125. School feeding programme (mid-day meals).
126. Integrated child development schemes.
127. Special nutrition in urban slums of intensive child development schemes.

*APPENDIX-II*

## METHODOLOGY OF ARRIVING AT THE SHARE OF THE DISTRICT UNDER EACH CRITERION IN MAHARASHTRA.

The total outlay meant for district level schemes is distributed on the following basis:

**Criterion-I: Population**

The benefits of the development efforts should reach the people in general and population of the weaker sections in particular. In view of this, the size of population including that of urban population as well as Scheduled Castes, Neo-Budhists and Scheduled Tribes population, is given the weightage. Sixty per cent of the district total outlay is thus allocated on population basis.

**Criterion-II: Scheduled Castes and Scheduled Tribes**

Since Scheduled Tribes, Scheduled Castes (including Neo-Budhists) are the weakest section of the society, special consideration and weightage is given to enable the district planners to take up special programmes so as to bring them on par with other sections of the society. In effect this section of the population gets additional weight, since they are also included in the distribution of allocation under criterion 1. Population of Scheduled Castes, Scheduled Tribes and Neo-Budhists is adopted as revealed in the 1971 census. The backward class population of the districts is expressed as a percentage of the backward class population of the state and 5 per cent is distributed on this basis.

**Criterion-3: Urban population**

Some weightage is necessary because urbanization or concentration of longer cluster of population in the cities and towns presents some special problems such as housing, sanitation, water supply, slum clearance, power supply, transport etc. They also throw considerable strain on social services like education, medical and public health services. As indicated in 1971 Census, urban population of the district is considered and is expressed as percentage of the urban population of the state. Five per cent is distributed on this basis.

**Criterion-4: Agricultural backwardness**

Industrial and agricultural backwardness are the major indicators reflecting the level of economic development. Agricultural backwardness of the districts is decided on the basis of two criteria, namely (1) value added by agriculture per hectare in the district, and (2) value added by agriculture per agricultural worker (cultivators and agricultural labourers).

For working out this criterion, the figures pertaining to the year 1967-68 were taken as this was more or less a normal agricultural year. The value added by agriculture per hectare was worked out by dividing the value added in each district by gross cropped area in the district and the value added by agriculture per agricultural worker was worked out by dividing the value added by agriculture in each district by the total number of agricultural workers i.e. the cultivators and agricultural labourers. Since these two independent criteria were worked out, the indicators for each district were pooled by working out the geometric mean of the figures for value added per hectare and value added per agricultural worker. This geometric mean is worked out by multiplying the value of the two factors and working out the square root of the product.

The ratio of the geometric mean of value added per hectare and value added per agricultural worker for the district and the corresponding state average was worked out. For all the districts, the allocation was given in inverse proportion to the ratio for the state. This was used because this method gives proportionately higher allocation to the backward district in proportion to its backwardness as compared with the state average. Thus, the district which has 10 per cent higher value of its geometric mean than the state average, is given 10 per cent less allocation and on the other hand a district having 10 per cent less value of its geometric mean than the state average is given 10 per cent larger allocation per agricultural worker. This was worked out by means of a deviation formula.

**Criterion-5: Backwardness in communication**

The development of communication is an important aspect of the economic infrastructure and for this purpose 5 per cent was distributed on this basis. For working out backwardness in this sector, the length of railways and the lengths of the national highways, state highways, major district roads and other district roads were considered. Here also, while deciding the district allocations, the geometric mean of the indicators regarding road and railway mileage per 100 sq. km. and per lakh of population has been worked out. The share of each district has been calculated by using the deviation formula as was adopted for working out the distribution under agricultural backwardness.

**Criterion-6: Backwardness in irrigation**

4 per cent of the allocable sum is distributed on this basis, agricultural development to a very large extent depends on development of irrigation. In view of this, 4 per cent of allocation was distributed to the districts on the basis of level of irrigation development in the district. For this purpose, the likely irrigation potential for each district by June 1974 through Major, Medium and Minor projects (state sector) was considered. The percentage of this potential to the gross cropped area in each district was worked out. Similarly, the percentage for the state as a whole was worked out. Allocable sum was distributed to each district by using the deviation formula as is used in the case of agricultural and communication backwardness.

**Criterion-7: Industrial backwardness**

Alongwith other indicators, the level of industrial development for each district was also considered and on this basis, 5 per cent was distributed to the districts in the following manner. The districtwise value added by manufacturing industries as revealed by the Annual Survey of Industries for the year 1969-70 has been used. Per capita value added by the industries is worked out for all districts as well as for the state excluding Greater Bombay. Greater Bombay was excluded since the per capita value is very high as compared to the per capita value in other districts. Moreover, if Greater Bombay is included this will distort the whole picture. The districtwise average worked out to Rs. 55.66. Districts having per capita value added higher than this figure are excluded. These districts are Bombay, Thane, Pune and Nagpur. For the remaining districts, the allocation was made in the inverse proportion of per capita value added by industries in the districts. For Nasik district, for example, the value added per capita was Rs. 40.78 which was 26.74 per cent less than the average. Similarly, for Aurangabad district, the per capita value added was Rs. 2.12 which was 96.17 per cent less than the state average. Thus, backwardness of Aurangabad district was 3.6 times as compared to that of Nasik district. Hence, per capita entitlement of Aurangabad district too was (Rs. 24.45) 3.6 times that of Nasik district (Rs. 6.80). This per capita allocation was then multiplied by 1971 census district population to arrive at the total allocation for each district.

**Criterion-8: Special Problems: six per cent**

(a) 3 per cent of funds is distributed to meet the special problems of drought prone areas. The share of each district is worked out on the basis of rural population in drought prone areas as identified by Sakthankar Committee.

(b) 1.50 per cent of the allocable sum is distributed to meet the special problems of coastal districts. Again the share of district is based on rural population.

(c) 1.5 per cent of the funds is allocated to meet the special problems of forests areas. The amount is distributed in proportion to the area under forests held by the Forests Department in each district.

# SELECT BIBLIOGRAPHY


**Reports and documents**

Bank of Maharashtra, *Annual Action Plan for Thane District*, 1982.

——, *District Credit Plan, 1983-85 and Annual Action Plan*, 1983, Thane District.

Government of Gujarat, *Report by a Team of Senior Officers on District Planning Machinery*, 1973.

Government of Haryana, *Development Plan of Karnal District* (*Fifth Plan and Perspective*), Chandigarh.

——, *Guidelines for the Formulation of District Plans*, *Economic and Statistical Organisation*, 1972.

——, *Statistical Handbook of Haryana*, Economic and Statistical Organisation, 1983.

Government of India, *Fifth Estimate Committee, Sixty Nineth Report, Development of Backward Areas*, Lok Sabha Secretariat, New Delhi, 1974.

——, *Guidelines for Formulation of District Plans*, Planning Commission, 1969.

——, *Interim Report on Credit Services for Small and Marginal Farmers and Agricultural Labourers*, 1971.

——, *Report of the All India Rural Credit Review Committee*, Bombay, 1979.

——, *Report of the Committee on Panchayati Raj Institutions*, New Delhi, 1978.

——, *Report of the Committee on Special Multi-purpose Tribal Blocks*, *Ministry of Home Affairs*, New Delhi, 1960.

——, *Report of the Committee on Tribal Economy in Forest Areas, 1967*, Department of Social Welfare, Delhi, 1970.

——, *Report on Evaluation of Study of Small Farmers, Marginal Farmers and Agricultural Labourers Projects, 1974-75*, 1979.

——, *Report on Formulation of Area Development Plan*, Committee on Plan Projects, New Delhi, 1966.

——, *Report of the Working Group on Block Level Planning*, 1978.

——, *Report of Working Group on Conceptual Framework on Multi Level Planning and Special Analysis* (*mimeographed*), *Planning Circular No. PC (p) 9/46WG (ef)/72-MLP, 22.1.1973.*

——, *Report of the Working Group on Fiscal and Financial Incentives for Starting Industries in Backward Areas*, Ministry of Industrial Development, Internal Trade and Company Affairs, Development Commissioner (Small-Scale Industries), New Delhi, 1967, (Chairman, N. N. Wanchoo).

——, *Report of the Working Group on Identification of Backward Areas*, New Delhi, 1969 (Commission Leader, B. D. Pande).

——, *Report on Scheduled Areas and Scheduled Tribes Commission*, Delhi, 1960, (Chairman, U. N. Dhebar).

——, *Study Team on District Administration*, Administrative Reforms Commission, Delhi, 1966.

Government of Maharashtra, *A Report on Reorganisation of Maharashtra Administration*, 1971.

——, *Detailed Statements of Outlays Provided for District Level Schemes in the Annual Plan*, 1983-84.

——, *Draft Sixth Five Year Tribal Sub Plan, 1980-81, to 1984-85 and Annual Plan, 1981-82, Integrated Tribal Development Projcct, Thana-II*, Bombay.

——, *Economic Survey of Maharashtra*, 1977-78, Bombay.

——, *Economic Survey of Maharashtra*, 1982-83, Bombay.

——,*Handbook of Basic Statistics of Maharashtra State*, 1981, Bombay.

——, *Indicative Framework of Proposed Perspective for District Development* (*draft*), Bombay, 1973.

——, *Report of the Committee on Relief from Rural and Urban Indebtedness.*

——, *Report of the Evaluation Committee on Panchayati Raj*, Bombay, 1971.

——, *Statistical Abstract of Maharashtra State for the year 1978-79*, Bombay.

——, *The Socio-Economic effects of Prohibition in Thane and Surat Districts*, Bombay, 1963.

*Socio-Economic Review and District Statistical Abstract of Thane District, 1979-80*, Bombay, Directorate of Economics and Statistics.

Government of Punjab, *Guidelines for the Formulation of District Plans*, Planning Department, July, 1974.

——, *Report of the Punjab Administrative Reforms Commission*, 1966.

National Institute of Community Development, Hyderabad, *Perspective on Tribal Development and Administration, Proceedings of the Workshop held at the National Institute of Community Development*, Hyderabad, 1975.

National Institue of Rural Development, Hyderabad, *A Manual for Formulation and Implementation of Block Plan.*

——, *Country Report on Integrated Rural Development*, India, 1981.

——, *Draft Gudelines for Local Level Planning (ESCAP)*, 1981.

Punjab National Bank, *District Credit Plan (1980-82)*, Karnal.

Reserve Bank of India, *District Credit Plans. Guidelines for the Third Round, Lead Bank Schemes*, Bombay, 1982.

——, *Report of the Working Group on the Role of Banks in Implementation of New 20*-Point Programme.

United Nations Asian Development Institute, Bangkok, *A Report on the Expert Group Meeting*, An Approach to Evolving Guidelines for Rural Development.

**Books**

Advani, B.T., *Influence of Socialism on Policies, Legislation and Administration in India*, Sterling, New Delhi, 1976.

Arora, Ramesh K., *Comparative Public Administration: An Ecological Perspective*, Associated, New Delhi, 1972.

AVARD, *Association of Voluntary Agencies for Rural Development, Neitei Villages, Imphal (East Block), Manipur*, Rural Development Plan, New Delhi, 1975.

Banerjee, M., *Planning in India*, Oxford, New Delhi, 1981.

Bansal, Prem Lata, *Administrative Development in India*, Sterling, New Delhi, 1974.

Bapat, N.G., *Economic Development of Ahmednagar District*, 1881-1960, Bombay Progressive Corporation, 1973.

Bengtson, M. I., *Rural Development Research and Agricultural Innovations: A Comparative Study of Agricultural Changes in a Historical Perspective and Agricultural Research Policy for Rural Development*, Swedish University of Agricultural Sciences, Uppsala, 1983.

Bhat, L. S. *et al*, *Micro-Level Planning: A Case Study of Karnal Area, Haryana, India*, K.B. Publications, New Delhi, 1976.

Chaturvedi, H.R., *Bureaucracy and the Local Community: Dynamics of Rural Development*, Allied, Bombay, 1977.

Clay, E.J. and B.B. Schaffer (Eds.), *Room for Manoeuvre: An Exploration of Public Policy Planning in Agricultural and Rural Development* (*Mimeo*), I.D.S., 1983.

Coale, A.J. and Hoover, E.M., *Population Growth and Economic Development in Low-income Countries*, Inter-India, New Delhi, 1983.

Dayal, Ishwar *et al*, *District Administration: A Survey of Reorganisation*, Macmillan, Delhi, 1976.

Desai, Vasant, *A Study of Rural Economics*, Himalaya, 1983.

Dubey, S.N., *Administration of Social Welfare Programmes in India*, Somaiya, Bombay, 1973.

Haldipur, R.N., *Local Government, Rural Development and Micro-Level Planning*, Cabinet Secretariat, Department of Personnel and Administrative Reforms Training Division, New Delhi, 1974.

Heginbotham, Stanby J., *Cultures in Conflict: Four Faces of Indian Bureaucracy*, Colombia University, New York, 1975.

Heredero, J.M., *Rural Development and Social Change: An Experiment in Non-formal Education*, Manohar, New Delhi, 1977.

Iqbal Narain, *et al*, *Panchayati Raj Administration: Old Controls and New Challenges*, I.I.P.A., New Delhi.

Ishwar Dayal *et al*, *Dynamics of Formulating Policy in Government of India Machinery for Policy Development*, Concept, Delhi, 1976.

Jain, D.K., *Project Planning and Appraisal in Planned Economy, The Indian Context*, Uppal, New Delhi, 1981.

Jetley, Surinder, *Modernising Indian Peasants*, New Delhi Asian Educational Services, India, 1977.

Kabra, Kamal Narayan, *Planning Process in a District*, Indian Institute of Public Administration, New Delhi, 1977.

Kistaiah, M., *Regionalism in India*, Hyderabad, Book Links Corporation, 1977.

Krishnamachari, V.T., *Fundamentals of Planning in India* Orient Longmans, Bombay, 1962.

Kurien, C.T., *Poverty, Planning and Social Transformation*, Oxford, 1978.

Malhotra, R.C., (Ed.), *Local Level Planning and Rural Development: Alternative Strategies*, Concept, New Delhi, 1980.

Mathur, B.C., *Bureaucracy and the Local Community: Dynamics of Rural Development*, Allied, New Delhi, 1977.

Mathur, K. and Bhattacharya, M., *Administrative Response to Emergency: A Study of Scarcity Administration in Maharashtra*, Concept, Delhi, 1975.

Mehta, B., *Bureaucracy and Change*: Centre for Administrative Change, Jaipur, 1975.

Mehta, V.D., *Economic Change in Rural India*, Progressive, Bhopal, 1979.

Minhas, B.S., *Planning and the Poor*, Sultan Chand, New Delhi, 1974.

Mundle, Sudipto, *District Planning in India*, Indian Institute of Public Administration, New Delhi, 1977.

Muttalib, M.A., *Development Administration in Rural Government for Agricultural Production*, Osmania University, Hyderabad, 1973.

National Council of Applied Economic Research, *District Planning-Moradabad*, New Delhi, 1968.

Nigam, Raj, K., (Ed.), *Management of Public Sector in India*, Vora, Bombay, 1971.

Pai Panandiker, V.A., *Development Administration in India*, MacMillan, Madras, 1974.

Pai Panandiker, V.A., Bishnoi, R.N. Sharma, O.P., *Development Bureaucracy*, Oxford and Indian Book House Publishing Company, New Delhi, 1983.

Pandey, S.M. and J.A. Sodhi, *Developing the Rural poor*, Shri Ram Centre for Industrial Relations and Human Resources, New Delhi, 1977.

——, *The Planning Commission Re-organized*, Indian Institute of Public Administration, New Delhi, 1971.

Patankar, Mamatha, *Economic Planning*, Sultan Chand, New Delhi, 1981.

Patel, M.L., *Dilemma of Balanced Regional Development in India*, Progress, Bhopal, 1975.

Patnaik, Nityananda and Saradindu Bose, *An Integral Tribal Development Plan for Koonjhar District, Orissa*, National Institute of Community Development, Hyderabad, 1976.

Paul, Streeten, *Development Perspective*, MacMillan, London, 1981.

——, *The Frontiers of Development Studies*, MacMillan, London, 1979.

Pradhan, Prachanda (Ed.), *Aspects of Development Administration*, Centre for Economic Development and Administration, Kirtipur, 1971.

Prasad, Awadesh, *Portrait of Bureaucracy in India*, Associated Book Agency, Patna, 1976.

Prasad, Nageshwar, *Decentralisation in Yugoslavia and India*, Navchetna, Varanasi, 1972.

Puttar Swamaiah, *Aspects of Planning*, Oxford, New Delhi, 1977.

Rakshi, Gangadhar, *Poverty and Planning in India*, World Press, Calcutta, 1977.

Rao, P.U.R., *Public Servant in Modern India*, Administrative Training Institute, Mysore, 1975.

Ray, Amal, *Organisational Aspects of Rural Development, Taluk-Level Admnistration in an Indian State*, World Press, Calcutta, 1976.

Reddy, Y., Venugopal, *Multi-level Planning in India*, Vikas, New Delhi, 1979.

Saroop, A., *District Planning for Integrated Development*, Planning Commission, (Mimeographed), New Delhi, 1972.

Sathe, Madhusudan, Dattatraya, *Regional Planning: An Area Exercise*, Saraswat, Poona, 1973.

Schultz, Theodorew, *Investing in People the Economics of Population Quality*, Hindustan Publishing, Delhi, 1981.

Sen, L.K., *Planning Rural Growth Centres for Integrated Area Development*, Hyderabad, 1971.

——, *Growth Centres in Raichur An Integrated Area Development Plan for a District in Karnataka*, National Institute of Community Development, Hyderabad, 1974.

Sen, Lalit K., and Abdul L. Thaha, *Regional Planning for a Hill Area*, National Institute of Community Development, Hyderabad, 1975.

Seshadri, K., *Agricultural Administration in Andhra Pradesh: A Study of the Process of Implementation of Intensive Agricultural Development Programmes*, Popular, Bombay, 1974.

Shah, S.M., *Rural Development Planning and Reforms*, Abhinav, New Delhi, 1977.

Shah, Vimal, *Planning for Talala Block, A Study in MicroLevel Planning*, The Gujarat Institute of Area Planning, Ahmedabad, 1974.

Sharma, A.N., *Spatial Approach for District Planning*, Concept, New Delhi, 1981.

Sharma, G.B., *Social Administration in India*, Madhav, Jaipur, 1970.

Sharma, S.K., *Deputy Commissioner in Punjab*, Indian Institute of Public Administration, New Delhi, 1971.

——, *Panchayati Raj in India: A Study of Reforms at Centre and State Level since Independence*, Trimurthi, New Delhi, 1976.

Sharma, S.K., (Ed.), *Dynamics of Development: An International Perspective*, Concept, Delhi, 1978.

Shukla, J.D., *State and District Administration in India*, National, New Delhi, 1976.

Singer, H.W., *Strategy of International Development: Essays in the Economics of Backwardness*, MacMillan, London, 1975.

Singh Tarlok, *India's Development Experience*, MacMillan, Delhi, 1974.

Singhi, Narendra Kumar, *Bureaucracy: Positions and Persons*, Abhinav, New Delhi, 1974.

Sinha, P.R.F., Kotte, N.V., and Arya, H.P.S., *Communication in Development Administration: A Study of International Communication in three Indian States*, National Institute of Community Development, Hyderabad, 1976.

Sinha, Vishwa Nath Prasad, *Chota Nagpur Plaeau: A Study in Settlement Geography*, K.B. Publications, New Delhi, 1976.

Srinivasa Murthy and Rameswari (Eds.), *Agricultural Prices and Economic Development*, Himalaya, Bombay, 1983.

Srinivasan, N., *Agricultural Administration in India*, Indian Institute of Public Administration, New Delhi, 1969.

Thakur, Srinivas, Y., *Indian Economic Development Retrospect and Prospect*, Sterling, New Delhi, 1982.

Todaro, Michael, P., *Economic Development in the Third World*, Longman, New York, 1981.

——, *The Struggle for Economic Development: Readings in Problems and Policies*, Longman, London, 1983.

Tripathy, R.N. *et al*, *Block Plan in the District Frame*, National Institute for Rural Development, Hyderabad, 1980.

United Nations, *Development Administration, Current Approaches and trends in Public Administration for National Development*, United Nations, New York, 1978.

——, *New Approaches to Personnel policy for Development*, United Nations, New York, 1974.

Uppal, J.S. (Ed.), *India's Economic Problems*, Tata McGraw-Hill, New Delhi, 1975.

Varma, S.C., *India's Attack on Rural Poverty*, Ministry of Rural Reconstruction, Government of India, New Delhi, 1981.

Venkatappiah, B., *District Development and District Administration*, Institute of Public Administration, Mysore Branch, Bangalore, 1968.

Waldo, Dwight (Ed.), *Temporal Dimensions of Development Administration*, Duke University Press, Durham, N.C., 1970.

Waidner, Edward, (Ed.), *Development Administration in Asia*, Duke University, Press, Durham, N.C., 1970.

——, *Technical Assistance in Public Administration: The Case for Development Administration*, Public Administration Service, Chicago, 1964.

**Research Papers and Articles**

Aiyar, S.P., "Planning in Indian Democracy", *Indian Journal of Political Science*, 24 (4) Oct.-Dec., 1961, pp. 337-46.

Alagh, Yogender K., "District Planning in India, Some issues", *Journal of the Lal Bahadur Shastri National Academy of Administration*, Spring, 1975 pp. 43-54.

Ali, S.Nasir, "Plan Implementation through District Administration", *Indian Journal of Politics*, July-December, 1972, pp. 67-90.

Balakrishna, S., *Calculation of Population Threshold in Regional Planning Exercises: An Alternative Method Behavioural Science and Community Development*, Sept., 1976 pp. 87-89.

Banerji, Shyamdas and H.Benjamin Fischer, "Spatial Analysis for Integrated Area Planning in India", *Urban and Rural Planning Thought*, Jan., 1974 pp. 1-45.

Bhalerao, C.N., "Changing Pattern of Development Administration in the District", *Indian Journal of Public Administration*, Jan.-March, 1966, pp. 123-31.

Bhattacharya, Asit Kumar, "Economic Regions in the Context of Development: Some Basic Considerations", *Artha-Vijnana*, March, 1973, pp. 57-90.

Bose, A.N., "Institutional Bottlenecks: The Main Barrier to the Development of Backward Regions", *Indian Journal of Regional Science*, 2 ( I ) 1970, pp. 45-63.

Brahme, Sulabhe, Kumud Pore and S.H. Pore, "Regional Planning: A Case Study of Marathwada Region", *Artha-Vijnana*, March-June, 1975, p. 187.

Chatterji, M., "Regional Economic Planning, Importance for India", *Economic Weekly*, 15 (3), March 30, 1963.

Chattopadhyay, B.K., "Project Selection and Promotion in Backward Areas", *Management Accountant*, August, 1975, pp. 511-14.

Chopra, R.N., "Administrative Organization for Regional

Development: The Experience of Punjab", *Indian Journal of Public Administration*, Oct.-Dec., 1965, pp. 737-49.

——, "Removal of Poverty: Some Suggestions and Administrative Implications", *Indian Journal of Public Administration*, April-June, 1972, pp. 216-26.

Dar, R.K.,"Some Notes on District Planning", *Journal of the Lal Bahadur Shastri National Academy of Administration*, Spring, 1975, pp. 179-90

Das Gupta, B., "Socio-Economic Classification of Districts: A Statistical Approach", *Economic and Political Weekly*, August 14, 1971, pp. 1763-74.

Dass, Kaushal, K., "India's Economic Growth and the Civil Service", *Journal of the National Academy of Administration*, Dec., 1968, pp. 1-8.

Deshpande, R.A., "Planning Machinery and Administration in India," *Public Administration*, Kanpur, April, 1964, pp. 15-21.

Deva, Raj., "Multi-Level Planning and Local Government Structure," *Indian Journal of Public Administration*, July-Sept., 1973, pp. 338-49.

Dharia, Mohan, "Planning for Development of Backward Areas and Weaker Sections of the Society," *Indian Journal of Public Administration*, July-Sept., 1973, pp. 259-68.

Dhar, P.N., "Strategy to Industrialize Rural and Backward Areas," *Kurukshetra*, Dec. 1, 1973, p. 8.

Diwan, Romesh, "Planning for the Poor," *Economic and Political Weekly*, Aug. 1971, pp. 1809-14.

Dube, P.N., "Plan Formulation at Grass Roots," *Economic and Political Weekly*, April 20, 1968, p. 649.

Dubey, S.N., "Tribal Welfare Programmes: An Analysis of their Organisation and Administration," *Indian Journal of Social Work*, Oct., 1971, pp. 207-20.

Dubhashi, P.R., "Gaps in the Indian Process of Planning: Importance of Regional Planning," *Indian Journal of Public Administration*, July-Sept., 1973, pp. 299-307.

Gadgil, D.R., "Regional Planning—What it means and involves," *Kurukshetra*, March, 1969, pp. 3-5.

Ghiare, B.M., "Financing of the District Plan," *Journal of the*

*Lal Bahadur Shastri National Academy of Administration*, Spring 1975, pp. 97-100.

Ghosh, A., "Development of Co-operatives in Backward Areas, National Co-operative Development," *Council Bulletin*, April, 1975, p. 14.

Gogoi, P.D., "Political Structure of the Adi people of Arunachal Pradesh," *Quarterly Journal of the Local Self Government Institute*, April-Sept., 1975, pp. 467-76.

Gopalakrishayya, "An Integrated Approach to Command Area Development Programme," *Indian Journal of Public Administration*, Jan.-March, 1979, pp. 74-85.

Guha, Sabita, "District Level Planning," *Yojana*, Nov. 16, 1978, pp. 15-17.

Gupta, L.C., "Decentralized Implementation: Some Administrative Problems," *Indian Journal of Public Administration*, April-June, 1965, pp. 251-73.

Hanson, A.H., "The Administration of Planning," *Indian Journal of Public Administration* April-June, 1963, pp. 149-61.

Hood, Christopher, "Using Bureaucracy Sparingly," *Public Administration, Summer* 1963, pp. 197-208.

Hooja, Rakesh, "District and Regional Planning: Some Aspects with regard to India", *Journal of the Lal Bahadur Shastri National Academy of Administration*, Spring 1975, pp. 191-204.

——, "The District as a Planning Unit: Style and Locus," *Indian Journal of Public Administration*, July-Sept., 1973, pp. 69-74.

——, "Planning for Rural Development by Field Staff—A View from Rajasthan," *Indian Journal of Public Administration*, Oct.-Dec., 1980, pp. 1089-99.

——, "State Level Planning—The Rajasthan Case," *Indian Journal of Public Administration*, July-Sept., 1976, pp. 549-62.

Hoyle, H.R., "The Role of the Civil Service in the Development Planning Process," *Journal of Administration Overseas*, Jan., 1972, pp. 45-52.

Inamdar, N.R., "Planning in Maharashtra," *Indian Journal of Public Administration*, July-Sept., 1973, pp. 320-37.

Irani, J.K., "Backward Areas in India and Development Programmes," *Finance and Commerce*, Jan., 1972, pp. 15-22.

Jathar, S.N., "Tribal Sub-Plan of Maharashtra State", *Cooperative Prespective*, Oct.-Dec., 1975, pp. 28-33.

Jain, P.C., "Gaps in the Plan for Industrialisation of Backward Areas", *Capital*, 14, Dec. 1972, pp. 986-87.

Joshi, N.D., "Integrated Area Development with Reference to District Planning", *Indian Journal of Agricultural Economics*, Oct.-Dec., 1973, pp. 8-16.

——, "Review of the Policy for the Development of Backward Regions in India", *Artha-Vikas*, Jan.-July, 1973, pp. 11-24.

Joshi, V.H., "Concept of Regional Analysis, Its Application to the Study of the Development of Backward Areas", *Artha-Vikas*, Jan.-July, 1973, pp. 64-68.

Kade Kodi, Gopal and V.S. Singh, "Regional Disparities and Areas with Special Problems in Uttar Pradesh", *Indian Journal of Regional Science*, 7 ( 1 ) 1975, pp. 53-68.

Krishna Swami, O.R., "Area Development Approach and District Planning", *Kurukshetra*, June 15, 1974, pp. 4-5.

Laxminarayan, H., "Long-way to Development of Nagaland" *Economic and Political Weekly*, Dec. 15, 1970, pp. 1971-74.

Lavania, G.S., "Approach to Integrated Area Development", *Indian Journal of Agricultural Economics*, Oct.-Dec., 1973, pp. 22-26.

Mac Nair, R.H. "Citizen Participation in Public Bureaucracies: Foul-weather Friends", *Administration and Society*, Vol. XIV, 1983, pp. 507-24.

Mann, R.S., "Leadership and Planned change in Tribal Rajasthan", *Khadi Gramodyog*, Dec., 1969, pp. 292-96.

Mathai, P.M., "New Strategy for Backward Areas", *Yojana*, July 1, 1972, pp. 483.85.

Mathur, Om Parkash, "National Policy for Backward Area Development: A Structural Analysis", *Indian Journal of Public Administration*, Jan.-March, 1974, pp. 73-90.

——, "Planning for Districts: Some Problems in Developing and Analytical Systems", *Journal of Lal the Bahadur*

*Shastri National Academy of Administration*, Spring 1975, pp. 21-34.

Mathur, Subodh, "Decentralisation of Development Planning: The Economic Area Approach", *Development Policy and Administrative Review*, July-Dec., 1975, pp. 127-30.

Mathur, V.K., Concept of Area Development as applicable to Tribal India", *Social Welfare*, Sept., 1968, pp. 8-9.

Misra, Girish, K., "Evaluation in Integrated Area Development Planning", *Behavioural Science and Community Development*, Sept., 1976, pp. 90-95.

Mozumdar, C., "Eastern Zonal Council: Its Possible Role in Regional Planning and Development", *Nagerlok*, July-Sept., 1976, pp. 41-53.

Nagaiya, D., "Growth Centres Approach to Regional Planning: A Case Study of Vidarbha", *Journal of the Lal Bahadur Shastri National Academy of Administration*, Spring 1975, pp. 75-84.

———"Methodology of Identification of Growth Centres: A Case Study of Vidarbha Region", *Journal of Lal Bahadur Shastri, National Academy of Administration*, Spring 1975, pp. 85-96.

Nath, Ashok, "Regional Development and Public Sector: A Case Study on North-Eastern Region", *Lok Udyog*, Dec., 1976, pp. 21-24.

Nath, V., "Area Development: Planning at District and Block Levels", *Indian Journal of Public Administration*, April-June, 1965, pp. 174-93.

———Progress of Rural Development Programmes: Regional Differences", *Economic Weekly*, Feb., 1963, pp. 175-77 (Annual Number).

———"Regional Development Politics", *Economic and Political Weekly*, July, 1971, pp. 1601-08, (Special Number).

———"Regions for Planning", *Indian Journal of Public Administration*, Jan.-March 1966, pp. 1-17.

———Suitability of a District as a Unit for Formulation of Integrated Area Development Plans", *Indian Journal of Agricultural Economics*, Oct.-Dec., 1973, pp. 38-40.

Nayar, Vaneet, "Methodology of Area Planning: The Karnal

Case Study", *Management in Government*, Oct.-Dec., 1969, pp. 44-53.

Pal. M.K., "Regional Disparities in the Level of Development in India", *Indian Journal of Regional Science*, 7(1), 1975, p. 35.

Pandey, M.P., "Regional Planning in Bihar" *Eastern Economist*, August 7, 1974, pp. 243-47.

Paranjpe, H.K., "Planning from Below: Why and How" *Economic weekly*, Dec. 19, 1964, p. 1993.

Patel, G.D., "District Area Development", *Indian Journal of Public Administration*, July-Sept., 1966, pp. 586-98.

Patel, M.L., "Land Problems of Scheduled Tribes in India," *Economic Studies*, Sept.-Oct., 1975, pp. 162-64.

Pathak, H.N,, "Developing Enterpreneurship in Backward Regions," *Arthavikas*, Jan-July, 1973, pp. 25-46.

Patnaik, S. and R.N. Chattopadhyay, "Spatial Variation in Levels of Development in Orissa", *Indian Journal of Regional Science*, 7(1), 1975, pp. 89-110.

Prabhakar Rao, P. and K.V., Sundaram, "Regional Imbalances in India: Some Policy Issues and Problems", *Indian Journal of Regional Science*, 5(1), 1973, pp. 61-80.

Prasad, Kamta, "Planning in India: Some Basic Issues Relating to Operational and Strategic Aspects", *The Indian Economic Association*, Bangalore, Dec., 28-30, 1983.

Prasad, L.B., "Three Tier Panchayat System of Santhals", *Vanyajati*, Jan., 1972, pp. 46-49.

Prasad, Tribhuvan, "Concepts, Significance, and Limitations of District Planning," *Journal of the Lal Bahadur Shastri National Academy of Administration*, Spring 1975, pp. 35-42.

Purnik, A.D., "Consumption Finance for the Tribals in Maharashtra", *Co-operative Perspective*, March 1977, pp. 15-20.

Rai, Haridwar, "Coordination of Development Programme at the District Level with Special Reference to the Role of District Officer in Bihar," *Indian Journal of Public Administration*, Jan.-March, 1966, pp. 28-59.

Raghaviah, Y., "Theory and Practice of Local Planning in

India", *Journal of the National Academy of Administration*, Dec., 1968, pp. 69-83.

Rai, Haridwar and Sakendra Prasad Singh, "The Green List Area Coordination and Agricultural Development: A Study in the Role of Area Development Commissioner in the Kosi Region," *Journal of Political Studies*, Feb., 1971, pp. 49-77.

Ramamurty, S.V., "Role of Administrator in Planning," *Commerce* 91 (2339) Annual Number, 1955, p. 18.

Rao, G.V.K., "Assault on Rural Poverty," *Yojana*, August 15, 1979, pp. 10-12.

Rao, Hemlata, "Identification of Backward Regions and the Trends in Regional Disparities in India," *Artha-Vijnana*, June, 1977, pp. 93-112.

Rao, M. Anand, "District Development Officer in Andhra Pradesh", *Quarterly Journal of the Local Self Government Institute*, Bombay, Vol. LIV, 1983, pp. 74-78.

Rao, S.K. "A Note on Measuring Economic Distance Between Regions in India," *Economic and Political Weekly*, April 28, 1973, pp. 793-800.

Rao, V., Nageswara, "Integrated Area Development with reference to the District Planning," *Indian Journal of Agricultural Planning*, Oct.-Dec., 1973, pp. 17-21.

Reddy, Y., Venugopal, "Multi-Level Planning with Special Reference to District Planning: Some Issues," *Journal of the Lal Bahadur Shastri National Academy of Administration*, Spring 1975, pp. 55-70.

Rieger, H.C., "Bureaucracy and the Implementation of Economic Plans in India," *Indian Journal of Public Administration*, Jan-March, 1967, pp. 32-42.

Sadasivan, S.N. "District Level Coordination in India: The Madras Experience" *Indian Journal of Public Administration*, Jan.-March, 1972, pp. 78-96.

Sain, K. and B. Bagchi, "New Strategy of Comprehensive Area Development Programme in West Bengal: An Analytical Study", *Indian Journal of Agricultural Economics*, Oct.-Dec., 1973, pp. 41-46.

Sarup, Anand, "District and Block Plans", *Yojana*, Jan. 26, 1978, pp. 43-46.

Satya Sundaram, I., "Strategy to Develop the Backward Areas", *Khadi Gramodyog*, May 1977, pp. 368-73.

Sen, Biman, "Planning for Poverty," *Yojana*, Aug. 15, 1979, pp. 29-38.

Seshadri, K., "Administration of Rural Small Scale Industry Development Schemes in Andhra Pradesh," *Journal of Local Administration Overseas India*, Oct. 1965, pp. 260-69.

Sethi, Harsh, "A Methodological Note on Area Development Programming: Some Reflections on Western Rajasthan,", *Development Policy and Administrative Review*, Jan.-June 1975, pp. 65-71.

Sharma, B.D., "Environmental Context and the Personnel System: Its implications for Tribal Areas," *Indian Journal of Public Administration*, Jan.-March, 1976, pp. 27-47.

——, "Planning from below with Special Reference to Tribal Areas," *Community Development and Panchayati Raj Digest*, July 1976, pp. 12-19.

Sharma, K.L., "Spatial Disparities in Rajasthan: A Comparative Study of Levels of Development Between Two Points of time", *Indian Journal of Regional Science*, 7 (1) 1975, pp. 88-98.

Sharma, P.N. and P.C. Katiyar, "Identifying Under-developed Districts in Uttar Pradesh," *Indian Journal of Regional Science*, 6 (1), 1974, pp. 30-38.

Sharma, P.V., "Regional Integration in Andhra Pradesh," *Artha-Vijnana*, Sept. 1974, pp. 298-313.

Shukla, Tara, "Integrated Area Development with Special Reference to District Planning," *Indian Journal of Agricultural Economics*, Jan.-March, 1974, pp. 16-18.

Singh, Ajit Kumar, "Integrated Area Development: Concepts and Issues," *Indian Journal of Agricultural Economics, Oct.-Dec., 1973*, pp. 27-31.

——, "Regional Economic Growth and Planning" *Eastern Anthropologist*, Oct.-Dec., 1973, pp. 329-37.

Singh, Daulat, "Dynamics of Integrated Area Development in India", *Indian Journal of Agricultural Economics*, Oct.-Dec., 1973, pp. 32-38.

Singh, Kartar, "Approach to Integrated Area Development,"

*Indian Journal of Agricultural Economics*, Oct.-Dec., 1973, pp. 1-7.

Singh, Radha Raman, "Multi-Level Planning for Achieving Integrated Development," *Khadi Gramodyog*, Jan, 1971, pp. 208-16.

Singh, Tarlok, "Development and Disparities: 1. Analysis and Approach, 2. Implications for Policy and Planning," *Yojana*, March 29, 1964, pp. 10-13 and April 12, 1964, pp. 5-7.

Singh, V.S., "Development Strategy for the Backward Regions of Uttar Pradesh," *Kurukshetra*, March 16, 1974, pp. 4-6.

Singhvi, U.C. "Panchayati Raj in India: Retrospect and Prospect," *Indian Journal of Public Administration*, July-Sept., 1976, pp. 478-492.

Sinha, R.K., "Novel way of Dispersing Industries in Backward Areas," *Khadi Gramodyog*, March 1974, pp. 284-87.

Somasckhara, N., "Identification of Less Developed Regions: A Case Study of Mysore," *Indian Journal of Regional Science*, 2 (2), 1970, pp. 157-74.

Sundaram, K.V., "District Planning: The Case of Maharashtra," *Indian Journal of Public Administration*, Jan.-March, 1979, pp. 57-73.

Swarup, Anand, "District Planning," *Journal of the National Academy of Administration*, Oct.-Dec., 1970, pp. 35-39.

Thompson, Victor A, "Administrative Objectives for Development Administration," *Administrative Science Quarterly*, June 1964, pp. 91-108.

Tiwary, K.N., "Planning at the State and District Level," *Journal of the National Academy of Administration*, Oct.-Nov. 1970, pp. 145-54.

Vasudevaraju, V.A., "Growth Centres Research and District Planning," *Indian Institute of Public Administration Bulletin*, (Pondicherry), Sept., 1972, pp. 7-10.

Vyas, V.S., "Nature and Role of Works Programme for Economic Development," *Indian Journal of Industrial Relations*, July 1974, pp. 95-112.

Wanmali, Sudhir, "Lessons of Work on Growth Centres for Micro-Level Planning," *Indian Journal of Public Administration*, July-Sept. 1973, pp. 308-19.

Yadav, Kirpa Nath, "Regional Planning in Bihar" *Khadi Gramodyog*, July 1976, pp. 425-31, Aug. 1976, pp. 466-72.

Zaheer, M., "Regional Planning for Integrated Area Development," *Community Development and Panchayati Raj Digest*, Oct., 1975, pp 43-46.

# INDEX